✔ KU-535-001

THE ART
OF FIELDWORK

LIVERPOOL JMU LIBRARY

3 1111 01359 3734

Malinowski explicitly discussed the difference between his data and those used by his predecessors. Indeed, in some respects much of his work has to be seen as an intellectual battle waged against his predecessors and many of his contemporaries, the successful outcome of which was to raise ethnographic fieldwork itself to a professional art.

—Max Gluckman
Introduction to *The Craft of Social Anthropology, xiii*

The Art of Fieldwork
Harry F. Wolcott

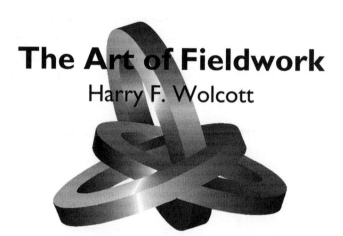

ALTAMIRA
PRESS

A Division of
ROWMAN & LITTLEFIELD PUBLISHERS, INC.
Walnut Creek • Lanham • New York • Oxford

ALTAMIRA PRESS
A Division of Rowman & Littlefield Publishers, Inc.
1630 North Main Street, #367
Walnut Creek, CA 94596
www.altamirapress.com

Rowman & Littlefield Publishers, Inc.
4720 Boston Way
Lanham, MD 20706

12 Hid's Copse Road
Cumnor Hill, Oxford OX2 9JJ, England

Copyright © 2001 by AltaMira Press

All rights reserved. No part of this publication may be reproduced,
stored in a retrieval system, or transmitted in any form or by any
means, electronic, mechanical, photocopying, recording, or otherwise,
without the prior permission of the publisher.

British Library Cataloguing in Publication Information Available

Library of Congress Cataloging-in-Publication Data
This book was previously cataloged by the Library of Congress as follows:

Wolcott, Harry F., 1929–
   The art of fieldwork / Harry F. Wolcott.
     p. cm.
   Includes bibliographical references and index.
   ISBN 0-7691-9100-X. — ISBN 0-7691-9101-8 (pbk.)
   1. Ethnology—Fieldwork. 2. Ethnology—Methodology. 3. Ethnology—Philosophy. I. Title.
GN346.W65 1995
305.8'00723—dc20   95-32480

ISBN 0-7619-9101-8 (pbk. : alk. paper)

Printed in the United States of America

™
The paper used in this publication meets the minimum requirements of American
National Standard for Information Sciences—Permanence of Paper for Printed Library
Materials, ANSI/NISO Z39.48–1992.

Interior Design and Production by Labrecque Publishing Services
Cover Design Inspired by Ben Hill
Cover Design by Ravi Balasuriya

TABLE OF CONTENTS

PART ONE
FIELDWORK CONTEXTS

CHAPTER ONE
INTRODUCTION

By all means the move to increase the general research sophistication of ethnographers should be encouraged. But at the same time, it would be tragic to lose what some converts call "soft," "unscientific," or "fuzzy" research. Much of the world we seek to understand has just those characteristics, including our own involvement in it as researchers.

—Michael H. Agar
The Professional Stranger, 197–198

Without the continued grounding in the empirical that scientific aspects of our tradition provide, our interpretive efforts may float off into literary criticism and into particularistic forms of history. Without the interpretive tradition, the scientific tradition that grounds us will never get off the ground.

—Roy A. Rappaport
"Cultural Anthropology's Future Agenda," 76

This book is about fieldwork and the art of doing it. It is not a book about art, and, although I intend the discussion to be helpful to fieldworkers, it is not a fieldwork manual. I do look at "artists" and how they go about their work, but I do so for the sake of analogy, to gain a perspective on what fieldworkers do that is like what artists do. My purpose is to encourage fieldworkers past, present, and future to reflect on how fieldwork, as contrasted with simply "collecting data," is an artistic undertaking as well as a scientific one.

I will not argue, nor do I believe, that fieldwork *is* art, any more than I believe that fieldwork *is* science. One often hears it described with cautious phrases that implicate *both* art and science by locating it tenuously between them, art as well as science, a "strange" or "gentle" science, a "rigorous" art, an activity requiring the artistic rendering of behavior systematically observed. The nexus between fieldwork and data collection is a central issue to be considered. So, too, is the relationship between the scientific aspects of the fieldwork tradition on the one hand, and what the anthropologist Evans-Pritchard has described as the "imaginative insight of the artist which is required in interpretation of what is observed" (1952:82) on the other.

Underscoring the *complementarity* of art and science has a certain appeal, especially in recognizing that fieldwork is not *only* science or that it should not be restricted by the canons of science. Nevertheless, the case on behalf of fieldwork as a science has been better served than the case for fieldwork as an art. In these pages you may find me "pushing" for the artistic dimensions of fieldwork as though I am redressing a wrong or correcting an imbalance. The notion that art and science are contradictory may have originated with Nietzsche (who considered art as the highest form of human activity), but Americans, among others, are noted for thinking in dualities, and the "Art vs. Science" dichotomy is well institutionalized in everyday thinking. It is amply reinforced in the existence of parallel but differentially revered (and funded) agencies like the National Science Foundation and our two national "endowments," one for the arts, the other for the humanities. An international journal, *Leonardo*, is devoted exclusively to the arts/sciences/technology dialogue. I have not set out to address the issues underlying that dialogue.

The focus of this discussion is restricted to artistic and scientific aspects in the doing of fieldwork, with fieldwork taken in a somewhat restricted sense to refer to a form of inquiry in which one immerses oneself personally in the ongoing social activities of some individual or group for the purposes of research. My position is that fieldwork of this sort is best regarded as its own thing, neither as potentially creative as art nor as typically systematic as science. Rather than seem to be left hanging somewhere between the two for being discernibly neither, fieldwork deserves a place of its own, an activity incorporating elements of both art and science yet slightly apart, in the way one might envision three interlocking rings. Fieldwork combines elements of art and science; it has no need to "become" one or the other. In the hands of any particular fieldworker, however, one or the other invariably receives the greater emphasis, for unless there is a compelling reason, they need not be in equilibrium. Something presented as a "scientific" account ought to be satisfyingly so.

Collecting data can be satisfyingly scientific, but fieldwork as presented here consists of more than collecting data. Whatever constitutes that elusive "more" makes all the difference. That needs to be stated emphatically, for a crucial aspect of fieldwork lies in recognizing when to be *unmethodical*, when to resist the potentially endless task of accumulating data and to begin searching instead for underlying relationships and meanings.

Portrait of the Author as a Not-so-Young Man

The book is not about fieldwork as art, as I am not an artist at either conducting or reporting fieldwork. No one kind enough to commend me for something I have written, either as a result of—or about—fieldwork, has gone so far as to suggest that I am an artist—and you aren't an artist until someone says you are. On the other hand, I would never deny unabashed efforts to approach my work "artistically." Nor have I felt much urgency about defending the research I have done as "science." I have, however, endeavored to tell it like it is, so my lack of preoccupation with doing good science does not necessarily leave me doing bad science, either.

My purpose in this book is to examine how fieldwork not only invites but also requires something of an artistic approach. How can we capitalize on that potential? And how, like other art forms, including even the fine arts, does fieldwork exhibit satisfactions, constraints, conceits, and deceits comparable to those of the art world? After all, artists live and work in a real world, too. What can we learn from examining that world?

I say that I am not an artist. I do not look for anyone to come forward to argue the contrary. Yet in ways both cultural and "cultured," art plays a significant role in my life, not merely in terms of what I enjoy and appreciate aesthetically, but as well in what I have been able to create, in spite of the absence of any recognizable talent. I like to think there is something of the artist in me, some capacity not only for appreciating but for creating, just as I assume there is something of the artist in you, and in everyone.

For example, the home in which I now live is a home I designed myself. That may, of course, speak more for my sense of space than for my artistic capacity, for even professional architects are inclined to set themselves apart from other artists. Whatever the case, the house is the handsomest one, aesthetically as well as practically, that I will ever have or need, and I feel a sense of artistic pride in the accomplishment.

In the past 50 or more years I have taken thousands of photographs, admittedly amateur in nature but certainly including some splendid ones. I have written several books, the academic kind that earn me the cautious accolade of writer rather than the more imposing one of author, but even academic writing is something of an art. I have been a regular theater-goer for five decades, a concert-goer for four, and an opera buff for almost that long. Like most Americans, I learned too early and too well that as an uneducated layman—and I have endeavored to retain that status by avoiding those art, music, and literature appreciation courses and programs constantly placed in my path—I am not expected to understand or fully appreciate "real" art. As part of that understanding, I am forgiven for recognizing what does and does not appeal to me personally, as long as I keep my opinions to myself.

None of these activities alone, nor all of them collectively, makes an artist out of me or links me in a recognizable way to an art world. It is not unknown for people to design their houses, take photographs, or go to concerts. Probably the best case I could make on behalf of art in my life would fit under a broad category of appreciation for what one might call "the art of living." (While I was writing this book, someone was writing that one. See Sartwell 1995.)

Among the activities I include in the art of living, I have conducted and reported fieldwork. As noted, I am not an artist at that, either. We have no category for the "artistic" fieldworker, and if we did, I am not sure I would want to be known as one—the words seem ill-suited for each other. Nor am I likely to be singled out as a "scientific" fieldworker. I have endeavored to make my fieldwork experiences and the accounts that followed from them careful and accurate, but I have also endeavored to make them reflective and deeply human. The longer I have been doing fieldwork, the more important this seems to become.

Although I doubt that I will advance the cause of scientific fieldwork in what follows, neither do I mean to diminish that effort nor to argue against fieldwork's becoming even more scientific in the near future, as it most surely will. My argument is that fieldwork can become more artful at the same time, with the important reminder that, in its own ways, art is every bit as rigorous and systematic as science. I do not argue on behalf of a "soft" or "fuzzy" approach to fieldwork, only against a fieldwork in which there is no allowance for fuzziness or ambiguity. I do argue on behalf of an approach that keeps humans always visibly present, researcher as well as the researched.

Where there is the ever-present temptation to play art off against science, one might give more than passing thought to the philosophical notion that science itself is but an art form, one among many aspects of art rather than the complement to it. But science, or more accurately the technology derived from it, has come to take the upper hand, and we look to it in support of programs and policies calling for swift action, with a bias toward intervention and treatment based on what can be done rather than judgments about what is worth doing. Fieldwork evolved out of a different tradition, as "naturalistic" observation over extended periods of time with as little intervention as possible and an underlying premise that other systems, other ways of knowing and doing, are worthy of sustained attention and efforts to understand. Not everything needs to be counted and measured, or changed and improved to conform to our standards, our ways. Artists portray. That is also what fieldwork is all about. Or was. Maybe it's time to review how fieldwork has been evolving and to contemplate what might be lost in our ready tilt toward science.

About the Title and Contents

The title *The Art of Fieldwork* is intended to convey two ideas central to this writing: first and foremost, that it is a book about fieldwork; second, that its focus is not with scientific techniques but rather with whatever else fieldwork entails in addition to technique. Out of curiosity, I searched the title "The Art of . . . " in our library's now computerized card catalog. I was dazzled to discover that the university has 1,516 entries that begin that way. And that does not include books with compound titles from A to Z, or Z to A, such as *Zen in the Art of Archery*, or *Zen and the Art of Motorcycle Maintenance*.

I was relieved to discover that, to the best of my knowledge, no one had yet written *The Art of Fieldwork*, yet distressed to discover long after I was committed to it that my title was so undistinguished. It is, however, a proper title for what follows. I assume that it immediately won some readers—new recruits willing to take up the call on behalf of the art of fieldwork—but I realize that at the same time I may have lost others who are already concerned about the fieldwork image.

I hope to present the case well enough that those who regard fieldwork as requiring both art and science will find further support on behalf of strengthening its artistic dimensions and potential. I will, in fact, argue that fieldwork is not merely a blend of the two, but a mode of inquiry in its own right, unique unto itself. Those not so inclined to emphasize artistic aspects or to separate fieldwork from science might at least be induced to reflect on whether being regarded as scientists is all that critical, and whether they may have internalized too rigid a view of how scientists themselves go about their inquiries. Would anything be lost if we were to insist that *fieldwork is fieldwork*, and only that? On the other hand, what might be lost were we completely to lose sight of fieldwork's artistic potential? Should we endeavor to suppress evidence of *imagination* or *emotion* in our own work, or should we be encouraging our colleagues and our students (especially our students) about the critical role such elements play in the mindwork that must accompany fieldwork? Read any particularly *un*imaginative studies lately? Are they our model?

I am challenged by the notion and delighted with the phrase "the art of fieldwork." I wish I could claim the idea for the title as my own, but I cannot. It came in correspondence with Robert Trotter at Northern Arizona University. Like many of his colleagues in the social sciences today, Trotter is an anthropologist who finds himself drawn almost too exclusively to the scientific side of fieldwork, both by the kind of research he has been conducting (folk healing and minority health problems, including AIDS research) and by the academic company he keeps. In other writing I was doing at the time, I sought his help in tracking down adaptations of the so-called "rapid" or "time-effective" data gathering techniques like Rapid Rural Assessment that have found their way into fieldwork practice. Applied anthropologists in particular see themselves as facing the reality that, if traditional fieldwork invariably takes so long to accomplish, someone else will be called whenever a short time is all the time available.

Trotter's response directed me toward the kind of resource I was seeking (for example, van Willigen and Finan's 1991 bulletin *Soundings*). He went on to note how his own work makes increasing use of such time-effective techniques—lots of data, quickly gathered and fed into computer programs already instructed as to how the analysis is to proceed.

> Analysis seems to be winning at the present time, because it is safer than interpretation. It is harder to get sued for analysis; you take fewer risks, reap fewer benefits. (Robert Trotter, personal communication, April 1993)

His comment prompted a further note of reflection: that the way he was currently conducting fieldwork somehow seemed to lack a ring of ethnographic authenticity:

> I feel that you have hit on a central issue; namely, how systematic can we become before we destroy the type of understanding that we are fundamentally seeking through ethnography? We have not had a good book on ethnography, and how it can be approached, for a number of years.

That is not to say there are *no* books on the topic, he hastened to explain, but rather that the books we have are too dated, too "cookbook oriented," or focused too exclusively on systematic approaches. H. Russell Bernard's splendid new (1994b) *Research Methods in Anthropology* is an example of a very good but also a very systematically oriented introduction to fieldwork. What we do not have, Trotter observed, is a book on the *art* of ethnography.

The art of ethnography? An idea begins to form. But why focus exclusively on *ethnographic* research, when qualitatively oriented researchers in many fields now conduct field-based studies. How about *The Art of Fieldwork* instead? Voilà! A book idea is conceived, title and all, to be devoted to exploring dimensions of fieldwork not well served by a preoccupation with data gathering alone.

This volume is devoted to that exploration. Most of the discussion turns on an examination of what it is about fieldwork that resembles what artists do and how what artists do differs from (and is similar to) what scientists do; it is not a treatise on what art is intended to accomplish.

Many of my references and examples come from cultural anthropology, my discipline of orientation. An ethnographic bias toward cultural interpretation will be evident throughout the account. That is where fieldwork got its start, and it helps to keep before us the cross-cultural and comparative basis on which it was founded. This aspect of fieldwork has become especially problematic for those being introduced to, or encouraged to pursue, qualitative approaches in settings totally familiar. On the other hand, some of my own illustrations come from research conducted in educational settings not all that different from other too-familiar settings in which researchers find themselves today.

About Art

Ultimately, of course, each researcher must strike a working balance to draw appropriately on both art and science in conducting any particular study. Although I intend to make a case for the art of doing fieldwork, and to proselyte on its behalf, I will also subject such efforts to critical examination. Art worlds have their own problems and peculiarities, and fieldworkers share some remarkably similar concerns with them. As well, we engage in some "darker" arts that need to be identified and addressed. Part One, "Fieldwork Contexts," takes a look at art and art worlds to provide perspective for what follows. In Part Two, I address what I call "The Fieldwork Part of Fieldwork," including both its basic arts and these darker arts. The conceptual aspects undergirding fieldwork are dealt with separately in the chapters that comprise Part Three, "Fieldwork as Mindwork." Eventually I get around to discussing some of the satisfactions in a final section, Part Four, "Fieldwork as Personal Work."

I do not see the relationship between art and science as a zero-sum game in which one side must lose so that the other may win. As fieldwork gets better—or, better stated, as we get better at it—my hope is that we will find ourselves doing both better art and better science without becoming too preoccupied about doing either. More attention seems to be going these days toward measuring and counting. I turn attention here to looking at what counts. The real genius in fieldwork lies in knowing how to answer that seemingly simple question: *What counts?*

No succinct, unifying concept or definition of art emerges in these pages. I did not begin with one. I have such faith in the power of writing to help think through complex ideas that I hoped one would evolve as I worked through drafts of the text, but that never happened. Instead, I look at some facets of art, ranging from how art, viewed as a social institution, works in its own strange ways, to suggestions for pursuing fieldwork more "artfully." That led to a working definition I propose here, stated in terms of what artists seek to do, rather than what art is. I should caution that the definition is well suited to my purposes but may lack qualities that would make it universally noteworthy:

> *Art is achieved when the addition of an idiosyncratic human touch in any production, whether performance or artifact, is recognized by a discriminating audience as achieving an aesthetic quality exceeding what is expected by the exercise of craft skill alone.*

That "art" remains somewhat ambiguous throughout these pages proved discomforting at first, especially since I was playing it off against the powerful forces of science. Yet science thrives on that same ambiguity—it has come to mean too much to too many who accept its findings too uncritically as our Ultimate Salvation, our Truth, our reliable Western Way of Knowing. Science does indeed offer *a* way to know the physical world, including the physical bodies, human and otherwise, in that world, but it is not the *only* way.

Fieldwork as discussed here involves the study of human beings in social interaction. The physical properties of those beings can explain only part of what goes on in everyday discourse. Measurement data and probabilities do not take on significance until the samples become large enough to support claims of representativeness. Fieldwork involves (literally) research in which the numbers are small, the relationships complex, and nothing occurs exactly the same way twice. The artistic challenge is to preserve, convey, and celebrate that complexity, even to the point of "messing up" science the way humans seem capable of doing. If, as Kirk and Miller suggest (1986:49), a fieldworker must be "ready to look a fool for the sake of science," the question addressed in these pages is, "What should a fieldworker be willing to do for the sake of art?"

19

art, Art, The Arts, The Fine Arts

Although most fieldworkers seem pleased to have their endeavor recognized as art, they are not at all pleased with the complementary yet uncomplimentary suggestion (whether stated or implied) that their work is not scientific or, far worse, that it is patently *un*scientific. A century of effort, after all, has been devoted to making fieldwork more scientific.

The ability to do successful fieldwork does indeed include the capacity for systematic work but also requires a sensibility that recognizes when systematic data are not called for, or are not *all* that is called for. Michael Agar, quoted in an epigraph to this chapter, is anything but a soft or fuzzy ethnographer; what he warns against is fieldworkers who are unaware that they themselves have their soft, fuzzy, "unscientific" side. Similarly, Roy Rappaport reminds us that without the interpretive tradition, we would be grounded forever by our own solid, empirical grounding. Perceived thus, science is perhaps best recognized as a critical aspect in the art of fieldwork. That is a different view from one that holds science to be kingpin in the fieldwork endeavor.

Fieldwork can also be regarded as a "fine" art, in the sense that it can be achieved and reported brilliantly. But it is not a fine art in the sense we customarily associate with music, painting, sculpture, architecture, and so forth. Great fieldworkers can produce great studies but they are not recognized as great artists. Come to think of it, academics are not ordinarily regarded as artists; the roles seem antithetical. And fieldwork is *by definition* an academic undertaking, to be judged by standards of academic competence. Academic performance can be likened to artistic performance; it is never confused for it. The course I pursue here looks for comparisons with art, and particularly with the work of artists, without the least suggestion that fieldwork *is* art.

Art has multiple meanings. Some of those meanings will be examined for the light they shed on fieldwork contexts, some for their more direct bearing on fieldwork practice, some for the meaning they give to the activity itself. Let me begin by sampling a range of meanings, emphasizing those of special relevance for this discussion. I am guided in this review by my trusty second (unabridged, 1987) edition of the *Random House Dictionary:*

• Art may express what is beautiful, appealing, or of more than ordinary significance.

• Art may refer to "a class or collection of objects" subject to aesthetic criteria, as in reference to paintings as an art form, or to a museum of art that houses such a collection.

• Art may refer to a field, genre, or category recognized as one of the arts, as in dance as an art.

• Art may refer to the fine arts collectively, sometimes with architecture singled out separately, as in a school or college of fine arts and architecture.

• Art may refer to any field using the skills or techniques of art (particularly in graphic design), such as industrial art or computer graphics.

• Art may refer to the principles or methods governing any craft, or to the craft or trade using them, as in the art of baking, the art of quilting.

• Art may refer in general to skilled workmanship or execution, or to skill in conducting any human activity, as, for example, the art of observing, an activity critical to participant observation. Thus art can be a component of craft.

• Art may refer to a branch of learning or specialized study, especially one of the fine arts (e.g., music) or the humanities (e.g., philosophy, literature) or to such studies more generally (e.g., the humanities collectively, the liberal arts).

• Art may refer to trickery, cunning, or artificiality in behavior.

Taken in reverse order, these various definitions form an ascending scale, from craftiness, to craft in everyday skills, to recognized craft skills, to the artful representation associated with the fine arts. Since fieldwork aims at representation, it cuts across these various meanings without having to become confused with the restricted meaning of the "fine arts" or denying fieldworkers the possibility of achieving fine art in their inquiries.

For example, the completed accounts that result from fieldwork are sometimes recognized for achievement "of more than ordinary significance." We can, and do, identify or debate our own shelf of "classics," models for others to admire and emulate. There is no danger of Our Classics' being confused with The Classics, but we do have our fieldwork idols and what we more or less agree among ourselves to be our master-pieces. And we, too, stumble over distinctions between art and craft. Fieldwork is likened as often to a craft as to an art. Social anthropology itself has been portrayed as a craft (Epstein 1967). Fieldwork can also involve deception or foster misunderstanding, so even this aspect needs to be addressed. I use the term "darker arts" to identify some pressing issues confronting fieldworkers along these lines and devote an entire chapter to the topic (Chapter 6). Before getting too involved with the activities of fieldwork itself, however, for perspective let me turn attention to works of art and the work of artists.●

CHAPTER TWO
FIELDWORK AS *ART?*

If it is true that the main task of art is the assertion of the authority of intuition to counterbalance the discursive method, it might appear at first sight that the artist is a natural opponent of the scientist. . . .

—E. L. Feinberg
Art in the Science Dominated World, 147

I would not go so far as to say that fieldwork is an "art"; but like an art there are basic rules of the form within which the artist-anthropologist is working. The research anthropologist in the field must know, respect, and play with these rules. Beyond that, fieldwork is a creative endeavor, with some anthropologists more creative than others, and this is true in any discipline.

—Charles Wagley
"Learning Fieldwork: Guatemala," 16

As I began planning this book, I quickly discovered that I needed to think about everything the title *The Art of Fieldwork* might imply and the emphasis to give here. Did I intend to delve into philosophical issues defining art or arguing whether art is a consequence of creative urges or the need to dominate? Did I want to get into a discussion of "art" at all—what it is, what it does, how it is achieved—or was art to serve only as a metaphor to prompt a different way to look at qualitative inquiry? Was the emphasis to be on what we already do that reflects the artistic element in our work, or on trying to inspire fieldworkers to new heights of artistic achievement? I was dismayed to discover more ambiguity in my self-imposed task than I had anticipated.

Consider how we customarily approach the work of the scientist and the work of the artist. We neither expect nor need to meet the former—the work stands apart, aloof, and we assess it the same way: coolly, objectively. By contrast, a first question related to a work of art is often, "What can you tell me about the artist?" That seems a relevant question to ask of the fieldworker as well. Recall how quickly I put myself in the scene in this writing—by the sixth paragraph of Chapter 1. Perhaps that was too soon, too self-absorbed on my part. Yet I felt it important for you to know something about the person presenting all this. I guess if I thought of myself as a scientist, that shouldn't matter. My sense is that it does matter. A lot!

Keeping in mind that my purpose is to examine fieldwork processes, not to create some noteworthy breakthrough in the philosophy of science, I was not altogether certain how sharp a distinction is needed to distinguish between art and science. In looking at fieldwork analogs for the science-versus-art contrast, I considered examining the root word -*graph*, which comes from the Greek -*graphos*: something drawn or written. In a broad sense, then, -*graph* refers to a kind of "picture." One might contrast the artistic touch of the *ethno*grapher, who composes a picture reflecting the lifeway of some group, with the scientific result produced by the *photo*grapher, who renders exactly what the (camera) eye "sees" as a result of variation in reflected light.

Yet the distinction is too slick. True, the photographer records, the ethnographer renders, but art and science are superbly melded in the best effort of either. The work of amateur photographers who lack an artistic eye is paraded constantly before us, the new point-and-shoot cameras having crystallized the placement of subjects at dull dead-center by dictating that readings of both light and distance be taken there. Dead-center photographs are no less interesting than the work of the ethnographer or other qualitatively oriented researcher whose account lacks balance between the extremes of an overdose of empirical data or a seeming disdain for them. Further, with darkroom and computer magic, the photographer can super-impose, add or subtract elements, change shapes and sizes, and do any number of wondrous tricks; there is no guarantee that a photograph depicts a real-world event.

In writing recently completed (HFW 1994b), I proposed that qualitatively oriented researchers distinguish between *analysis* and *interpretation* rather than regard the two as synonymous. I meant to set the two dimensions apart and treat them equally. Although I probably built a better case for the one with which I feel in closest sympathy (interpretation there, as with the artistic aspects of fieldwork here), I had no intention of casting my allegiance totally with one at the cost of the other.

Analysis, as portrayed in that writing, seems to fall within the parameters of the scientist at work, leading to "findings" not ordinarily contested, even in the case of fieldwork approaches in which it sometimes seems that everything can be contested. As others point out, there *is* a "there" out there, and it can be counted or measured and reported within limits of accuracy generally acceptable to all. That gives to analysis a certain *undeniability*, to be matched only by the *plausibility* with which we assess interpretive effort. The artistic potential may be more obvious in matters of interpretation, but questions of what gets analyzed, and how the analysis is to proceed, can also be viewed as artistic choices.

It is tempting to drag *creativity* into the discussion, as Charles Wagley does in an epigraph to this chapter, "Fieldwork is a creative endeavor." This can lead to a subtle implication that creativity is what distinguishes the artist from the scientist. Such an argument risks losing the ear of anyone who identifies closely with science and who sees creativity as essential to the progress of that work. Similarly, *imagination* or *intuition* is not easily given up as belonging solely to artistic endeavor. Although there is an implied playfulness in both terms that I do not ordinarily associate with my own stereotype of the scientist at work, one can wonder where science would be without them. As the philosopher of mathematics Imre Lakatos once noted (1978:99), "The direction of science is determined primarily by human creative imagination and not by the universe of facts which surrounds us."

No, art and science are not so easily separated; there is opportunity aplenty for good science in the work of the competent artist, good art in the work of the competent scientist. Temperament or "style" might be drawn into the argument, but the exceptions challenge rather than prove the rule.

Surely there are high-strung, temperamental scientists, just as there are staid artists for whom the tantrum is not a correlate of talent.

Perhaps it makes more sense simply to inventory the kinds of artistic endeavor that come easily to mind and to assess whether or how they offer a useful analogy for looking at the fieldworker as artist. Let me turn to a consideration of that possibility.

A Fieldworker Is (Most) Like A . . .

How far to press any analogy? For every type of art form and artist, an analogy can be drawn with fieldwork highlighting some aspects and obscuring others. One analogy I find appealing is to contrast a fieldworker with either the potter who works with clay or the carver whose medium is wood or stone.

Fieldworker and potter alike are intent on shaping and molding some object out of formless raw material. I found the work of a potter expressed beautifully in these words:

When Mud Woman Begins*
Electricity
down my arm
through this clay
forming into
spirit shapes
of men
women
and children
I have seen
somewhere before.
—Nora Naranjo-Morse

---

* "When Mud Woman Begins" is from *Mud Woman: Poems from the Clay*, by Nora Naranjo-Morse, copyright 1992 by the University of Arizona Press. Used with permission.

26

This vision of the potter—inspired by the poet—represents the artist's task as a building-up from previously collected material, fashioning something dependent on the artist's skill, whether intended as original or replica. Contrast that with an artist—or fieldworker—who perceives the task as one of revealing something already present but covered or hidden. I think particularly of the (perhaps romanticized) Eskimo carver whom I heard anthropologist Edmund Carpenter describe years ago:

> As the carver holds the unworked ivory lightly in his hand, turning it this way and that, he whispers, "Who are you? Who hides there?" And then: "Ah, Seal."
>
> He rarely sets out, at least consciously, to carve, say, a seal, but picks up the ivory, examines it to find its hidden form and, if that is not immediately apparent, carves aimlessly until he sees it, humming or chanting as he works. Then he brings it out: Seal, hidden, emerges. It was always there: he didn't create it; he released it; he helped it step forth. (Carpenter 1971[1961]:163)

This is not unlike a story attributed to Michelangelo. When asked to describe how he carved the magnificent David, his explanation was, "I took a block of stone and chipped away everything that was *not* David." His famous set of statues, the Prisoners of Stone, suggests something of the same. Once the figures were freed, Michelangelo did not return to "complete" the works; *his* task was finished, in spite of the fact that the statues were not.

This second type of artist—like some fieldworkers—views and engages in a task perceived differently from that of the potter. This one does not attempt to fashion something anew but only to reveal for others what is already there, so they may see what he or she sees. Perhaps anthropologist Carpenter overstates the case with his phrase "carves aimlessly." Although there are moments in fieldwork when each of us may worry about working aimlessly, such moments of thoughtful reflection about how next to proceed may mark another striking similarity between artist and fieldworker.

I like these different analogies. Not only are they powerful and dramatic in themselves, they also illustrate two dramatically different ways through which fieldworkers may approach a new assignment: to shape and mold something that has never been, or to uncover and thus reveal what was there all along.

Hardly surprising that provocative analogies can be drawn between fieldworkers and artists when we realize how connected with life fieldwork can (should?) be, and how all-encompassing the term *fieldwork* is. Although I did not supply a crisp definition of fieldwork, you do need to keep in mind that as used here it refers not to all on-site research but to on-site research involving a long-term relationship and direct personal involvement. (See also Agar 1980:69–70, who characterizes ethnographic relationships as "long-term and diffuse.")

Let me turn the tables to ask: When I use the terms *fieldwork* or *fieldworker*, what image comes to your mind? In whatever mental picture you create, do you include yourself? Alone, or with a team of researchers? Or is your imagined fieldworker drawn from some well-known photograph, such as that of Gregory Bateson and Margaret Mead on the jacket of *Fieldnotes*, or Steve Tyler on the jacket of *Writing Culture*? While you may imagine someone sitting on the veranda of a tropical hut, or walking briskly down the corridor of the local hospital, and another reader imagines interviewing sherpas in Nepal or assembly-line workers in Detroit, all the while I had in mind a 33-year-old doctoral student standing before his classroom of Kwakiutl Indian children on an island along the coast of British Columbia in the fall of 1962 (HFW 1967). Today's fieldworkers may turn up anywhere.

When I prompt with the term "artist," what vision pops into your head? My immediate impression is both literal and caricature: the painter standing before an easel, brush in one hand, palette in the other, and wearing the essential paint-spattered smock and dark beret. No reason my painter cannot be outdoors, capturing on paper or canvas—or even in a notebook of quick sketches—some natural scene or group activity, thus strengthening my analogy between an engagement with the fine arts and the fine art of fieldwork.

My Random House unabridged dictionary leads me on a merry chase this time as I try to tease out all-inclusive categories to describe everything artists can do or be. If "painter" or "sculptor" occur most frequently as examples, I am reminded that we have categories and subcategories for fine arts and applied arts, for plastic arts and graphic arts, for commercial art, performing arts, and, most recently, performance art, fusing such artistic media as dance, drama, film, music, painting, and video, derived in part from the 1960s invention of the performance "happening." I am reminded as well that whether we are thinking of the artist as recluse painter or public performer, there is an expectation of advanced skill, so that whenever boundaries blur between art and craft—as for example, in the graphic arts involved in engraving, etching, woodcuts, or lithography—the individual whose work exhibits *exceptional* skill may be recognized as an artist. Of course, that includes the con artist as well—the trickster "adept at lying, cajoling, or glib self-serving talk," as my dictionary summarizes it.

Artists and Artisans and "All That Is Required"

A distinction is sometimes made between the *artist* engaged in one of the fine arts and the *artisan* engaged in a craft or applied art. In practice, however, artisans can win accolades for achieving high *art* in their *craft*. A crisp distinction between art and craft would have served well here, but the differences must instead remain blurred.

Perhaps that is for the best. To attend adequately to the "art" of fieldwork, it is necessary to consider how it is viewed as both *craft* and *art*. I do not mean to diminish the craft aspect of fieldwork. No disservice is done by using that label. Note such works as Kimball and Partridge's fieldwork dialogue presented under the title *The Craft of Community Study* (1979), or Epstein's earlier fieldwork manual, *The Craft of Social Anthropology* (1967). On the other hand, I do want to point out how, in fulfilling *and exceeding* craft dimensions, those who perform well are often recognized, and emulated, as artists.

Perhaps the resolution of the tension between fieldwork as art and fieldwork as science—a unifying purpose in which all parties recognize a common objective—lies in efforts to refine fieldwork as craft. I was both surprised and pleased to find two strong proponents of *systematic* fieldwork and ethnoscience methodology arguing on behalf of craft as *that part of the whole enterprise that can be taught:*

> We have to separate the craft of ethnography from the art. The craft can be taught. Art can be taught—up to a point—and practice is an

29

important dimension of becoming a good artist. But great art is ultimately dependent on the talent of the artist. (Werner and Schoepfle 1987b:16)

In their very next sentence, however, these authors explain what they had set out to do in preparing their two volumes on *Systematic Fieldwork* (1987a, 1987b) that set a course quite different from the one I pursue here:

> For many applications of ethnography a master craftsman-ethnographer is all that is required. These volumes address the problem of becoming such a master craftsman. (P. 16)

I admire and respect the work of master craftsmen. (With today's gender-sensitive language, I will refer here to master *craftspeople*, or a master *craftsperson*. However, I will use the term *craftsmanship*, rather than the cumbersome *craftspersonship*.) Whether I am having my automobile repaired, new lenses ground for my eyeglasses, or my income taxes prepared, skilled craftspeople are the ones I seek out. But I want to encourage, and to some extent inveigle, committed fieldworkers to think beyond and to reach beyond skill—to regard themselves not only as craftspeople, but as artists as well. If, as Werner and Schoepfle suggest, the artistic side can be taught only *up to a point*, then we need to consider how that dimension can be nurtured, coaxed, teased out, fanned—whatever it is that any one individual can do to encourage another to do by way of providing experience, advice, ideas, illustrations, anecdotes, resources, or sometimes simply great expectations.

The point is to encourage fieldworkers to regard the fieldwork enterprise not merely as a craft, in the sense that Kimball and Partridge, Werner and Schoepfle, and others use that term, but as an approach to research in human groups that involves *more* than technical skill, *more* than a time-consuming way to conduct thick surveys. Surveys are fine when the objective is to know how everybody does it: frequencies, distributions, average or "typical" behavior. Fieldwork ought to inform us about how—and to some extent why—*somebody* does it, somebody whose way of thinking about things and doing things promises in some significant way to help us understand similarities and differences between their ways and our own.

30

E. L. Feinberg, quoted in an epigraph for this chapter, suggests that the main task of art is "the assertion of the authority of intuition" (1987:147), with intuition understood to include both sensory and intellectual elements (p. 21). What can be done, or done more of, to encourage fieldworkers to exercise the authority of their intuition, and thus to capture their artistic insight rather than subjugate it to a determined objectivity?

One way to provide such encouragement is to remind fieldworkers of the many ways in which their forbears exercised intuition, regardless of whether they called attention to it. Another is to ensure that artistic sensitivity and endeavor in fieldwork and reporting today are recognized and applauded rather than discouraged or trivialized. We have to take it upon ourselves self-consciously and publicly to commend qualitative researchers for artistic as well as scientific accomplishments. That is an attitude and activity in which everyone interested in qualitative inquiry has a role to play. If we really want to see fieldwork carried out and written up more artfully, the first step is to give adequate recognition to what is already being done and encouragement to anyone willing to venture (risk?) doing even more. As readers, reviewers, critics, or users of qualitative research, our efforts can have an immediate effect.

With colleagues or students, a slight push in the right direction may be all that is needed, with a well-timed question as to whether one might be more daring with an interpretation or with the way a research problem has been framed. Perhaps fieldworkers need only to feel less cowed by demands for rigorous science that may in fact be neither as demanding, nor as rigorous, nor even as prevalent as generally assumed. We make it all right for others to think about and practice fieldwork as an art as we ourselves demonstrate that it can be done and see that others are rewarded for the doing.

The potential each of us has *individually* to influence and literally "bring out the best" in another may get lost in the discussion that follows. I close this chapter with a vignette to serve as reminder of that potential, a brief account related by an 83-year-old woman recalling how she learned to quilt. The story* originally appeared in *The Quilters: Women and Domestic Art*, by

---

* Used here with the permission of Doubleday, a division of Bantam Doubleday Dell Publishing Group, Inc.

Patricia Cooper and Norma Bradley Allen (1989[1977]:52) and was the basis for a Broadway play, *The Quilters*. It came to my attention while reading Howard Becker's *Art Worlds*, to which I turn in the following chapter.

> Mama was a beautiful quilter. She done the best work in the county. Everybody knew it . She never let nobody else touch her quilts. . . .
>
> I always longed to work with her and I can tell you how plain I recall the day she said, "Sarah, you come quilt with me now if you want to."
>
> I was too short to sit in a chair and reach it, so I got my needle and thread and stood beside her. I put that needle through and pulled it back up again, then down, and my stitches were about three inches long.
>
> Papa come in about that time, he stepped back and said, "Florence, that child is flat ruinin' your quilt."
>
> Mama said, "She's doin' no kind of a thing. She's quiltin' her first quilt."
>
> He said, "Well, you're jest goin' to have to rip it all out tonight."
>
> Mama smiled at me and said, "Them stitches is going to be in that quilt when it wears out."
>
> All the time they was talkin' my stitches was gettin' shorter.

That may be all it takes if you are putting together your first fieldwork account and you have the support of a discriminating audience—people willing and able to offer the help you need and patient enough to let you develop your account within an appropriate framework without stifling you in the process. That kind of support is reflected in an appreciation that my colleague Duncan Waite at the University of Georgia found in the words of Shelley Mishoe in acknowledging the help of members of her qualitative dissertation study dealing with respiratory care practice. She thanked him specifically for "teaching me to trust my instincts, value my experience, and go with what I know."

If you have done, or are planning to do, fieldwork, you are already engaged in what is potentially an artistic as well as a scientific endeavor. You need a capacity for careful observing and reporting, but you need as well to trust your instincts, value your experience, and have a clear sense both of what you do and what you do not know. You also need that audience of others standing by—not all that big an audience, but an audience, nonetheless—with help and encouragement and patience as you find your way into an activity that cannot achieve its full potential through the exercise of technical skill alone.

These chapters—necessarily more impersonal but intended to provide help and encouragement nevertheless—may serve in the interim until you find your own supportive audience, but find it you must. There are always people around to take the role that Papa so readily assumed with Sarah's first efforts at quilting, critics determined to uphold standards and make sure that your work conforms. Systematic approaches to fieldwork demonstrate such conformity through adherence to established procedures, but that is not to suggest that artists—or fieldworkers—are ever completely free to do-their-own-thing. A look at some of those "others" and the collective influence they wield on the doing of art is the focus of the next chapter.●

LIVERPOOL JOHN MOORES UNIVERSITY
LEARNING SERVICES

CHAPTER THREE
HOW ART WORKS

All artistic work, like all human activity, involves the joint activity of a number, often a large number, of people.

—Howard S. Becker
Art Worlds, 1

No matter how much care an ethnographer devotes to his or her project, its success depends on more than individual effort. It is tied to outside social forces including an anthropological community that accepts the project as meaningful and international relationships that make fieldwork possible.

—Barbara Tedlock
"From Participant Observation
to the Observation of Participation," 78

In chapters to follow, you may find me writing about fieldwork as though each fieldworker were the center of the universe, a free agent who delves into the social life and social contexts of everyone else, unencumbered by social contexts of his or her own. That serves well enough for reviewing how fieldworkers go about their tasks, for considering the artistic dimensions of the tasks, and for inventorying some of the professional problems and personal satisfactions of these endeavors.

In that writing, I will relate what I have observed and experienced and learned from others, and I will offer whatever insight or advice I can, the old hand passing on his own version of a tradition. I must leave it to you to distinguish between the art of fieldwork and "Harry's version of fieldwork" if at times I seem to confuse the two. Before getting to the basics, however,

I want to take a step back and examine the social milieu in which fieldwork is conducted, drawing upon the social milieu of art worlds for perspective.

In a paper written years ago and recently revised (HFW 1994a), I examined several of the extraneous forces that influence the doing and reporting of fieldwork. In that writing, I drew upon time for my perspective, identifying influences past, present, and future. The *past* exerts its influence through the accumulated lore and literature of the various traditions in which we work. In pointing a way, it often points *the* way for studies we undertake. The *present* exerts its influence not only by the nature of the particular assignment and setting but also through the resources (time, energy, funding) available for getting the work completed. There is never enough time to realize the infinite potential of fieldwork; by constantly threatening to run out on us, time forces us to recognize limits on what we can accomplish. In that important sense, our works are never "completed." Rather, as Clifford Geertz suggests, citing Paul Valéry (Geertz 1983:6), what we really do is *abandon* them. *Future* influences take into account the relatively narrow range of options we have for reporting our work. Our various audiences, both professional and public, hold rather rigid expectations about how, where, and what we report.

In this chapter I want to return to an examination of these external—and in some ways seemingly irrelevant—constraints, this time from a socially interactive perspective. Maintaining a focus here on art, I draw an analogy between the art of fieldwork and other creative endeavors in which the term "artist" is more customarily heard. To draw these parallels, and for a general outline in the discussion that follows, I also draw heavily on sociologist Howard S. Becker's *Art Worlds*, published in 1982.*

A personal note is in order. Both in person and through his writing, Howard Becker has often come to my rescue in helping me find a perspective or procedure for working through data or thinking about how to write up research. (For examples of that advice, see Becker 1986, or a

---

* Copyright for *Art Worlds* is held by the Regents of the University of California. Quotations are used with permission of both the author and the publisher, the University of California Press.

compilation of his writings edited by Burgess, 1995.) He was also one of the earliest researchers to conduct fieldwork in schools, beginning with his 1951 dissertation study of the role and career problems of Chicago teachers (see Becker 1980), following what is known as the Chicago School or Chicago "tradition" of hands-on sociological studies.

For several decades, Becker has been a source of wise counsel for qualitatively oriented researchers, particularly in the fields of education and sociology. By the time I caught up with him in person in the mid-1960s, his interests had taken him into other arenas. One of those was a sociological inquiry into the world of art, prompted in part by the combination of his sustained interest in photography and his experiences as an accomplished jazz musician.

I did not follow Becker in his pursuit of art worlds. Not until this writing did it occur to me that his excursion into the aesthetic realm might provide valuable insight for my own examination into the art of fieldwork. But indeed it has!

In Becker's view, social systems of art *worlds*—comprised of many more people than only artists themselves—are the real *producers* of art works. As he explains, "I have made art worlds my central concern, treating them as the producers of art works, looking at their careers, workings, and results, rather than at those of individual artists" (Becker 1982:351).

Becker describes his approach to art as conventionally sociological, which in this case means a focus on the art worlds of our own everyday experience with High Culture rather than the cross-cultural perspective that might lead an anthropologist into comparative studies. His influence should be apparent throughout this chapter as I borrow from his text about those other art worlds to lend perspective on the art of fieldwork.

I found striking parallels. I could not help wonder why Becker had not turned his mirror back on himself to examine the artistry in his own professional career as a field-oriented sociologist. He does make occasional reference to writers as artists, although I doubt that he was thinking of himself as one of them. I had to remind myself, however, that the preoccupation with finding parallels between fieldwork and art is my own. Any inquiry must have boundaries. Becker's examination of artists at work in their social milieu was not intended to embrace his own artistry as an astute observer of, and writer about, the social scene.

Defining Art and Artists

Taking the role of the conventional sociologist—to whatever extent that is possible for such an unconventional one—Becker describes his intent in *Art Worlds* to approach art by focusing on "the social organization of people who work at art and of the audience which responds to it" (p. 352). That is not to suggest a simple two-way arrow between individual artist and receptive patron, however. The audiences are multiple and complex; an artist *never* works entirely alone. As Becker explains:

> Whatever the artist, defined as the person who performs the core activity without which the work would not be art, does not do must be done by someone else. The artist thus works in the center of a network of cooperating people, all of whose work is essential to the final outcome. (P. 24–25)

This perspective that Becker brought to his discussion is the one I borrow here in drawing an analogy to the social organization that supports the conduct of fieldwork. Obviously that network must include fieldworkers themselves. Perhaps less obviously, it also includes a wider circle of individuals whose efforts and interactions are essential to the final outcome, and includes as well the varied audiences that fieldworkers hope to reach and other audiences that, like it or not, will reach them.

A moment's reflection reveals how extensive are the strands that link, and in important ways bind, seemingly lone and independent researchers, in the field or at their desks, to larger and more embracing social systems. We all must contend with the literature of the past, the fads and fancies of the day. (In a paper presented in 1992, Frederick Erickson characterized the current era in social research as "Post Everything.") We contend as well with the critiques of reviewers, the interests of publishers or funding agencies, the influence of colleagues who either do or do not cite our works or assign them as texts, and the potential outcry from unseen masses ready to remind us when, on the one hand, we overstep our bounds or when, on the other hand, we avoid issues to which we *ought to* be giving attention.

The point of Becker's inquiry is to show how these multiple contexts define an art world. Artists do not and cannot control that world, nor are they its gatekeepers. And there never could be enough room at the top for everyone who aspires to be recognized as an artist to be awarded that recognition. Creativity or genius that we applaud in the abstract gives way before a powerful insistence upon conformity in practice. Our recognized artists themselves must recognize how hard to push, and their pushing is reassessed with the unveiling of virtually every new art work, performance, or public showing in the perpetual swing between extremes, here too little, there too much. ("That's not art!" exclaims a character strolling through a gallery exhibition in Jesse Green's novel *O Beautiful.* "That's someone skipping therapy." I have read or listened to fieldwork accounts that prompted a similar response in me.)

Becker takes the paintings hung on motel walls to represent a broad category he refers to as *canonical art.*

> Imagine, for any particular organized art world, a canonical art work, a work done exactly as the conventions current in that world dictate. A canonical art work would be one for whose doing all the materials, instruments, and facilities have been prepared, a work for whose doing every cooperating person—performers, providers of supplies, support personnel of all kinds, and especially audiences—has been trained. Since everyone involved would know exactly what to do, such a work could be created with a minimum of difficulty . . . Such a work might bore everyone involved. By definition, it would contain nothing novel, unique, or attention getting, nothing that violated anyone's expectations. It would create no tension and arouse no emotion. The paintings on motel walls are just such canonical works. (P. 228)

There are similar phrases to "motel art" that one hears bandied about, such as *airport art, bank art, tourist art.* Although Becker does use *hack* as a descriptor, I do not think he means to denigrate such art as much as to suggest that although it is acceptably competent and conforming, it is "just what one would expect." More charitably we sometimes label it *decorator art,* acknowledging the work of those who produce art that makes no pretense at being great art. Becker proposes the term *integrated professional* to describe such people. We can draw parallels between the integrated professional artist and what we might describe as the integrated professional fieldworker whose work also can be characterized as competent and acceptable, conforming but uninspired.

Imagine, too, a canonical artist, fully prepared to produce, and fully capable of producing, the canonical art work. Such an artist would be fully integrated into the existing art world. He would cause no trouble for anyone who had to cooperate with him, and his work would find large and responsible audiences. Call such artists integrated professionals.

Integrated professionals have the technical abilities, social skills, and conceptual apparatus necessary to make it easy to make art. Because they know, understand, and habitually use the conventions on which their world runs, they fit easily into all its standard activities. (Pp. 228–229)

Integrated professionals—artist and fieldworker alike—turn out conventional studies. In art worlds, Becker notes, both the works and the professionals who produce or participate in them are treated as interchangeable (p. 231); whatever their distinctive differences or unique abilities, they can more or less be substituted for one another.

To our wider audiences, fieldworkers probably exhibit that same interchangeable quality. Nuance we cherish within a particular discipline or orientation is shrugged off as too minor to be of concern, as, for example, the cavalier disregard sometimes exhibited by qualitative researchers for distinguishing ethnography from related but nonetheless distinguishable allies. Conversely, differences cherished across disciplines may be quickly rationalized away when a hasty call goes out to recruit researchers ready and willing to accept an assignment. I remember receiving a telephone call from an official in Washington, D.C., inviting my immediate participation in a funded project that sought my perspective "as a sociologist." When I pointed out that any contribution I might make would be from an anthropological perspective rather than a sociological one, the project officer replied, "That's just fine, too." My name was already on the approved list of those to be contacted. A disciplinary affiliation I had endeavored to establish for the previous twenty years was of virtually no consequence. (I might note that I accepted the assignment anyway. As an old saying goes, "I ain't cheap, but I can be had.")

A central question Becker addresses, of relevance here, is how *some* activities get defined as art and others do not. I turn next to his insight on that issue, which leads as well to examining the nexus between arts and crafts.

Art vs. Craft as a Public Decision

When does an activity become defined as art? The judgment is not left for artists to decide among themselves. "Whenever an art world exists," Becker writes, "it defines the boundaries of acceptable art, recognizing those who produce the work it can assimilate as artists entitled to full membership, and denying membership and its benefits to those whose work it cannot assimilate" (p. 226). That is the tough reality of art worlds. It is also the experience of those who have produced great art without being recognized in their own times as great artists.

Being able to claim one's work as art offers advantages that some seek self-consciously and others modestly eschew. Household or folk arts that sometimes become cottage industries—cooking and baking, needlework, basketry—or hobbies and recreational activities pursued seriously, such as social and folk dancing, flower arranging, and singing, are examples of activities in which it seems of little consequence among those who engage in them how they are perceived by others (p. 37). Naive artists enjoy a similar independence, often having no connections with any art world, typically working alone (pp. 258–259).

Becker points out that art worlds "frequently incorporate at a later date works they originally rejected, so that the distinction must lie not in the work but in the ability of an art world to accept it and its maker" (p. 227). Furthermore, he suggests that most contemporary high arts started out as some form of craft (p. 298), noting by way of illustration that the making of paintings was once thought of as no more than skilled work (i.e., craft) that became redefined during the Renaissance as something special (p. 17).

Drawing a line between arts and crafts is, therefore, a function of art worlds. When the distinction is made, it is done in recognition that "making art requires technical skills that might be seen as craft skills" (p. 272). However, Becker notes—and here you may detect his influence on my working definition of art offered earlier—there is something *more* that artists contribute beyond craft skill, "something due to their creative abilities and gifts that gives each object or performance a unique and expressive character" (p. 272). In some cases, skilled personnel who support the work of the artist may be recognized as craftspeople who do craft, while other activities may be called by either title.

The histories of various art forms include typical sequences of change in which what has been commonly understood and defined by practitioners and public as a craft becomes redefined as an art or, conversely, an art becomes redefined as a craft. In the first case, participants in an art world borrow from or take over a craft world; in the second, a mature art world begins to exhibit some of the characteristic features of craft worlds. (P. 272)

In the previous chapter, I raised the question of knowing where to draw the line that distinguishes fieldwork as craft from fieldwork as art. Following a suggestion by Werner and Schoepfle (1987b), I relegated to craft those aspects of fieldwork procedures and techniques that can be taught. That leaves to art whatever it is beyond those teachable elements that allows some fieldworkers to carry out and report their inquiries in a fashion clearly exceeding the guild average. And we, too, sometimes discover provocative and superbly executed studies that failed to draw attention or acclaim in their day, as, for example, Gregory Bateson's *Naven*, rediscovered 22 years after its original publication, or Paul C. P. Siu's *The Chinese Laundryman*, unpublished (and deemed unmarketable) until after his death (see Sanjek 1990:408).

I continue to search for terms to describe that special something that sets art apart from craft. Social scientists have long had a fascination with the term *innovation*, but their attention has been directed toward issues of social or technological change rather than to purely artistic invention (see, for example, Barnett 1953; Spicer 1952). "Creativity" might seem an obvious choice, except that some attributes associated with creativity are not ones we relish in association with fieldwork, particularly the suggestion that, unlike researchers in any other field, those of us who do fieldwork "create" our own data. As Ottenberg notes, "Historical scholars working with archives do not usually employ materials that they themselves have written!" (1990:152). Similarly, there is an ever-present caution not to become "too creative" in the retelling and, especially, in the interpreting of one's fieldwork.

Perhaps the word *genius* serves better, used here in the broad sense of "extraordinary natural capacity." On the other hand, genius in another sense, in reference to extraordinarily high intelligence, may not signal any special advantage; fieldwork can easily disarm anyone gifted with what intelligence tests measure but lacking in common sense. One kind of common sense in fieldwork, for example, is the art of knowing how to "catch on" without catching on too quickly and thus appearing "too smart," a know-it-all.

Becker offers an alternative to problems of trying to distinguish between art and craft by looking instead at a category combining them, the "artist-craftsman." Cumbersome as it is, that label also seems well suited for fieldworkers who, like artist-craftspeople recognized in other lines, sometimes demonstrate extraordinary natural capacity, yet neither are nor desire to be recognized as "artists."

Art worlds customarily look for something "unique and expressive" in performance or product that sets the artist apart, while craft pride customarily derives from a consistency of both product and quality. Thinking of fieldwork as the work of "artist-craftspeople" allows us to keep our claims modest in terms of outcomes (qualitative inquiry is relieved of the responsibility to demonstrate its capacity to achieve "great art"), while at the same time acknowledging that some fieldworkers, and the accounts their work generates, clearly stand apart from and above the rest: there *are* better and worse accounts. As Becker states the case:

> Crafts ordinarily divide along the line between ordinary craftsmen trying to do decent work and make a living and artist-craftsmen with more ambitious goals and ideologies. Ordinary craftsmen usually respect artist-craftsmen and see them as the source of innovation and original ideas. (P. 276)

The "Minor Art" World of Fieldworkers

Becker makes another useful distinction that examines the development of certain "minor arts" and minor art worlds. These labels pertain to crafts in which artist-craftspeople are recognized and rewarded for superior achievement on criteria like "beauty" that differ from criteria ordinarily employed (usefulness, for example) to judge a competent level of craft skill.

The recognition that minor arts and minor art worlds coexist with major arts and major art worlds invites another perspective on the art of fieldwork. Fieldwork, too, can be pursued as a sort of "minor art," one in which highly accomplished individuals are recognized and generously applauded, although their work does not presume to be "great." That would preclude us from having to claim that there have been—or ever will be—Great Fieldworkers, comparable to recognized Great Painters, Great Sculptors, or Great Composers. (Bronislaw Malinowski probably comes closest; one can search far to find higher praise than this from Margaret Mead, who once wrote, "I am convinced all over again that Malinowski was perhaps the most thorough field worker God ever made" [quoted in Sanjek 1990:217–218]. However, that same thoroughness, redefined as "haphazard" documentation, is also a major criticism leveled at both Mead and Malinowski's work.)

Becker's description of the "apparatus" of art worlds invites further comparisons. What do fieldworkers have by way of analogy to the shows, prizes, sales to collectors, and teaching positions associated with both major and minor art worlds?

> Artist-craftsmen develop a kind of art world around their activities, a "minor art" world. The world contains much of the apparatus of full-fledged major arts: shows, prizes, sales to collectors, teaching positions, and the rest. Not all craft worlds develop such an artistic, beauty-oriented segment (plumbing has not). But where an art segment develops, it usually coexists peacefully with the more purely utilitarian craft segment. (P. 278)

Shows. With the exception of fieldworkers who report through visual media—photographic exhibits, film—and do actually have something to exhibit that can be "seen" by viewer or critic (and increasingly by participants-turned-critics as well, as Burns points out [1993]), we cannot display our results in any form comparable to the gallery or art show. Individually, our output is too slow. A fieldwork-based monograph produced every few years would represent a prolific output, yet the cost of renting a tuxedo to go look at four or five books on a table hardly seems worth it. Conversely, the collective outpouring from *all* the fieldwork reported from even *one* year would be far too great to assemble or display, especially if one were to try to include, in addition to published books and monographs, all the papers presented in graduate seminars or read at regional and national meetings, plus all the accounts submitted to funding agencies.

We do not have the equivalent of art shows, but that does not mean we lack critics ready to pick us off, one at a time, in the constant outpouring of published reviews. We also "vote with our feet" in attending the volunteered sessions or invited addresses of author-researchers deemed to be at the cutting edge of our various disciplines or momentarily able to capture the public spotlight. "Academics attending seminars have impeccably subtle ways of assessing colleagues' opinions before deciding whether to respond to the presentation of a visiting speaker with praise, contempt, or silence," observes anthropologist Sally Price in a chapter titled "The Mystique of Connoisseurship" (1989). We are expected to *know* who is current, who is passé. Should we display a momentary lapse in our powers to discriminate, the person sitting next to us may quickly bring us up to date. "Good grief, she's still pumping the same stuff from a chapter she published years ago," mumbled the stranger sitting next to me when I appeared too enthusiastic in my applause for a speaker at a national meeting.

Prizes. As professionals we are, of course, above such things as prizes: we take no "firsts," covet no ribbons. But there are other ways to reward fieldworkers and their works. Acceptance by a publisher or professional journal—especially a refereed journal—is not the least among such rewards. Some organizations regularly announce committee-based selections of outstanding new studies. Workshop organizers and presenters promote professional lives and works by the mere mention of particular studies, or by identifying researchers whose work and "promise" should not be overlooked. Many organizations make official recognition of exemplary dissertation studies or the work of scholars early in their careers. Most old, established institutions have named awards to bestow on researchers making a particularly noteworthy contribution or in recognition of distinguished careers in teaching, service, and, especially, published works. An example is the Society for Applied Anthropology's annual Malinowski Award, which does double duty by recognizing the achievements of a contemporary social scientist while keeping Malinowski's name before us as a scholar/fieldworker worthy of emulation. The early founders of Anthropology and Education are similarly honored anew with each successive awarding of the Solon T. Kimball Award and the George and Louise Spindler Award; the American Educational Research Association now gives annual recognition to the best qualitative dissertation; and so on.

Sales. Our works are not one of a kind, so we have nothing comparable to those well-publicized "sales to collectors" that occasionally bring fame (usually without the accompanying fortune, to be discussed below) to producing artists. Nevertheless, there is a discernible "market" in qualitative research, and its assorted gatekeepers play key roles in determining what gets printed in the journals, what gets published commercially. At least two acquisitions editors of my acquaintance, the late David Boynton of Holt, Rinehart and Winston, and Mitch Allen, who now publishes under his own imprimatur, AltaMira Press, have played major roles as gatekeepers in deciding what was to be published and as enthusiastic advocates for authors fortunate enough to be tapped. These two editors, and their counterparts in other publishing houses favorably inclined toward qualitative works (such as Falmer Press; Harcourt, Brace; Sage; Teachers College Press), also have worked in concert with a number of formal or informal academic advisers and consultants who exert an influence on the selection and development of materials for publication.

Under the direction of Neil Rowe, Waveland Press carved a niche in the qualitative market by *reissuing* studies that originally appeared during a heyday of case study publishing in the 1960s and 1970s. With typically thin markets, more and more monograph-length studies were going out of print as harsh realities of increased publishing and distribution costs, coupled with a sudden preoccupation with corporate profit-making, turned venerated old publishing houses into corporate footballs. Able to bypass the expensive outlay for initial publication, Waveland was able not only to revive promising titles but even to set many of them on the road to becoming "minor" classics.

The original intent in developing the case study format was to keep costs low so that instructors could assign several monograph-length studies in lieu of having students purchase a single traditional text. The quality of the monographs in these series was high: attention was given to writing, and manuscript length was carefully monitored. (See, for example, Solon Kimball's Anthropology and Education Series, the Spindler-edited Case Studies in Cultural Anthropology as well as the Case Studies in Education and Culture, the Kiste-Ogan Social Change Series in Anthropology, and series published by several university presses.) Except in a few cases—with the success of Napoleon Chagnon's study *Yanomamö: The Fierce People*, first

45

published in 1968, undoubtedly topping the list—demand never quite met expectations. The potential of the case study approach requires a sophisticated level of teaching neither easily achieved nor easily adapted to the lecture hall. The unanticipated recycling of used copies by university bookstores cut deeply into the anticipated market costs for new ones, dampening publisher enthusiasm and driving up unit costs. Nevertheless, Spindler is quick to remind me that today, 35 years after its inception, the original Case Studies in Cultural Anthropology series is "alive and well," with some 58 titles in print and new cases being added every year (personal communication, May 1995).

Publishers are not bashful in informing their purchasing publics about text adoptions (sometimes listing all the institutions that have adopted a particular work) or boasting of how many "printings" their more successful texts have undergone. Beyond the boundaries of cultural anthropology, where ethnographies continue to hold their own, the market for texts dealing with issues of *method* far outstrips that for descriptive accounts. As a consequence, some of us who do not think of ourselves as "methodologists" find that our publication lists suggest otherwise. We are free to write what we want, of course. But there is a certain satisfaction in the assurance that what one is writing has some chance of being published and read.

A visit to the book exhibit at the national meeting of professional associations provides a good indicator of what publishers in each field believe is being used, particularly in classroom adoptions. Publishers try simultaneously to "read" their markets and to cultivate them. Like their artist counterparts, fieldworkers do not and cannot control the publishing world. Nor do we instruct publishers about "the market." Right or wrong, publishers instruct us. And like any art dealer, when a publisher tells you "Nobody's buying that stuff anymore," rest assured that particular publisher is not interested in what you are doing. Quite up to you if you want to keep on producing it, of course, and perhaps you should. Not all academics are concerned with being "in fashion." Just maintain your perspective and recognize your problem for what it is.

Teaching positions. Interesting that Becker includes mention of teaching positions as part of the "apparatus" of the arts. In doing so, he draws attention to the impact of teaching as *an occupation for practitioners of art* as well as a means of selectively recruiting new members. Not at all incidentally, teaching helps maintain a solid corps of enthusiastic followers more likely to exert their influence as *consumers of the works of others* than through what they themselves produce. Becker refers collectively to these enthusiastic neophytes as *trainees*:

> People study the arts seriously and semiseriously, taking courses, practicing difficult disciplines, devoting large amounts of time and other resources, often making substantial sacrifices and requiring them of their families and friends as well. Few of them ever become full-time professional artists. No art has sufficient resources to support economically or give sympathetic attention to all or any substantial proportion of those trainees in the way customary in the art worlds for which they are being trained. (1982:52)

The effect of costs incurred against potential income generated is important in the selection of art worlds, particularly among those dependent on self-support:

> Artists who lack substantial financial resources cannot do work which requires costly materials, equipment, personnel or space. Media like poetry and photography, requiring relatively small investments, thus attract many practitioners. (P. 95)

Clearly a gatekeeping function is at work here. Many hear, or believe they hear, the call; few are chosen. On the other hand, the status of beginner, hobbyist, or amateur offers a protective aegis; beginners often escape the harsh judgments directed at the serious devotee. There is tolerance, a certain spirit of encouragement shown toward promising "first works." That protective aegis extends to proto-ethnographers as well. The ethnographic endeavor has been joined by individuals making the most modest of claims, especially those who substitute experience and intuition for formal credentials. The oft-alluded-to accounts of "travelers, missionaries, and explorers" are a case in point. Such authors are better off to let others do their claims-making for them rather than presume to encroach on the sacred ground of the professional.

I have urged the same restraint on qualitative researchers who sometimes appear too eagerly to have embraced an "ethnographic method" they may not fully understand or have appropriated a label their work may not warrant (HFW 1987b). When in doubt as to whether one has produced genuine ethnography, my advice is to select a more cautious label (for example, case study) so that the work is not faulted simply on the basis of an ill-chosen descriptor. Should it prove subsequently to warrant the label "ethnography," let others confer it.

I do not skip lightly over the role of *training* in preparing fieldworkers. Pursuit of a graduate degree with the intent of making social research a career focus—today requiring the doctorate if one seeks a university position—must be among the more expensive career routes in terms of time commitments and tuition costs, especially given current occupational uncertainty. If one is unable to locate a source of funding, there are additional travel and living expenses to anticipate in meeting the requisite stint of fieldwork.

As with those who would pursue careers in art, researcher ranks, too, lack sufficient resources to lend more than partial support to any "substantial proportion" of the trainees who enroll in such courses. Yet the research requirements for many advanced degrees now allow, and sometimes require, a brief excursion into qualitative research. Students who pursue an extended field study may unexpectedly discover that they have lengthened the duration of their graduate program by a year or more, thereby increasing the risk of never completing it at all. For students in those social sciences where fieldwork can become an integral part of the career, such a risk is a calculated one. For students in the professional schools, the extra time may only prolong student status while involving them deeply in acquiring research skills they are never likely to use again. That does not mean the effort is necessarily wasted; to the contrary, the experience may prove one of the highlights of graduate studies and possibly of one's professional life, a point I will take up later. Nevertheless, Becker's observation is germane: There are many more trainees in qualitative research, all devoting large amounts of time and making substantial sacrifices, than will ever have opportunity to conduct further field research as "professionals."

The relationship between teacher and taught invites further comparisons between the "training" of artists and the "training" of fieldworkers. With the strong bias toward research that characterizes graduate programs, students can be batched in large numbers through introductory courses in both quantitative and qualitative approaches. Beyond such basic courses, however, opportunities for further study are constrained by the limited size of most graduate faculties, limited time of faculty members, and limited faculty experience in qualitative work. Some students develop a formal or informal mentoring relationship with faculty, but over the years I have spoken with numerous doctoral students well into a descriptive study who felt ill prepared and quite vulnerable in working entirely on their own. They do not speak lightly of the "sink or swim" position in which they find themselves. There are limited opportunities for graduate research assistantships, but even in those cases, fieldwork does not lend itself to apprenticing in a way that apprentices actually "see" the master at work. Further, wary faculty may attempt to redefine the professor-student relationship as a seemingly collegial one ("You really know as much about that as I do") to keep students from becoming overly dependent.

By comparison, "training" in the art world is set up on a model of close, almost intimate supervision. Not all trainees gain access to that intimacy, although even in institutions given to huge lecture classes, studio courses tend to be small, with a preference for hands-on instruction and individual tutoring. Master craftspeople and artists take on "apprentices" and "pupils," terms seldom heard in reference to the learning of fieldwork. Neither are our various schools, periods, or distinguishable styles named after the masters, part or present. There is no Michael Agar School, or Clifford Geertz School, or Malinowski School of fieldwork. We might look askance upon anyone committed too wholeheartedly to one successful field scholar, wondering if perhaps a young colleague mistakenly—or too enthusiastically—"apprenticed" rather than sought to gain intellectual independence.

The Patron Effect

Many years ago, anthropologist Alfred G. Smith proposed a contrast between two major and distinctly different audiences to whom his colleagues address their studies, audiences whom he labeled "peers" and "patrons" (Smith 1964). He illustrated the differences between the two audiences by providing a series of paired statements contrasting the research-oriented reports written for peers (that is, other anthropologists) with more popularly focused accounts addressed either to the public as patron-at-large or to some subset within it, such as introductory texts written for class adoptions, or papers addressed to professionals in other

49

fields (e.g., educators, public health specialists, sociologists). Briefly summarized, the contrasts he posed included the following:

- Regarding other cultures for their own sake, vs. offering cultural alternatives for the patron's way of life

- Analyzing the constants and variables between cultures, vs. emphasizing what is unique about each

- Presenting peers with a maximum amount of data, vs. assuming that patrons prefer a high ratio of explanation to information

- Linking past to present, providing explanations to peers in terms of causes, vs. presenting patrons with "value-oriented formulations and goal-directed explanations" involving evaluative criteria for judging how to make things better, thus anticipating how the future must inform the present

- Emphasizing a uniquely anthropological approach to cultural analysis, vs. the blending of disciplinary perspectives, especially including psychology and sociology

- Offering technical analyses and discrete conclusions warranted by scientific evidence concerning subsistence patterns, kinship systems, or material culture in reporting to peers, vs. presenting patrons with broad, aesthetically satisfying interpretations

Smith's writing was prompted not so much to pose the peer/patron contrast itself as to examine the impact of Ruth Benedict's widely-read anthropological classic, *Patterns of Culture* (1934) and what he described as Benedict's "Dionysian Innovation." Smith proposed his peer/patron distinction as a way of explaining why Benedict's book continued to enjoy a wide readership outside anthropology, yet found constantly diminishing support within it.

I found the peer/patron distinction provocative and useful, particularly in trying to understand the nature of the dialogue in "anthropology and education." As with any interdisciplinary endeavor, the audience for that dialogue is mixed. Anthropologists working in education who persist in "doing their own thing" have often missed the mark in efforts to reach their educator audiences; anthropologically oriented educational researchers fail to pass muster among their anthropology colleagues when they write for a patron audience of professional educators. The peer/patron distinction has also helped me read the literature and listen to the dialogue in other disciplines (psychology, as a prime example) in which my patience and interest are quickly lost in peer-oriented discussions but can sometimes be rekindled in more "pops"-oriented presentations addressed to patron audiences unimpressed with collegial in-talk.

In delving into art worlds, the "patron" notion takes on a different connotation, one more closely related to the concept of patronage. Although we do not recognize or refer to "patrons" as an influence on fieldwork, we most certainly have our equivalent of them. A patronage system, Becker points out, makes "an immediate connection" between what the patron wants and what the artist does. "Patrons pay, and they dictate— not every note or brush stroke, but the broad outlines and the matters that concern them. They choose artists who provide what they want" (p. 103). That places patrons in a powerful position vis-à-vis the artists they patronize. In turn, Becker observes,

> The ability to pick the best artists and commission the best work shows the nobility of spirit and character the powerful and wealthy think they possess, so that being a good patron supports the claim to high rank. (P. 100)

The education of the powerful and wealthy thereby becomes an important influence on what they will pay the artist to produce. In turn, their tastes stand to influence the taste of others. When they succeed at that, they enhance their claim to status and thus gain further recognition as patrons of the arts. Sometimes power and wealth foster an independence of spirit; when they do, patrons are in a position to indulge their personal tastes, oblivious to the acclaim of others:

> Stubborn patrons, sure of their own judgment, often ignore public criticism, and have supported much innovative and unpopular work. In any event, politically, financially, and socially powerful patrons often control opportunities to exhibit or to have performed the work they commission. (P. 100)

51

From the artist's perspective, the expectations are clear even when not necessarily every artist's dream: "The artist with a patron need only please that patron" (p. 100). The cost may seem high to the artist who feels constrained by a patron's fancy, but the artist with a patron has the comfort of knowing that there *is* a client. Whether commissioned on a piece-by-piece basis or through continuing sponsorship, such art is virtually guaranteed a market, with time and expenses negotiated in advance to the agreement, if not always to the total satisfaction, of both producer and patron.

We do not have "patrons" to support field-based research, but we have our equivalent in the funding agencies that support our work. It is more than a little disconcerting to recognize similarities between the sources for funding fieldwork and those "politically, financially, and socially powerful patrons" who exert their influence in art worlds.

Funding agencies announce what they are interested in funding, sometimes with broad goals and loosely administered grants, more often with narrowly defined objectives and tightly monitored contracts. Researchers reply, under some circumstances presenting their credentials, submitting formal proposals in others, in either case placing their skills at the bidding of those in control of the purse strings. Paradoxically, the more determined you are to carve out a role as an "independent" researcher, the more likely you are to find yourself conducting your work at the bidding of others.

To be truly "independent," you would have to join the unenviable ranks of struggling artists everywhere who attempt to support their own work. Like struggling artists, researchers who wish to maintain their independence usually support themselves through teaching, sandwiching research interests between full-time duties and short periods of unpaid leave, or accumulating paid leave through the institution of the academic sabbatical.

A seemingly ideal arrangement would be to garner funding that allows full time to devote to research of one's own choosing. There are funds that allow such freedom to a few fortunate recipients (for example, the five-year carte blanche grants of the MacArthur Foundation), but most unrestricted grants are for small amounts and limited time, such as summer research grants awarded by universities to their own faculties, or competitive grants like the Fulbright awards that support periods of up to a year of work overseas. Most funding comes with strings attached, so one is not really free at all. The funding agency, rather than the researcher, is in a position to dictate what is to be studied, in what fashion, for how long.

The successful grant-getting researcher is also likely to be drawn into a never-ending cycle in which the ability to continue a line of work is contingent on further funding, so that scrambling for grants becomes part of the work cycle. Time must be "borrowed" from present projects to seek out new announcements (the RFA or RFP, Request for Application/Proposal) and to prepare and submit bid-like proposals on future work. And just as artistic success can lock one into a particular style or medium, success in grant writing can doom one to writing similar grants forever. Satisfactory prior performance provides a strong basis for renewed funding, but it tends to lock one into following *essentially* the same line of inquiry in project after project.

For many years the so-called research universities have been recruiting some researchers on a self-sustaining basis, offering promotion in rank without the corresponding security of indefinite tenure: The position disappears when the researcher is no longer able to garner funds adequate to support continuing work. Although that does not create cohorts of starving researchers, it does create cohorts of anxious ones whose uncertain futures are linked to game-playing in the politics of grant-getting. Like their struggling-artist counterparts, "soft money" researchers nervously anticipate a future in which they may be able neither to please their former patron nor to find a new one.

The patron-researcher relationship is not restricted to those who conduct fieldwork, of course. It prevails throughout the research world, within academia, and among for-profit and not-for-profit agencies and independents alike. For qualitatively oriented researchers, the relationship poses a two-edged sword. Relatively speaking, fieldwork is difficult to monitor yet inexpensive to fund. Seasoned bureaucrats know that the time and costs to oversee modest little projects are about the same as for costly large ones. From a funding agency's point of view, big, expensive projects are preferable. In addition, fieldwork is not likely to produce the kind of dramatic results that reflect well on a sponsoring agency.

If patronage seems an unfortunate way to fund research (or art), the absence of such support is even worse! These days we may also be experiencing a bit of waffling among earlier supporters of qualitative inquiry. Some agencies seem to run hot and cold in their enthusiasm, at one moment insisting that every proposal include a qualitative or ethnographic "component" (frequently unspecified), and at the next moment funding only tightly designed studies that produce hard data rather than the sort generated by participant observation and open-ended interviews.

In days when funding went to academic institutions, rather than to named individuals in them, the oscillating between qualitative and quantitative orientations was less critical, for one could pull together teams of colleagues with requisite skills. Today's qualitatively oriented researchers—the younger ones, at any rate—must be more nimble-footed, able to conduct their work in quantitative or survey modes, if that is the order of the day, and able to contribute to a large-scale qualitative study if allowed or required. As noted, the trend has been for fieldworkers to add some "rapid" techniques to their fieldwork repertoire. It is not only art patrons who "choose artists who provide what they want" (p. 103); our patrons, too, call the shots.

Observing Conventions

Thus far I may seem to have indicted every source of restraint in the art worlds and, by analogy, every source of restraint on the lone fieldworker, except the restraint that artists impose upon themselves through too-well-internalized traditions or "conventions." I must correct that impression, for in practice the consequences of these dynamics are known to and tacitly accepted by everyone involved. As Becker observes (p. 29), "People who cooperate to produce a work of art usually do not decide things afresh. Instead, they rely on earlier agreements now become customary, agreements that have become part of the conventional way of doing things in that art."

I underscore this important point: Contemporary art worlds, both in Becker's sense and in the way I employ the phrase here, consist of *all* the people whose activities are necessary to the production of works that world defines as art. Thus works of art "are not the products of individual makers, 'artists' who possess a rare and special gift. They are, rather, joint products of all the people who cooperate via an art world's characteristic conventions to bring works like that into existence" (p. 35).

Although a *particular* convention may be revised for a particular work, the fact remains that artistic conventions cover *all* the decisions that must be made with respect to works produced. Becker inventories several of them:

- Conventions dictate the *materials* to be used, as when musicians agree to base their music on the notes contained in a set of modes, or on the diatonic, pentatonic, or chromatic scales, with their associated harmonies.

- Conventions dictate the *abstractions* to be used to convey particular ideas or experiences, as when painters use the laws of perspective to convey the illusion of three dimensions, or photographers use black, white, and shades of gray to convey the interplay of light and mass.

- Conventions dictate the *form* in which materials and abstractions will be combined, as in music's sonata form or poetry's sonnet.

- Conventions suggest the appropriate *dimensions* of a work, the proper length of a performance, the proper size and shape of a painting or sculpture.

- Conventions regulate the *relations* between artists and audience, specifying the rights and obligations of both. (P. 29, paraphrased)

Recognition of such conventions operating in art worlds prompts an examination of comparable conventions that impose upon both performance and product in fieldwork. Such conventions become especially apparent in the reporting phase, when others *must* be involved in order to realize the final product. Our *materials* prepared for publication, for example, include an adequate descriptive account presented in standard written English, with legible typed copy appearing on one side only of letter-size (A-4 size outside the USA) 16 lb. or better white paper, today one or more "ribbon" copies ordinarily accompanied by a perfectly-matched computer disk. The exact specifications here, as with conventions pertaining to "form," may vary slightly from one occasion to the next, but any researcher-author knows roughly what they entail *without ever having to give them a thought*. And that, of course, is precisely how conventions exert their

55

influence: We don't think about them because there is no need to; we simply observe them.

The fieldwork equivalent for conventions of *abstraction* include showing proper deference to our forebears as well as attention to theories and concepts currently in vogue. Better still, of course, to catch sight of the next wave. This task of "staying ahead of the curve" becomes more formidable every year, for today's fieldwork scholars, as Van Maanen points out, "must now know not only their Marx, Weber, and Durkheim but also be familiar with the works of Gramsci, Bakhtin, Habermas, and Rorty and *au courant* with the fashionable French such as Bourdieu, Derrida, and Foucault" (1995:27n).

Conventions for the *form* in which material and abstractions are combined have been drilled into us since kindergarten: Keep your work neat, provide ample margins, and give evidence of the niceties you have picked up along the way regarding the placement of footnotes, reference style, distinctions between first, second, and third order headings, and a logical exposition and flow of the account from a well-constructed problem statement to a well-thought-out, clearly warranted conclusion.

Similarly, you should give evidence of having internalized the *dimensions* appropriate for the kind of account you are preparing. In academic writing, for example, you need a sense of how long a sentence should be to lend an element of erudition; short, readable sentences can raise suspicion that you yourself seem not to grasp the complexity of the issues you address. You need a similar feel for paragraphing and for stringing paragraphs into coherent subunits and units. One of the finer sensibilities in this regard is in bringing the length and proportions of a journal article into proper alignment, or recognizing when a piece of writing simply must be of monograph length (and substance) to achieve your intended purposes.

Casually discussing this topic of article length with my colleague Phil Young, we found ourselves in easy agreement that fieldwork reported as ethnography must be of monograph length; anything less substantial than that (e.g., article, chapter in an edited volume) can be "ethnographic" but cannot be ethnography. We doubted that any ethnographer would disagree with us—though of course they well might—and yet we realized that neither of us has ever heard the question raised. Right or wrong, we just "knew." (Similarly, Allan Burns tells me that among ethnographic filmmakers, convention holds that to be genuinely ethnographic a film has to exceed 40 minutes in length.) We also recognize that there is no authority to which we can turn to confirm our convictions. Technically length is, or ought to be, as irrelevant as time spent in the field, in defining a proper ethnography. There are unstated, yet generally acknowledged, standards about such things, the very kind of "tacit understandings" that fieldworkers search out in other settings but take largely for granted in their own.

Finally, we can find parallels in conventions that regulate *relations* between the producers of fieldwork accounts and the consumers of them— their reciprocal rights and obligations. For example, we can withstand, expect, and sometimes even relish a degree of thoughtful criticism from those who read our accounts carefully, but we brook no nonsense from anyone who exercises the role of critic without meeting a prior obligation to be well informed.

Similarly, the producer of an account does not expect it to be plagiarized, or to be duplicated (in the literal sense) without credit. The technological ease of duplicating material—the making of *exact* copies—today raises thorny issues that confound another unresolved one: Should artists be entitled to a proprietary interest in their works after being compensated for them initially? If an art work gains in value after it leaves the artist's hands, should the artist receive additional compensation, or does appreciation in its tangible form belong only to a patron or dealer? Philosophically the question is interesting to ponder when we hear the astronomical prices paid to the resellers of art treasures, but anyone who has ever bought a secondhand book has similarly deprived its author of the benefit from that resale. The pleasure of finding my own fieldwork accounts for sale in secondhand bookstores carries with it the ambivalence of realizing that the shopkeeper will take more profit from each resale than I originally received as royalty. Becker's point—one I seem not to heed in this case—is that secondhand booksellers are part of my authorly world; both literally and figuratively, the "shelf life" of my fieldwork publications is entirely in their hands.

Audiences expect artistic works not only to be original but also to be worthy of time and money, which, after all, they must invest largely on faith. Whether paying for a book, ball game, or ballet, the consumer pays up front. Only afterward—usually too late to do anything about it—can audience members know for sure whether they have had their money's worth or have simply been "had." (Are you old enough to remember a time when you could actually listen to a musical recording *before* you purchased it? Maybe *those* were the good old days everyone talks about.) Truth in advertising is important to consumers and audiences alike; audiences do not like to be deceived. A study advertised as being fieldwork-based must be just that; a study claiming to be ethnography will be judged on that claim. Admittedly, we live in a world of media hype; we do not necessarily feel cheated if we purchase an account "destined to become a classic" that fails to meet such expectations. But stand clear of any audience led to believe it was going to be privy to a spectacular but has just been presented with a spectacular flop.

The Limits of Convention

Knowing the conventions must not be confused with observing them all to a T. To do that is to risk losing one's audience after all, paradoxically by being perceived as too conventional. Here might be another way to distinguish the craftsperson from the artist, for the former is recognized for consistently achieving the same standard of quality, time after time, while we may allow, and even expect, the artist to achieve something "unique and expressive." Conventions place a multitude of constraints on the artist, yet successful artists sometimes find ways to tweak convention's nose—in just the right amount, at just the right time:

> Though standardized, conventions are seldom rigid and unchanging. They do not specify an inviolate set of rules everyone must refer to in settling questions of what to do. Even where the directions seem quite specific, they leave much to be resolved by reference to customary modes of interpretation on the one hand and by negotiation on the other. (Becker 1982:31)

Becker cautions that artists tempted to free themselves from the constraints of the art world "lose or forego all the advantages the integrated professional more or less automatically enjoys" (p. 236).

> Remember that the conventional way of doing things in any art utilizes an existing cooperative network, which rewards those who manipulate the existing conventions appropriately in light of the associated aesthetic. (P. 306)

These seem strange words of caution, when one might instead expect Becker to exhort artists to free themselves from their cultural trappings, strike out on their own, and let the world beat a path to their doorstep. Bear in mind, however, that he is describing the system as he believes it actually works, offering a cool analytical look instead of an impassioned plea for creativity. In Becker's assessment, the fate of most artistic mavericks shows what happens to those who ignore the "crucial importance of organizational development to artistic change" (p. 300). He develops that theme:

> Artistic mavericks show what happens to innovators who fail to develop an adequate organizational support system. They can make art, but they do not attract audiences or disciples, and found no schools or traditions. . . . The history of art deals with innovators and innovations that won organizational victories, succeeding in creating around themselves the apparatus of an art world, mobilizing enough people to cooperate in regular ways that sustained and furthered their idea. Only changes that succeed in capturing existing cooperative networks or developing new ones survive. (Pp. 300–301)

Becker goes so far as to argue that artists can "predict accurately" the likely responses of others, that they more or less create the effect they want, because the artistic process itself is so conventionalized (p. 203). Obviously some artists are unusually canny in their powers of prediction. Others are simply more daring:

> The limitations of conventional practice are not total. You can always do things differently if you are prepared to pay the price in increased effort or decreased circulation of your work. (P. 33)

I am not so easily convinced that artists are endowed with the power of accurate prediction; in fact, that may be an important criterion that distinguishes successful (that is, recognized) artists from the rest. (Becker hedges his position, suggesting not that recognized artists always predict accurately but that they "guess wrong less often than non-artists do" about the effects they will create in others [p. 203].) I do think he is correct that, right or wrong, artists engage in prediction in the choices they must make throughout their careers. Anyone who has temporarily set an idea on the "back burner," or who has selected the less innovative but more-likely-to-succeed alternative between two ways of conducting or writing up a study, may recognize a comparable element of prediction in choices confronting the fieldworker. Becker proposes that we might track how artists make choices intended to enhance their reputations:

> It would be interesting to compare, for a variety of artists during different periods, the work they made and threw away, the work they made and kept but did not feel it safe, politic, or wise to show to anyone else (each choice reflecting the social constraints they operated under), and the work they actually displayed to the public as characteristic, the work they were willing to let decide their reputations and professional fates. (P. 207)

For some artists—and some fieldworkers—there is another side to this issue: the individual who rises above personal career deliberately to produce something unconventional, or who intentionally takes a risk that puts reputation in jeopardy on behalf of some personally felt higher purpose. In fieldwork, this sometimes occurs when our characteristic in-depth study reveals circumstances in which the researcher feels that some group is being oppressed, that some individuals are at risk in ways they themselves do not recognize, or that the public trust has been betrayed. Qualitatively oriented researchers have been noted for a tendency to link their approach with sociopolitical causes and to pursue openly ideological inquiries.

Similarly, an established artist might make a foray into new territory in order to pave the way for talented but unrecognized younger artists, stepping aside to let others have the spotlight. On a personal level, that might be summarized by noting that not all *prima donnas* are prima donnas. Art worlds are peopled by individuals, not a few of whom take delight in being different, free of convention rather than constrained by it. Such individuals face what Becker calls the "interesting and difficult dilemma" of being creative as well as reflective, innovative as well as repetitive and routine:

> To produce unique works of art that will be interesting to audiences, artists must unlearn a little of the conventionally right way of doing things they have learned. Totally conventional pieces bore everyone and bring the artist few rewards. So artists, to be successful in producing art, must violate standards more or less deeply internalized. (P. 204)

"Unlearning" may account for some artistic behavior, occasions when an artist deliberately goes against convention in striving constantly for ways to be interesting. Still, Becker may attribute too much uniformity to participants in art worlds, giving too much credit to the ability of cultures to replicate themselves, too little attention to the fact that no two individuals ever get exactly the same message or make sense of "culture" in exactly the same way. Whatever "explains" it, there is variation aplenty in all cultural systems. That variation is at once a source of internal tension in dealing with nonconformists and an impetus for change. Things may not change much, but neither do they remain exactly the same, no matter how much effort is devoted to trying to keep them so.

Artistic License Reconsidered

Among the dictionary definitions of license are ideas of intentional, exceptional, even excessive deviation from rule, convention, or fact, often for the sake of literary or artistic effect: thus, *poetic license*. I have followed Howard Becker's exploration of *Art Worlds* to draw comparisons between the real world of the recognized artist and the realities of the world of the fieldworker. Unlike subsequent chapters intended to underscore the creative, expansive side of fieldwork—as well as to point to some of the hazards and traps that await the unwary—this one looked for parallels in the way both artist and fieldworker move within complex, highly conventionalized, and rather restraining social networks.

If in some ways fieldworkers are engaged in an art form that allows them to indulge their artistic genius, they also are constrained by tacit rules—unspoken as well as spoken traditions imposed by myriad other social forces, past, present, and future. As native artists and craftspeople alike often explain to inquiring anthropologists, *of course* they do not have to follow the same patterns time and time again, *of course* they are free to think up a new design. They are free to do anything they wish. But they wouldn't consider actually doing so, not for a moment!

Fieldworkers are not so very different in the ways they regard their options. *Of course* they are (relatively) free to conduct their work any way they want. *Of course* they are (relatively) free to present it any way they want. But for the most part, they don't consider doing so, not for a moment. The traditions are firmly in place. If we do not observe them, how will others know that we ourselves recognize and understand them? Better perhaps to exhibit only a modicum of creativity. And if not just now, perhaps *after* the award of tenure or the success of a first and admittedly "somewhat more conventional" study. Timing is critical.

Taking stock of the expectations and conventions under which we operate, the artist-craftsperson does seem an appropriate analog for the fieldworker who, in the long run, must demonstrate that standards of rigorous scholarship have been observed in a work, rather than have it recognized only for demonstrating a certain artistic flair. Genius has been described as "1 percent inspiration and 99 percent perspiration." Fieldworkers can be guided by a similar ratio. There needs to be a spark. Just be wary that allowing as much as 1 percent for inspiration might prove a bit high.◉

PART TWO
THE FIELDWORK
PART OF FIELDWORK

I have a general idea about their life and some acquaintance with their language, and if I can only somehow "document" all this, I'll have valuable material.

—Bronislaw Malinowski
A Diary in the Strict Sense of the Term, 167

F ieldwork is correctly regarded as a time for gathering data, but it is not the only way or time for doing so, not the only label that points to field-based research, and not restricted to data gathering alone. Thus fieldwork has a broad meaning and a narrow one. For the title and scope of this book, I take the broadest of meanings: Fieldwork includes everything one does from outset to completion of a field-based study. Here in Part Two, however, fieldwork will be examined in its narrower sense, limited to that part of the research process when the fieldworker is actually "in the field."

Sociologists sometimes express a preference for the term "field study" (see, for example, Zelditch 1962) and leave "fieldwork" for their anthropological colleagues. Fieldwork never did belong exclusively to cultural anthropologists, or only to anthropology, and today it is sometimes used so broadly as to be synonymous with qualitative research in general, as in "taking a fieldwork approach." Anthropologists might once have preferred to be more protective of their special term "ethnography," but in some circles that term is used so widely as to be synonymous with the other two. Nevertheless, titling this book *The Art of Ethnography* might have suggested to some readers that I was writing only for anthropologists. Although I address fieldworkers more generally, it is worthwhile to keep in mind that for the activities described here in Part Two, "The Fieldwork Part of Fieldwork," how an anthropologist goes about it differs little, if at all, from

63

LIVERPOOL JOHN MOORES UNIVERSITY
LEARNING SERVICES

how any other fieldworker goes about it. The critical differences that distinguish among these orientations are in the mindwork that accompanies fieldwork, to be discussed in Part Three.

Today's researchers have been reared in an era when *everyone* has become more methodologically self-conscious—researchers in applied fields like education seem almost totally preoccupied with method—so it is not surprising that what was often referred to as ethnographic "research" in the past has become today's ethnographic "method." That fact is reflected in a course I have taught with a title already chosen for me: Field Methods in Cultural Anthropology. I was surprised to find myself teaching a cultural anthropology course with "methods" in its title. Younger colleagues, on the other hand, were uneasy when I proposed changing the course title to Ethnographic Research, concerned that students would not recognize that the focus of the class was "methods" nonetheless.

Part Two deals specifically with the art of the fieldwork-part-of-fieldwork. I examine fieldwork in terms of what I call its Basic Arts (Chapter 5) and then its Darker Arts (Chapter 6), the latter devoted to examining some disconcerting aspects of looking so closely into the lives of others. I begin the discussion (Chapter 4) by making a contrast between fieldwork and "just being in the field."◉

CHAPTER FOUR
FIELDWORK VS. (JUST) BEING IN THE FIELD

How ethnographic. In Morocco only several days and already I was set up in a hotel, an obvious remnant of colonialism, was having my coffee in a garden, and had little to do but start "my" fieldwork. Actually, it was not exactly clear to me what that meant, except that I supposed I would wander around Sefrou a bit. After all, now that I was in the field, everything was fieldwork.

—Paul Rabinow
Reflections on Fieldwork in Morocco, 11

In this chapter and throughout the book I make an important distinction between "being in the field" and doing fieldwork. I have added the word "just" to help mark the distinction. Fieldwork does, of course, require one to be "there"—in the field—but Rabinow's observation "Now that I was in the field, everything was fieldwork" notwithstanding, simply being in the field is not enough to make "everything" fieldwork.

For example, we might be reluctant to accept the idea of a telephone pollster calling coast to coast as fieldwork. But what about a survey researcher canvassing door to door? A mailed questionnaire may be sent from afar, but what about a face-to-face interview when someone begs and promises to take "only a moment or two of your time"? Newscasters touting live, on-the-spot coverage invariably include interviews held at the site of real or invented media events "in the field." By their very presence, can they be said to be doing fieldwork? And what about the individual who accepts an assignment away from the home office or local campus to learn what it is like to live abroad, or what it is like at the other end of the corporate ladder? Need one go far afield to do genuine fieldwork? Conversely, does any research conducted far afield qualify as fieldwork?

On five occasions in my professional lifetime I have spent the better part of an academic year living in another country. On only three of those occasions did I conduct fieldwork. I have also conducted fieldwork under circumstances where I traveled to my field site by automobile, almost without exception returning home every evening. One of those occasions was overseas, three were research inquiries conducted while I was in residence on my home campus, and all were within a 25-mile radius of where I resided. An additional study was conducted literally in my own backyard. Yet I consider them all to be bona fide examples of fieldwork. So, wherein lies the distinction between just being there and doing fieldwork?

To me, the essence of fieldwork is revealed in the intent behind it, rather than by the label itself. To repeat the working definition offered earlier, fieldwork is a form of inquiry in which one is immersed personally in the ongoing social activities of some individual or group for the purposes of research. Fieldwork is characterized by personal involvement to achieve some level of understanding that will be shared with others. There may be discomfort and hardship aplenty connected with the experience, ranging from the distractions of diarrhea or lost luggage to the despair of personal failure or lost hope, but the extent of one's suffering and sacrifice are not factored into judgments about the worth of the fieldwork *as fieldwork*. What does count is what others stand to learn as a consequence of the fieldworker's investigative effort *through the subsequent recounting of it*. Fieldwork in its narrow sense must become part of something more, something that catapults it beyond the range of personal experience, beyond simply "being there."

I take a firm position that there is no such thing as "unreported research." No one can claim to have "done all the fieldwork" who has not also written it up. Fieldwork is validated only through the requisite reporting that results from it. Fieldwork that does not get written is partial and incomplete; alone, it amounts to no more than what may have been anything from an intellectually rich to a psychologically devastating personal experience.

Taking the position that the information shared from the experience is what validates fieldwork activity, I do not intend to dwell in any great length on what kind of image a fieldworker should try to create, how to be a gracious guest in a strange place, or how to avoid giving offense by pointing, gesturing, or refusing food or drink. The travel guides can coach you as to how and how not to place your head, hands, and feet from one country to the next; I'll concern myself primarily with what's *inside* your head—and heart. By the time we get to Part Three we can leave the rest of your body out of it entirely and focus exclusively on what is going on in your mind. I must leave it to you to keep your mind in touch with your heart. Although I do press for more candor in fieldwork reporting, I will make only brief mention of the role of emotion, in the final chapter. Emotion is another aspect of fieldwork that has begun to receive special attention (see, for example, Ellis 1991; Kleinman and Copp 1993) as we come to regard it as a potential ally in our work rather than a sign of weakness in the worker. Here is where art can embrace as a treasured source of energy and insight what the more systematic approaches manage too often and too well to exclude.

That's what I mean by fieldwork; it may not be what you mean by it. You may have had something not quite so all-consuming in mind. For example, you might have been wondering about adding some unstructured interviewing to a field research project originally designed to gather information through a mailed questionnaire. Or you may have decided to encourage your field assistants to record *their own* impressions, as well as to record respondent comments, even when their comments are not related directly to the questions on the printed form.

Let me propose a critical distinction between *doing fieldwork*, a process that assumes a degree of wholehearted commitment, and simply *borrowing a fieldwork technique or two* to enhance or complement an essentially quantitative or survey approach. Admittedly this is a matter of degree, and of personal judgment and professional association as well. An anthropologist able to study in a group or setting only intermittently, or for an embarrassingly short period of time, may nonetheless refer to the research— even if it consists mostly of what Rabinow calls "wandering about"—as fieldwork. A quantitatively oriented researcher who spends an unusual amount of time doing essentially the same thing before initiating more systematic inquiry might insist, and rather indignantly, that the research—the *real* research, that is—didn't begin until some hard data were collected.

In the sense I use the term, fieldworkers are researchers who make the commitment that full-time—or at least longtime—on-site presence demands. As quoted in the epigraph to this chapter, Rabinow was not wrong to observe, "now that I was in the field, everything was fieldwork," but it was his *intent*, not his presence, that made it so. There were others (rather few, it seems) in that Moroccan hotel, but they were not "in the field" and they were not doing fieldwork.

At the same time, I have not meant to kindle or capitalize on interest in fieldwork, only to suddenly turn the tables and define it in such a way that few can meet rigorous criteria of time and commitment. I do not mean to disparage, or intend to discourage, the efforts of any quantitatively oriented researcher contemplating how to add qualitative dimensions to an inquiry, whether through observation, interviewing, or simply "wandering about." Nor do I disparage the work of qualitatively oriented researchers who may employ these techniques but whose research pursuits neither demand nor allow the level of involvement ordinarily associated with fieldwork. It certainly is not necessary to commit to fieldwork to want to be perceived as a sympathetic and humane researcher, interested not only in collecting information but interested as well in the people from whom one is collecting it. For the fieldworker, however, achieving some depth of human understanding provides the rationale for the whole endeavor. I restrict my use of the label *fieldwork* to research involving the intimate, long-term acquaintance necessary to gain that understanding.

Data Gathering as Technique

When I began to write anthropological texts, I followed the conventions of my training. I "gathered data," and once the "data" were arranged in neat piles, I "wrote them up." In one case I reduced Songhay insults to a series of neat logical formulas.

—Paul Stoller
In Sorcery's Shadow: A Memoir of
Apprenticeship among the Songhay of Niger, 227

FIELDWORK VS. (JUST) BEING IN THE FIELD

Field workers have started accumulating case material in somewhat the same fashion as the social scientist in modern communities, the influence of whose methods is perceptible in the newer techniques.

—Audrey Richards
"The Development of Field Work
Methods in Social Anthropology," 305

"If I can only somehow 'document' all this," Malinowski muses as he jots in his personal diary, "I'll have valuable material." That is certainly the crux of it—figuring out how to record and how to convey to others what the fieldworker has observed and experienced firsthand. Early anthropological fieldworkers were especially interested in the classification and distribution of "peoples." The kinds of data they sought lent themselves to categorical statements so that groups could be compared. (Radcliffe-Brown insisted that anthropology was in effect "comparative sociology.") Those early fieldworkers were unabashed data gatherers. What set them apart from an earlier generation of so-called "armchair anthropologists" was that they set out to collect their own data rather than preoccupy themselves with data gathered (and reported) rather more haphazardly by others.

Understandably enough, the practice of and pressure for gathering "hard data," thus to be assured of having *something* to report, persists today. The problem with such a focus is, as it has always been, that gathering data can become an all-consuming task. The first casualty of the fieldwork experience can be field experience itself. I have seen this happen even with students pursuing modest fieldwork exercises, when some slick technique turns their study around by offering (and delivering) nice, neat numbers that leave the people, and more creative original purpose, behind. Anthropologist Audrey Richards, quoted in the epigraph immediately above, noted this tendency of fieldworkers to start working "in the same fashion as the social scientist in modern communities." She was writing in 1939!

There will never be an end to the kinds of data-specific techniques to be developed, and computer capabilities now make it possible to handle previously unthinkable quantities of data. We have entered a data-obsessed era, and fieldwork practice has been affected accordingly. I peruse professional journals and newsletters apprehensively, aware that today's fieldworkers-in-the-making are being introduced to a far broader range of field-oriented techniques in courses taught by others than what they get in any course I teach.

For more than a quarter of a century, I have been teaching such courses, sometimes with a broad "qualitative" approach, more often with an anthropological emphasis on ethnographic research. At one time my course was designed primarily for doctoral students in education and related professional schools; more recently, as noted, it has been taught as Ethnographic Research in a department of anthropology. I have always been satisfied that the course is "solid." Students experience field-based research firsthand. They do not simply read about it or talk about it, they do it—at least to the extent possible within the time constraints of an 11-week term. Yet I cannot help wondering whether my students get too soft a version of fieldwork, a version gained largely on my own in the days before texts and courses on anthropological "methods" or qualitative research had become the vogue.

As I had suspected (and feared), what today's students are expected to know—at least when cultural anthropologists convene to set standards for what *others* should teach and *others'* students should know—the list of procedures and techniques is formidable. For example, from one widely distributed report (Plattner 1989), here is a sampler of what "a professional ethnographer, of any theoretical persuasion, specializing in any geographical area, ought to master " (p. 30), and thus, presumably, ought to have been taught in a comprehensive training program:

- Structured direct observation of events: time allocation analysis, interaction analysis

- Observation and recording of the physical environment, to include how to read (and preferably how to draw) topographical and other maps, and, as needed, skills in remote sensing, soil analysis, biomass transects, etc.

- Still photography and, increasingly, video recording

- Approaching informants, maintaining an interview situation, and "disengaging" from an interview in a manner that leaves open the possibility for further interviewing

- Designing and pretesting interview schedules—to include semi-structured interviews on both broad and narrow topics (e.g., child rearing for the former, a specific ritual for the latter); an open-ended life history/life cycle interview; an ethnogenealogical interview; a structured interview

- Systematic interview techniques to determine the limits of a domain of study (e.g., free listing), informant judgments of the similarity among items in a domain (e.g., triad tests, free pile sort, successive pile sort, paired comparison); belief frames and componential analysis; consensus analysis, cultural model research, analysis of decision making

- Data recording, coding, and retrieval skills, perhaps through a database management system

- Finding and using published and archival sources

- Specific training in the use of the Human Relations Area Files

- Thematic analysis of textual materials

- Use of microcomputers for word processing and data manipulation

- Translating and back-translating interview schedules and interview protocols

- Developing a research design for the quantitative testing of a hypothesis

- Designing a data codebook; coding and entering data into computer files

- Statistical processing of data and interpretation of statistical results (e.g., level of measurement, central tendency, dispersion, regression, significance levels)

- Using common multivariate methods such as factor analysis, cluster analysis, and multidimensional scaling

- Reading and interpreting graphs, plots, charts, and tables

71

- Understanding basic sampling theory and common sampling procedures

- Exploratory data analysis to produce and interpret stem and leaf plots, scatter plots, bar charts, cross tabulations

Such a list, rigorous as it may be, is only one among a number of forces urging—and in a sense, pressuring—me to become more data-oriented in thinking about, pursuing, or teaching fieldwork. My own microcomputer rests opposite me at my desk. I use the term "rests" advisedly, for if microcomputers pick up any vibes at all, mine surely suspects by now that I will never begin to tap into all its capabilities, even to present or display information. It will never have an opportunity to show me what it can do to list data, lay out frequencies, or produce spreadsheets or contingency tables. But it can—and does—taunt me with all that might be, were I a bit more computer literate. When I inadvertently clicked Grammar on a menu bar while working on a draft of this manuscript, my computer had the audacity to question my high percentage of passive constructions and lengthy sentences, habits my personally chosen reviewers have not had the heart—or nerve—to mention for years. And the manual accompanying my new laser printer exhibits an audacity of its own, contradicting the style requirements of my professional journals by admonishing me about under-lining, referring to such practice as a "throwback" to the typewriter that will make my work look unprofessional!

On the other hand, simply by sitting opposite it, the computer taunts me with a voracious appetite that makes me feel I am "wasting" not only its potential capabilities but its capacity as well. If nothing else, at least shouldn't I try to fill it up with data? Its kind of data, of course—which are not necessarily my kind of data. *The answers to my best questions do not lie in the accumulation of data.* John Seidel, author of the computer program The Ethnograph, has expressed the problem this way:

> My concern is that, because computer technology allows us to deal with large volumes of data, we will be lured into analytic practices and concep-tual problems more conducive to breadth analysis rather than depth analysis. We will start trading off resolution for scope. (Seidel 1992:112)

Breadth as a tradeoff for depth points exactly to the problem that concerns me as fieldwork appears headed once again to become a data-driven activity. And that is why I make the distinction between fieldwork and just being in the field. Neither activity achieves a higher purpose or confers more dignity than the other, but I think fieldwork demands a different mental set and achieves a different goal, one that is *qualitatively* different from a quantitatively driven study. You can have either, and you can have both. But they are not one and the same.

Not only do professional journals and my computer remind me of this preoccupation with data; the mails, the telephone, and the vexing research issues posed by students and colleagues serve as constant reminders of the tilt toward the more systematic and scientific aspects of our work. Colleagues representing other disciplines also gently goad me with the reminder that their data and mine differ. Theirs, they insist, are "real," at least in the sense of being external to themselves, while they argue that as a fieldworker I "make up" most of what I call data.

The telephone rings from near and far with authors or publishers seeking advice or critical review about how far to go in allowing qualitative inroads into territory once the exclusive domain of the psychometricians. I have the impression that today finds many "closet quantifiers" having to hold a brief for qualitative/descriptive approaches currently in vogue, approaches that they do not find sufficiently rigorous. Their resolution is a ceaseless effort to shore up qualitative research procedures and to perpetrate the same criteria for assessing them that have become standard in the dialogue of traditional quantitative researchers—for example, criteria like objectivity, reliability, validity—an issue to be taken up in Chapter 7.

The mails bring more of the same. Even "e-mail" boasts its own network of qualitative researchers in a dialogue of immediacy once reserved for the hard sciences. I receive announcements and flyers advertising workshops and summer institutes not only available to my students but offering to upgrade me! As someone who *teaches* fieldwork, I am encouraged to enroll myself as a student. At the moment of originally drafting this chapter, an announcement appeared on my desk about another of the highly regarded National Science Foundation-sponsored Summer Institutes on Research Methods in Cultural Anthropology. The workshop experience promised to upgrade my skills on topics not all that different from criteria listed earlier outlining minimal skills that I should be teaching my students:

- Structured interviewing techniques, such as free listing, pile sorts, ratings and rankings

- Using computer software for questionnaire construction, data analysis, and text management [Software programs familiar to qualitative researchers include ANTHROPAC, The Ethnograph, Folio VIEWS, NUDIST, QUALPRO, TACT, etc. These programs undergo constant revision and critical review. See, for example, Weitzman and Miles, 1995; or a helpful summary of software programs and characteristics in the appendix of Miles and Huberman 1994.]

- Direct observation data: coding behavior, time allocation

- Social network analysis: map structure, detect cliques, measure centrality, autocorrelation

- Detecting and visualizing relationships among variables: measures of similarity and distance, multidimensional scaling, cluster analysis, correspondence analysis, and loglinear modeling

A bit of content analysis suggests the shifting emphasis in the offering of this workshop in recent years. Everything familiar to an old-fashioned ethnographer like myself is getting tightened up, the focus shifting toward "neat" data—the kind that can be plugged into a computer program—rather than to neat (that is, intriguing) problems that only a fieldwork approach can address. Key informant interviewing, for example, has disappeared as a topic, as has open-ended interviewing. "Structured interviewing" has become structured interviewing *techniques*. More tellingly, "interviewing" itself has shifted toward *questionnaire construction* guided by a computer software program. "Principles" of direct observation yield to the collection of direct observation *data*. And whole new analysis-oriented facets have emerged, one focusing on social network analysis, another on detecting and visualizing relationships among "variables."

An aspect I initially found so delightful in the work of many field-oriented researchers, one that made it refreshingly different from the experimental and social psychology of the day, was the absence of those mysterious qualities called "variables." I never have figured out the logic in calling the variable you manipulate the independent one and the variables you leave alone as dependent, and I have never met a variable I liked. I share Michael Agar's preference for what he has termed the "holistic perspective," the belief that "an isolated observation cannot be understood unless you understand its relationships to other aspects of the situation in which it occurred" (1980:75). "From a holistic point of view," he continues, "the very idea of a variable is enough to make one skeptical" (p. 76).

I repeat that the purpose of this writing is not to rail against any such efforts to make fieldwork more scientific. Nor will I inventory excesses that sometimes seem intended to displace fieldwork rather than render it more effective, or to make fieldwork not only more efficient but virtually researcher-proof, safe from the foibles of fieldworkers themselves. But in drawing attention to the art of fieldwork, and contrasting fieldwork with data gathering, I hope that fieldwork's unique contribution as an interpersonal approach to seeking human understanding can be preserved and strengthened, even as the disciplines that have fostered it seek self-consciously to become more scientific and, in the process, to look more and more like each other.

Who Are Today's Fieldworkers?

I think a dramatic shift has been occurring that now finds many cultural anthropologists acting more like traditional social scientists—the very trend Audrey Richards detected more than half a century ago—at the same time that researchers from allied professional fields are drawn toward ethnographic or more broadly qualitative approaches. It is important to recognize that anthropological research has never been limited to fieldwork, although fieldwork has always been the *sine qua non* for anthropologists and remains so today. Efforts to make the study of anthropology more scientific, cultural anthropology included, have caught fieldwork in their sweep. The benefit is the positive influence this has on the data fieldworkers gather; the risk is that data gathering is being mistaken for fieldwork.

By making a crisper distinction when we speak of one or the other, fieldworkers of any persuasion ought to feel free to develop the artistic potential in their work, at the same time that many anthropologists are endeavoring to establish themselves more broadly as social scientists. Russ Bernard, himself a major force on behalf of a more rigorous anthropology, sums it up thus:

> In the past, cultural anthropologists were more concerned with description than with explanation and prediction . . . Many anthropologists today, however, are interested in research questions that demand explanation and prediction, questions like: Why are women in nearly all industrial societies, socialist and capitalist alike, paid less than men for the same work? Why is medical care so hard do get in some societies that produce plenty of it? (1994a:176)

These are, indeed, among the kinds of issues addressed by today's social scientists, and anthropologists have a contribution to make from their holistic, comparative, cross-cultural perspective. But it is crucial to realize that, while individual researchers can bring such a perspective to their inquiries, problems of such magnitude are not well suited to fieldwork approaches. Only by carefully rephrasing a question to ask, "What, if any, contribution toward understanding this issue might be made through fieldwork?" is there any possibility of a match between research question and research strategy when the issues addressed are so sweeping.

There is little question that the social sciences will turn more and more to systematic approaches to address such issues or to meet increasing demands for explanation and prediction. That should afford ample opportunity for those social scientists who find their identity as "scientists," but it is all the more reason to recognize fieldwork as a different form of inquiry attracting an ever-expanding network of qualitatively oriented researchers. The latter are less concerned with data per se, and more concerned with an approach that offers insight into the human experience through the fieldworker's own firsthand experience.

Fieldwork as Intimate, Long-Term Acquaintance

It is by intimate, long-term acquaintance with culture groups that one gains insight. . . .

—Robert Redfield
In Rubinstein, ed., *Fieldwork*, 126

Fieldwork takes time.

Does that make time the critical attribute of fieldwork? According to ethnographic tradition, the answer is yes.

In our hurry-up world, that tradition has been buffeted by time itself and has been steadily eroding. An ideal of two years (or longer) in the field as the standard, perhaps related to the success of Malinowski's inadvertently long fieldwork among the Trobrianders (he had to sit out World War I because of his Polish ancestry), has today been shortened to half that time at best. Realities of academic life make even 12 months a standard that few committed ethnographers can afford (often literally) to make, and old-fashioned fieldwork of any sort is almost out of the question for privately funded agencies that do not have the luxury of making "contributions to knowledge." Against the pressure to reduce the expectation of at least a year in the field is the compelling argument that anyone contemplating field-work should be present at least through a full cycle of activity. For most of the peoples among whom the earlier anthropologists worked, that cycle was related to the annual cycle of the growing seasons. The *ideal* of 12 months—minimum now having become maximum, as it often does—remains well entrenched.

That does not mean a 12-month minimum is always observed, but fieldworkers whose stay must be brief usually go to some length to explain their circumstances and shore up doubts raised by a shorter tenure. One way to do this is to pay close attention to identifying and observing through whatever constitutes a "cycle" of activity, and to recognize how short recurring cycles may be nested in larger ones.

In micro studies as well as in macro ones, fieldworkers often link brief visits that extend over a long period of time, so that the brevity of the periods when one is actually in the field is mollified by the effect of long-term acquaintance. Anthropologist Simon Ottenberg's review of his fieldwork among the Igbo (formerly the Ibo) of southeastern Nigeria provides an example:

> I spent 15 months in 1952–53 in a group of villages called Afikpo, another like period in 1959–60 at Afikpo and nearby Abakaliki Town, and brief visits to Afikpo in the summer of 1967, the winter of 1988, and in March and October 1992. (1994:91)

Ottenberg notes a paradox: "What is curious about my Igbo project is that the field research aspect has not been that extensive, but the writing has been." He goes on to explain, "Thus, long-term research has a somewhat different meaning for me than for others who have spent more time in the field" (p. 92). I suspect that many fieldworkers would admit to giving a "somewhat different meaning" to the time they have actually spent on site. What could ever be enough?

By whatever standard, Ottenberg's time in the field is extensive. Numerous others honor the same tradition—William Crocker, for example, whose fieldwork among the Canela, most recently reported in 1994, now extends through an accumulated total of more than five years and eleven trips that date back as far as 1957. Interestingly, however, the basis for Ottenberg's claim that his is long-term research is the duration of the period in which he has been *writing*. It might have been equally appropriate, although a bit unusual, for him to have staked his claim on the basis of *thinking* about the Igbo for a long time. If at first blush such a claim seems a bit strained, we might turn the tables to realize how seldom we are treated to studies that even mention the extent of deep and profound thought in reflecting on the fieldwork experience. Perhaps you already recognize some advantage in taking the broad view that takes fieldwork to be far more than only time spent in the field.

The question remains: Does time alone guarantee breadth, depth, or accuracy of one's information? I think not. Mere presence guarantees rather little, and most assuredly there have been fieldworkers and research problems that required less time to get the job done. Margaret Mead, for one, was neither bashful nor apologetic about the short duration of her fieldwork experiences. She was quick to note that she considered herself a quick study who could accomplish a great deal in a relatively short period. What might Redfield have meant by *intimate* long-term acquaintance?

How Intimate Is Intimate?

Many years ago I got to thinking about the crossover point in fieldwork when I felt I knew enough about even one individual—let alone an entire "people" such as the Kwakiutl—in sufficient depth that I could write with confidence because I felt I knew what I was talking about, beyond the relatively safe practice of quoting "informants" (or, reflecting current efforts

to be more collaborative, "participants") verbatim. I settled on three admittedly arbitrary criteria to serve as indicators of the adequacy of my personal
knowledge about another individual's life. Although strange in the telling,
they continue to caution me as reminder of how little any of us customarily
knows about others except for the most intimate of our *personal*—rather
than our professional—associates.

My first criterion asks, *What do I know of this person's sleeping arrangements?* Optimally, this means "sleeping" in both a figurative and a literal
sense. Figuratively, who are and who have been the person's "sleep with"
partners, at present and, preferably, in the past as well? Are there known
offspring resulting from any of these unions? As for sleeping in the literal
sense, where does this person sleep? What constitutes bed and bedding,
how many others share it, how many others sleep in the same area but not
the same bed, and where do others sleep who share the same quarters (for
example, do young children have a room, or rooms, of their own; what
accommodation is made for guests)?

I must admit surprise in discovering how my own assumption that
middle-class Americans all sleep in beds has had something of a jarring
effect. I was asked to stand in for a prospective out-of-town investor
interested in the purchase of a large old house near my campus that had
been remodeled to accommodate a number of profit-making rental units
for students. Master key in hand, an obliging manager insisted that we
inspect every apartment, following the courtesy of only the briefest knock
on the door. I was relieved that with what seemed his incredible invasion
of tenant privacy only one resident was at home early on a Sunday afternoon.
But my shock at the rudeness of the approach was matched by the surprise
of finding only one bed among some 15 apartment units. Everyone else
appeared to sleep on mattresses or air mattresses on the floor, almost as
many using sleeping bags as bedding. Nothing could better have underscored for me the transient nature of student life and cramped conditions
under which many students live—or how out of touch I am with their
lifestyle. The experience reminded me how much we assume, yet how little
we really know, about how others live, including others whom we perceive
as "just like us."

My second criterion asks, *What do I know about how this person's laundry
gets washed, dried, and put away?* Although the topic does not, at first blush

(a blush that might be literal as well as figurative), seem as intimate as knowledge about sleeping arrangements or sexual partners, laundry not only is an intimate item but is also revealing of personal relationships and/or the division of labor within a household. I first became aware of the social significance of laundry while reading Oscar Lewis's *La Vida*. As I recall, an older woman was "keeping" a much younger man, and one of the things she did to "keep" him was to look after his laundry. For her, that meant taking care to have clean underwear folded and tucked away in a drawer each day, ready for the following morning. As a single young adult I found the idea of having someone else look after your underwear surprisingly intimate. As a child, my laundering needs had been attended to by my mother, assisted at various times by a maid or "cleaning lady." After I began living away from home (summer jobs, other employment, the military, returning to graduate school), laundry was my own responsibility—at least whenever I was living too far away to "save up" and bring it home on intermittent visits.

Those who do their own laundry also reveal something of their lifestyle. When and where does the laundry get washed? And does the amount of laundry washed at one time provide an indirect measure of personal wealth? Ever notice a not-quite-dry white shirt on a young waiter or busboy in a Third World country and realize it was probably the only formal work shirt he owned? Even closer to home, I could not resist commending a student I encountered on the campus one brisk autumn morning for what I interpreted initially as robustness, as he was clad only in a T-shirt and what appeared to be gym shorts. He shook his head to the contrary. "Laundry day," he offered by way of explanation. I nodded in acknowledgment and revised my too-hasty interpretation. On whatever day he suddenly finds himself without clean clothes to wear, every possible item of clothing is taken immediately to a coin-operated washing machine at the local launderette.

Anyone who has resided where laundry is only done by hand has probably had to give undue attention to "getting the laundry done"—the task requires the cooperation of another human rather than simply the convenience and availability of a machine. During my first field experience, living and teaching as a bachelor on a Canadian Indian reserve, I washed (in an electric wringer-type machine powered by the school's own generator) and hung out my own laundry. That I did my own laundry amused the adults and baffled the children. "Where's you Mom?" the children asked whenever they caught me "hanging out the washing" to perhaps-dry in the damp coastal climate, reminding me that in their eyes certain tasks were properly the responsibility of a wife or mother. It was perfectly all right for males to *help* with the washing, even to *do* the washing when someone was indisposed. It was not all right, not "customary," for an adult male to live alone and have to do such things for himself. To the consternation of her male siblings, one of the older girls in my classroom offered to do my washing for me to save me from what she felt must surely be my ineptness or embarrassment.

On four subsequent occasions when I have lived overseas for extended periods, finding a way to get the laundry done has always made it necessary to have at least a part-time housekeeper. Although cooking and cleaning posed no serious problem, the very thought of having to wash laundry in cold water in a plastic tub on the floor posed an insurmountable one. Yet on my most recent assignment overseas, a young American male teaching in a rural area in southern Thailand insisted that local Muslim women wouldn't even *consider* washing underwear for him.

Laundry is but one of many possible indicators of the level of a researcher's intimate knowledge. How anyone's laundry gets done is itself curiously personal, something a researcher might learn about with no intention of reporting. I mention it as a reminder that our knowledge of everything or everybody else (and of ourselves as well) is invariably partial and incomplete. Part of the art of fieldwork lies in being attentive to and able to acquire ordinary everyday information, rather than letting our assumptions fill in the gaps or using a questionnaire as likely to elicit socially correct responses as honest ones. A related art is to be able to communicate to a reader what it is that we do know, with what degree of certainty, rather than to try to create the impression of seeming to know everything. We must also be able to communicate to those among whom we conduct our research the extent to which details of their ordinary daily lives are of professional interest, not because we necessarily intend to report them, but because having such detail at our command helps to ensure that what we do report is both accurate and properly contextualized. Accustomed as we are to the *role* of researcher, it is also difficult to realize how foreign that idea is in many groups. My Kwakiutl pupils helped me appreciate that point with their customary response to almost any question I posed, "What do *you* want to know for?"

To compensate for the seemingly mechanical nature of my first two criteria for gauging intimate knowledge, my third criterion tests a quite different domain. As researcher, I ponder for myself, *How much do I know about any of my informants' grandmothers?*

I have no particular set of questions in mind about grandparents, only the general issue of a researcher's familiarity with family members who, living or not, may be presumed to have had an influence on an informant's life. Grandparents play important roles in that regard, exerting an influence that a researcher would be unlikely to have observed firsthand but might reasonably be expected to know about as a consequence of extended life history interviewing or being privy to occasions for family reminiscing.

I have described three criteria that serve as a sort of personal litmus test and reminder of how little any researcher is likely to know about those among whom we work or study. They are not a guideline for conducting research, even for the sort of traditional person-centered fieldwork that most interests me; they are only a means for me to reflect on the depth of my knowledge. None of the three was relevant in problem-focused studies in which it was more important to try to represent multiple views on what the problem was or how it might be addressed. Yet a phrase like Redfield's, reflecting on "intimate, long-term acquaintance," is not to be shrugged off lightly. My criteria address the question of what one might expect to know as a consequence. Every fieldworker needs some kind of guidelines for assessing the adequacy of his or her expanding knowledge base. And even as a child, I became aware of how much more I felt I understood about my playmates or school chums whenever I had the opportunity to meet their parents, to visit their homes, or, especially, to meet their grandparents. (Come to think of it, that may have been the earliest hint that someday I might find my métier in the study of cultural acquisition.)

Some fieldworkers assess the adequacy of their accumulating knowledge by their ability to shop local markets and prepare local foods. The ability to make appropriate jokes, especially in a different language, is another measure. Redfield's own student, the late Sol Tax, took the challenge of negotiating the construction of a new house for his mentor as the opportunity "to test and expand his practical knowledge of Guatemalan culture" in the village where the two of them were conducting research (Rubinstein 1991:199).

In fieldwork we grapple constantly, both within ourselves and with our more objectifying colleagues, about how much we know and whether we ever know *with certainty*. On the basis of intimate, long-term acquaintance, however, we should be satisfied that even our conjecturing is well informed, regardless of whether we necessarily are able to produce evidence that might "prove" us right. While our critics may express concern about the paucity of our hard data, we find solace in knowing that we know more than we feel we need to tell. Part of the art of fieldwork is learning to live with such tension. And part is finding ways to distinguish what we can present as fact from what we only surmise on the basis of extensive firsthand experience.

Performance First, Then Script

In exploring analogies between fieldwork and art, fieldwork itself might be viewed as a performing art. In drawing that analogy, we find a paradox. In fieldwork, performance comes first, script comes later. The two may be totally unrelated.

Fieldwork—how one "acts" while in the field— is not a performance that all give well. Those who do give it well are unlikely to be applauded, for the audiences to one's performance in the field ordinarily remain unimpressed unless the fieldwork goes badly or interferes with perform-ances of their own. The audience that would be interested—one's critics or colleagues in research at the time, or one's students at a later date—are not privy to what is going on. Except for scrutiny by a tiny set of technical readers who must grant conditional approval—a funding agency, a disser-tation committee, an institutional review board, or a governing body with authority to grant or deny access—the *public* announcement of the perform-ance follows rather than precedes it, that section typically titled "Method" or "How I Proceeded with This Study."

One important rationale for, and benefit from, conducting extended rather than short-term fieldwork is that those in the study cannot maintain a pretense or pose forever. Sooner or later things will get back to normal, and the fieldworker will be able to observe the everyday life of real people, not an individual or group putting on an act to win favorable review. Time works the same for the fieldworker as well; one can play at being Mr. or Ms. Goody-Goody just so long. The "real" you will show through soon enough, even without the additional hazards of social or physical isolation, bureaucratic misunderstandings, or external factors over which you have no control. Fieldworkers may feel especially vulnerable to being "put upon." They want access to the knowledge those in the setting have. For the information they seek, how much should be given in return?

A further analogy with performance is with an actor's lot—of "waiting in the wings," awaiting one's cue to go on. Since the days of Franz Boas, experienced ethnographers have bemoaned time spent waiting for events to take place, or for informants who show up late or not at all. As one of my students noted in frustration in a written field report, "Anybody was never around during the interviews." "Waiting" is sometimes described as the primary activity in long-term fieldwork, waiting that is reckoned in weeks and months rather than mere hours or days. One might characterize fieldwork as an inquiry process in which the researcher's task is to *distill time*, his or her own endless waiting magically evaporating in the final account so that the reader jumps from one action to the next with a terse phrase such as "From 10 days to 2 weeks later . . ." "Not until they become adults . . . " or "In the *Winter* Ceremonial, by contrast. . . ."

I do not mean to make either a virtue or an art out of waiting, but time and timing are a genuine "cost" in fieldwork. Living as we do in a society predicated on the notion that time is money, I cannot escape a feeling that much of the effort ostensibly devoted to making fieldwork more scientific is really directed at making it more expedient, less time-consuming, and thus less "costly."

Is efficiency itself relevant here, or is this a problem created by confusing fieldwork with techniques of data collection? Time is what most modes of inquiry either compress or overlook. Perhaps the kinds of individuals drawn to fieldwork have an intuitive regard for the important workings of time in the present, just as historians have regard for the important workings of time in the past. Thus to hurry through is to miss the point of what both fieldwork and life itself are all about. Can anyone clearly demonstrate that efficient fieldwork is better than inefficient fieldwork? One way fieldwork might be allied more closely with art or science is with the calculated, intentional efficiency we associate with the latter. Fieldworkers, by contrast, often get caught in situations where they have no alternative but simply to tough it out and let time run its course. We cannot hurry the lives of those about us, only our own. Compare this with the determination on the part of the data-oriented researcher to get the data collection phase over and done with, in order to get on with the "real" work of analysis that lies ahead.

After the script is completed, the major performer in the fieldwork drama—the fieldworker—may appear to disappear from sight and site alike, as was the custom when accounts were rendered in the third person and left literally to tell themselves. Today's fieldworkers are encouraged to put themselves into their scripts, but we do not expect them to burden us with their hardships or regale us with self-reports of how splendidly they conducted themselves.

And thus the performance goes unremarked. We have only the account as rendered by the fieldworker for making our judgment as to the nature of the performance itself. That underscores the importance of what comes out of the experience rather than what one puts into it.

First things first, however. Part Two continues with two chapters directly concerned with the art of in-the-field fieldwork. There is a definite "work" cast to this part of the discussion, a sort of all-this-will-be-worth-it-someday approach. A review of some of the personal rewards and satisfactions of fieldwork is reserved for the book's final section.

CHAPTER FIVE

FIELDWORK: THE BASIC ARTS

There may be kinds of information that are in fact vital to the task of anthropological analysis but that are fairly consistently excluded from our field notes—in other words that we have conventional criteria for identifying observations as data that are inappropriate for the kinds of hypotheses and theories we wish to develop in our analysis. The frequent assertion that anthropology is an art as well as a science might depend precisely on the unsystematic or unreflecting way in which we accumulate part of our basic data.

—Fredrik Barth
Preface to *The Social Organization of the Marri Baluch,* x

This chapter is as close as I come to presenting a fieldwork manual. It brings me perilously close to dwelling on the techniques and strategies of fieldwork as craft, although I will focus on the less systematic aspects related to the experience rather than on data gathering per se. At the same time, behind every strategy or technique employed in fieldwork there needs to be sound human judgment—an artistic decision guided in large measure by what passes as ordinary courtesy and common sense. I have made "Courtesy and Common Sense" my first subheading, to precipitate out some pervasive elements in fieldwork before dealing with topics more customarily addressed in such discussions. Under the unconventional subtitles "Being There," "Getting Nosy," and "Looking Over Others' Shoulders," I then review fieldwork's major dimensions: participant observation, interviewing, and archival research.

Courtesy and Common Sense

On first thought, participant observation would seem to be the obvious choice as a starting place for discussing the basic arts involved in fieldwork.

On second thought, centering on participant observation hopelessly confuses whatever is unique to fieldwork with the display of everyday courtesy and common sense.

A fieldworker can easily offend through inappropriate behavior, comment, or question. But fieldworkers are not clairvoyant; they, too, are subject to making social errors. If it takes thoughtful explaining to get out of a tight or embarrassing predicament that one shouldn't have gotten into in the first place, that is certainly not an art limited to those who do field research. Nor are those who do fieldwork necessarily gifted in the handling of human relations. I have heard colleagues reportedly successful at fieldwork ask rhetorically, "Can you imagine *me* doing participant observation?" and a voice inside me whispers, "Well, frankly, now that you mention it . . . ."

Presumably the human relations aspect of fieldwork is enhanced for those to whom such qualities as empathy, sympathy, or at least everyday courtesy and patience, come naturally. I see no evidence that such qualities can be taught, or that they show themselves to be particularly abundant among the practitioners of certain disciplines to the exclusion of others. The consequence of anthropology's supposed humanizing message seems not, in my experience, to be any more or less evident in the everyday behavior of anthropologists than of ordinary folk. If it were, then to be a member of an anthropology department would be the envy of members of every other department on the campus.

The idea of "participant observation," which James Clifford characterizes as a predicament transformed into a method (1988:93), can raise a straightforward question: How does one go about being artful when assuming so obvious a role? I recall a colleague in the 1960s who flat-out rejected any proposal he was asked to review that explained, or attempted to explain away, the question of method with the simplistic response "participant observation." Michael Moerman, writing in the postmodern heyday, has observed that participant observation, "once anthropology's secret shame," had subsequently become "the fashionable focus of its self-absorption" (1988:68). Nevertheless, participant observation will surely continue to occupy the preeminent role Russ Bernard ascribes to it as the "foundation of anthropological research" (1988:148). It is all encompassing, yet, Bernard continues, it is "not really a method at all." Rather, it is "a *strategy* that facilitates data collection in the field—all kinds of data, both qualitative and quantitative" (p. 150). Employing it as a strategy requires common sense.

Viewed as a strategy, participant observation needs to be examined in terms of what it is that brings fieldworkers into a setting in the first place and whether they are well situated to learn whatever is to be learned. This is where many qualitative researchers get off on the wrong foot, somehow confusing the fact of their physical presence with the hope that simply by "being there" they will be able to observe or experience what they are interested in observing and experiencing. Two questions to ask in that regard are, "Can whatever I want to study be 'seen' by a participant observer at all?" and, if so, "Am I well positioned to observe those phenomena?" These questions need to be followed by a third one: "What are my own capabilities for participating and observing in this situation?" Many descriptive studies intended to be pursued through participant observation have elected a time-consuming approach with only an outside chance that the researcher proposing them will ever have the opportunity to "see" whatever purportedly is to be observed.

To illustrate: Years ago I remember talking with a student who had heard of an Alaskan village where television was about to be introduced. Intrigued with the possibilities of ethnographic inquiry and the tradition of village studies, the student asked whether I thought ethnography would "work" as the appropriate research strategy for a study of the impact of television on village life and, if so, how I would approach it.

My personal reaction was, "Why bother?" The broad sweep of a community study did not seem warranted with such a narrowly focused and poorly posed question. I replied that on a well-funded project one might assign an ethnographer to *every* family, or, lacking such generous funding, one might assign a lone researcher to any household willing to have a longtime observer. In either case, the purest observer would not want to influence the results and therefore would be hesitant to describe the study as one on TV's impact, yet a live-in observer in a village household might prove far more entertaining than TV fare, the researcher's presence creating the very kind of distraction that dedicated participant observers try desperately to avoid. It looked to me like a low-yield investment of researcher time to catch a few possible comments and to record some TV watching. Even then, at the end of the year how would anyone actually assess "impact"? The proposed project seemed to illustrate what Fredrik Barth has described as a tendency to confound *process* and *change* (Barth 1994a:76).

Granted that the village had been without TV before, was the occasion for introducing it all that interesting? It was not the inefficiency of the research strategy that bothered me so much as the mismatch between the magnitude of the problem and the magnitude of the investment in time and resources to study it. A year devoted to a study of village life in modern Alaska ought to be a provocative experience and rich source of data. A commitment of that sort seemed to warrant a more imaginative scope of work than tracking TV viewing and attempting to assess—or guess—its impact. I gently asked whether the student could think of any other ways to get relevant information if the social impact of TV was his burning issue?

Another example illustrates the complex cross-over (or heavy residue) from tightly designed quantitative studies to the creative use of qualitative ones. This time *sampling* was the bugaboo. A student in a seminar I was presenting overseas was interested in studying what she called "discovery learning." In my suggestion that participants engage in some modest field research during the course of the seminar, she saw an opportunity to try her skills at classroom observation. But she had become distraught over a major obstacle she foresaw and made a special appointment to discuss it with me. "I have always understood that any school or classroom in which I do observations must be selected by random sample," she explained. "What if the school and teacher I happen to draw isn't using discovery learning?" Her faith in sampling procedures for subject selection was as profound as her misunderstanding of when to apply them. Common sense should have guided her to a setting where she was likely to find the phenomenon of interest; questions of frequency and distribution were beyond the scope of her proposed inquiry.

I was intrigued that this student felt bound so rigidly to sampling procedures in spite of the fact that hers was to be an exploratory case study. It signaled that my explanations about qualitative research were not powerful enough to dispel her previously held beliefs about how "research"

89

is supposed to be conducted. There was room for some teaching here, but there was also a challenge for me to try to learn what I could about the beliefs associated with "research" from my workshop participant. Might that be where the real art is in all inquiry: recognizing what might be learned as situations present themselves? If so, then, as anthropologist Mariam Slater once caricatured it (1976:130), whether or not you eat soup with a chicken head floating in it is rather incidental to the business at hand. What counts in fieldwork is *what is going on in your mind.*

Even to describe participant observation as a "strategy" may be going too far, except to prompt researchers to seek an opportune vantage point for seeing what they want to observe. The element of strategy turns on two complementary questions to be reviewed over and over:

- Am I making good use of the opportunity before me to learn what I set out to learn?

- Does what I have set out to learn, or to learn about, make good use of the opportunity presenting itself?

What is going on in the researcher's mind is critical to all this. If nothing is going on, not much is likely to come out of the experience except experience itself, with a possible residue of "empathy, a rapport high, and headnotes," in Roger Sanjek's terms (1990:238). This is not unlike actors whom we criticize for simply "mouthing words" rather than getting into their role. (I address this issue more fully in Part Three, "Fieldwork as Mindwork.") It may seem strange thus to separate mind from body, but the distinction helps to underscore the difference between what others observe us doing as we go about fieldwork—how we get around and conduct ourselves—from what is going on in our minds as we go about it.

How researchers move their bodies around is not what makes art out of fieldwork. Nevertheless, one can offer suggestions as to how to move about with sufficient grace as to be perceived graciously by those with whom we hope to interact. I have identified four areas of social behavior that seem especially important for the successful and satisfactory conduct of field-work—its *performance* aspects, if you will. None is unique to fieldwork. I regard them collectively as no more than the demonstration of everyday courtesy and common sense.

1. *Gaining entrée and maintaining rapport.* These two terms, joined so often as to have become a single and sometimes trite phrase in fieldworker accounts, mask a great deal of the angst associated with fieldwork, especially among those who have never done it and who worry that they may not be successful in achieving its personal dimensions. I remember a young graduate student in anthropology who returned from a difficult (not impossible, just difficult) year of fieldwork in the Canadian Far North anxious to communicate to his fellow students not only how terribly important this aspect of fieldwork was but also that these were critical aspects for the *duration* of fieldwork, not just a pair of tasks to be attended to first thing on arrival.

Maintaining rapport presents a continuing challenge through the very presence of an intrusive and inquiring observer forever wanting to know more and to understand better. The long-term nature of fieldwork, and the likelihood of both physical and emotional/intellectual isolation, exacerbate interpersonal tensions: Fieldwork can be its own worst enemy. I know because I've been there. No one was stealing my mail during the year of my induction into fieldwork as village teacher on a Canadian Indian reserve. There simply were times when there was no mail for anyone to bring, or only unimportant mail when important mail hadn't been sent. A couple of families *were* regularly relieving the school of a few gallons of fuel oil; I needed to maintain perspective more than I needed to maintain rapport, for I had not been sent to the village as an agent of the government with a primary responsibility for safeguarding that fuel supply.

2. *Reciprocity.* There is an art to gift giving. There is something of an art to gift receiving. These arts are by no means unique to the conduct of fieldwork, but fieldwork entails a subtle kind of exchange, one that often involves gifting across cultural boundaries where exchange rates may be ambiguous or one wonders what to offer in exchange for intangibles such as hospitality or a personal life history. Whether, and how much, to pay key informants, for example, always presents a problem. Grant-rich investigators are concerned that they may offer too much, while resource-poor graduate students are concerned that any payment at all is a further drain on already overtaxed resources. Employing local field assistants, or choosing a dwelling to rent or a family with whom to reside, invariably puts

researchers at risk of siding with factions or otherwise being accused of being partial, parsimonious, or extravagant—and perhaps all of these at once.

Conventional wisdom cautions fieldworkers to remain as neutral as possible, especially when new to a site, but that option is not always open in the field. Conversely, one must learn how to manage being "put upon" by those who recognize the inherent fieldworker vulnerability to requests, when success depends on being able to make requests of others. If as fieldworker I am unsure what I may need from you by way of help or information at some future time, I have to be cautious in turning down requests you make of me at present. At the same time, I dare not fully reveal how vulnerable I feel, lest you impose unduly. Such decisions are not made easily. Along with extending the depth of one's understanding, long-term commitment extends both the depth and the duration of one's vulnerability.

One-shot interviewers or pollsters have it easy. At most, they may be hit up for a cigarette or a ride to town. They don't stay around long enough for requests to start escalating, as they inevitably do over time. Questions such as whether to pay a standard rate for interviewee time ought already to have been worked out as a matter of project policy. On the other hand, a request for food, money, medical assistance, or a job can put a resident fieldworker in an awkward bind, damned if you do, damned if you don't. In the abstract, a firm policy seems advisable ("Sorry, I just don't loan money—to anyone."), but in the world of diplomacy, everything remains negotiable, and fieldwork requires the art of diplomacy. One seeks knowledge in the professional role of researcher but prays for wisdom in the personal roles that make it possible.

3. *A tolerance for ambiguity.* Another admonition that becomes trite in the saying but essential in the doing is the need to remain as adaptable as one is humanly capable of being, to exhibit a "tolerance for ambiguity." In terms of priorities, perhaps this point deserves mention first, yet one can hardly claim that all fieldworkers exhibit this quality or that only fieldworkers need it.

There is no way anyone can train or prepare another for all the vagaries of fieldwork any more than one can train or prepare another for the vagaries of life. Of course, there is no way one can pass on to another the quality of tolerance, either: Merely saying it does not make it so. But there have been times in my own fieldwork (and life) that with nothing more than the cliché to sustain me, I have managed to eke out just a bit more patience than I thought I could muster. Someday the admonition to develop a "tolerance for ambiguity" may be helpful in your own work (and life). Simply suppressing a too-hasty comment or reaction is a good step in this direction.

Fieldworkers would hardly go wrong to take "tolerance for ambiguity" as their *professional* mantra if it is not by nature a personal one. I have seen it treated exactly that way in a summer workshop designed to help prepare teachers for assignments in the Alaskan bush. I was unable to think of any other phrase that might someday have proven more helpful. The workshop instructor used the expression so often that participants groaned every time he repeated it, and they presented him with a special T-shirt designed with that slogan on it. By the following winter, I assume that his message took on more significance as daylight hours and patience shortened and the realities of bush living began to take their toll.

I have heard the phrase "life shock" in reference to a related problem. Those of us who make our entry into the real world via protected mainstream lives and respectable academic routes—the usual pool from which fieldworkers are recruited—are not necessarily well versed in the harsher realities associated with life itself. During those years we spent in the library *studying* about life, everybody else was knocking about in it. We may never have witnessed anyone dying, the sort of thing genteel folk do in hospitals, out of sight. We were even less likely to have witnessed a birth, especially in my day. The ragged and deformed may also have remained out of sight. All those statistics we read—poverty, illness, accidents, violence, abuse—may suddenly materialize for a fieldworker whose most traumatic experience to date had been a ticket for speeding.

The ambiguity comes in the meaning of human life, which proves not to be endowed with such universal reverence as we ourselves have been schooled to believe. "How many children do you have?" you inquire of your Ndebele informant in southern Africa. "Six, maybe five," he responds, leaving you to wonder if he really does not know how many children he has. But that is exactly why he has answered with such calculated ambiguity. When he last saw his children, there were six. In the interim, something may have happened to one of them, even if they all were OK this morning. And anyway, one does not want to provoke fate by taking anything for granted.

Not even natural disasters—fires, floods, earthquakes—shake us from our Western belief, or faith, that essentially we humans remain in control. We have the proof. Even our language comforts us: fireproof, earthquake proof. Foolproof! Fieldwork can sorely test the belief that we exert such control. A tolerance for ambiguity is an essential element in the art of participant observation.

4. *Personal determination coupled with faith in oneself.* Self-doubt must be held in check so that you can go about your business of conducting research, even when you may not always be sure what that entails. In part this means being able to maintain balance in the face of what anthropologists have termed "culture shock." Michael Agar describes it this way:

> The shock comes from the sudden immersion in the lifeways of a group different from yourself. Suddenly you do not know the rules anymore. You do not know how to interpret the stream of motions and noises that surround you. You have no idea what is expected of you. Many of the assumptions that form the bedrock of your existence are mercilessly ripped out from under you. (Agar 1980:50)

And that's only half of it; whatever shocks you probably was not what you originally set out to understand. The complexity of your task grows before your eyes, with more and more you want to understand as you realize you understand less and less. At such times you cannot help wondering if any fieldworker before you has confronted anything quite like this!

Rest easy—no one about to undertake fieldwork can ever answer exactly what will be encountered or exactly what is to result from a descriptive inquiry. If they could, there would be no point in doing the research this way, for our studies are constructed in the doing. Even hard-nosed experimentalists recognize, as Ludwik Fleck observed 60 years ago, that if a research experiment were well defined, it should be altogether unnecessary to perform it (Fleck 1979[1935]:86). The more that is known about a topic, the less likely a qualitative broadside of the kind that results from fieldwork may be best suited to explore it further. There is a becoming level of uncertainty in this work, but you must be prepared for the unsettling experience of constantly having to set and reset your course.

Should you feel so baffled by what confronts you that the only recourse you see is to record "everything," you will realize that certain "everythings" take precedence over others. What do you see and hear that strikes you as most important? How might you direct the attention of a newcomer to this setting? How can you best distill its essence for a reader who will only be able to "see" through your eyes or "hear" through your ears? Description is the starting point, Square One. You need never be at a loss as long as you remember you can always go back to description when you feel stuck.

Being There

Used in its broadest sense, participant observation is so all-encompassing that it can refer to virtually everything qualitative researchers do in pursuing descriptive/naturalistic inquiry, cultural anthropologists do in pursuing ethnography, sociologists do in pursuing a field study, and so forth.

Here I take participant observation in a somewhat narrower sense that makes it the complement to interviewing rather than inclusive of it, although that still leaves it to cover any field activity not specifically related to some form of interviewing. Its essence is captured, although oversimplified, in the phrase "being there." In a chapter with that title, Clifford Geertz offers a lighthearted image of the "proper" role of the fieldworker:

> What a proper ethnographer ought properly to be doing is going out to places, coming back with information about how people live there, and making that information available to the professional community in a practical form . . . (Geertz 1988:1)

Somewhere between "going out to places" and "coming back with information . . . ," every fieldworker has to achieve some workable balance between participating and observing. There is always a question of whether those two processes constitute discrete functions or are hopelessly intertwined in the very act of anyone being anywhere, but it is comforting to have our own special label for what we do to reassure ourselves that *our* being there is different from anyone else's. That self-conscious role is what we examine when discussing participant observation—how we can realize the potential not simply of "being there" but of being so agonizingly self-conscious about it.

How to participate effectively, how to observe effectively (especially that), how to keep the one from interfering with the other, and how to get others to act "naturally" while we try to appear nonchalant about our own presence—those are the confusions and challenges of the *participant* dimensions of the participant observer role. They, in turn, are confounded by the perennial problems of the process of observation. Those include what to look at, what to look for, and the never-ending tension between taking a closer look at *something* vs. taking a broader look at *everything*.

Many sources are devoted to the topic of field observations and participant observation (two recent additions are Adler and Adler 1994, and Jorgensen 1989). I, too, have joined in efforts to demystify that which cannot necessarily be explained, in a recently revised paper, "Confessions of a 'Trained' Observer" (HFW 1994a[1981]). My purpose in that writing was to help neophyte fieldworkers recognize what the problems are, rather than to offer simple solutions for resolving them. Each of us addresses the problems in specific ways in specific cases; there are more-or-less appropriate adaptations, not definitive answers. But no old-timer is going to forsake an opportunity to offer a bit of advice. My suggestions here underscore the dilemmas and inventory the options that confront the participant observer.

Doing Better Participant Observation; Using Participant Observation Better

- You may tell others you are "just observing" and may satisfy their curiosity, but do not believe for a minute that there is any such thing as "just observing." A lens can have a focus and a periphery, but it must be pointed somewhere, it cannot "see" everywhere at once; in Kenneth Burke's aphorism, "A way of seeing is a way of not seeing" (1935:70). Our marvelous human eye has its scotoma, its blind spot; the analogy to fieldwork has been duly noted (for example, by Crapanzano 1980:ix).

  When you are not sure what you *should* be attending to, turn attention back on yourself to see what is it you *are* attending to, and try to discern how and why your attention has been drawn as it has. What are you observing and noting; of that, what are you putting in your notes, at what level of detail; and at what level are you tracking your personal reactions to what you are experiencing? Kleinman and Copp (1993) suggest that note taking is not complete until you go back over your notes to make "notes-on-notes." The point is to ensure that you are coupling your analysis to your observations (rather than putting that task off until later), and to help you remain attentive to your own processes as a human observer. Don't worry about all that you are *not* getting; focus on what you *are* getting: Observe yourself observing.

• Review constantly what you are looking *for* and whether or not you are seeing it or are likely to see it. You may need to refocus your attention to what is actually going on and discard some overconceptualized ideas you brought into the field (such as "watching" decision-making or "observing" discrimination). Begin by looking for recurring patterns or underlying themes in behavior or action. That should include patterns of things *not* happening as well as things that are happening. The latter kind of observations are most likely to be made comparatively, for example, "Back home this would be a major source of stress, but here no one seems to concern themselves." You will probably catch yourself becoming prematurely evaluative, particularly when righteous indignation tells you what people *should* be doing but are not. In case you don't recognize it, that's culture at work. Yours, not theirs! Tracking your own "shoulds" and "oughts" may provide valuable insight into your own processes as an observer.

Another kind of comparative question that can help focus your observations is to reflect on what a fieldworker of another persuasion within your discipline, or schooled in a different discipline entirely, might find of interest in a setting. Take the economist's concern for the allocation of scarce resources, for example. Questions addressing the distribution of resources can prompt fresh insight for a fieldworker who may not have thought about what is in short supply in a seemingly affluent community (for instance, time) or what seems to be in abundance (perhaps time, once more) in one stretched for resources.

In the course of opportunities for fieldwork, watch also for recurring themes in your own evolving career that lend focus and continuity to it. A common thread running through my own work is a focus on cultural acquisition. In any setting where I am an observer, I find myself asking, What do people (individually, collectively) have to know to do in order to do what they are doing here? And how do they seem to be transmitting or acquiring that information, especially in the absence of didactic instruction?

• I doubt that any observer can sustain attention for any great length of time. Be prepared to discover that observation itself is a mysterious process. At the least, it is something we do "off and on," and mostly off; we cannot meaningfully sustain passive attention. We compensate for that by "averaging out" our observations, reporting at a seemingly constant level of detail that implies we are keener at this than we are. A realistic approach for the fieldworker is to recognize and capitalize on the fact that our observations—or, more accurately, our ability to concentrate on them—are something comparable to a pulse: short bursts of attention followed by inattentive rests.

Capitalize on the bursts. Be especially observant about capturing little vignettes or short (but complete) conversational exchanges in careful detail. You could never capture all the conversation you hear about you, and you neither want nor need to. But what conversation you do record needs to be recorded in sufficient detail that you can report it verbatim. Beginners often gloss their observational efforts in a way that leaves them with no *reportable* data. Every statement they record is paraphrased *in their own words*, rather than in segments of conversation as actually spoken. A guideline I suggest is: What you do record, record in sufficient detail that, should the need arise, you would be able to report it directly from your notes. I am not suggesting that you actually report that way—fieldnotes don't usually make for great reading—but I urge you to record pertinent information at that level of detail. Otherwise, why bother?

• Try to assess what you are doing (that is, your participation), what you are observing, and what you are recording, in terms of the kind of information you will *need to report* rather than the kind of information you feel you *ought to gather*. (More on this idea of remaining goal-oriented is coming in Chapter 9.) If you think you might need certain information, by all means record it, but keep asking yourself whether or how you intend to use it.

- Reflect on your note taking and subsequent writing-up practices as a critical part of your fieldwork "work." There is a balance to be struck with writing up fieldnotes. For some, note taking is one (and perhaps the only) activity in which they feel they are really "doing" research. They may be tempted to overwrite because of the satisfaction note making brings. I worry about them less than I worry about those who resent the time that must be devoted to writing and who procrastinate and thus make the task increasingly formidable. If you are one of the latter, I suggest you try to discover how short you can make entries that nonetheless satisfy you for their adequacy, and then find a way to make that level of note making part of your daily routine (e.g., finishing up yesterday's notes while having your second cup of morning coffee). However you approach it, you must make note making sufficiently "doable" that you always do it, rather than put it off. It may prove to be a chore, but it need not become a dreaded one if you follow the simple rule of keeping your entries up to date. There isn't much sense to go out and get more if you haven't digested what you took in last time. (For more on fieldnotes, see Sanjek 1990; for more on writing them, see Emerson, Fretz, and Shaw 1995.)

Most of what you observe will remain in a form that Simon Ottenberg calls "headnotes" (1990:144-146), but some of it must make it into written jottings, whether simple or elaborate, that will eventually prove invaluable. Your elaborated note making also provides a critical bridge between what you are experiencing and how you are translating that experience into a form in which you can communicate it to others. Make a practice of including in your notes not only standard entries about day, date, and time, accompanied by a simple coding system for keeping track of entries, but also reflections on and about yourself—your mood, personal reactions, even random thoughts—that may later help you recapture detail not committed to paper but not "lost," either.

Note taking is not the only kind of writing for you to consider at this stage. There is something temporary about any kind of notes that effectively says the "real" writing will come later. What is to prevent you from doing some of that "real" writing as fieldwork proceeds? Instead of putting everything in an abbreviated note form, take time frequently to draft expanded pieces written in rich detail in such a way that they might later be incorporated into your final account. Disabuse yourself of any idea that as long as you are doing fieldwork, note taking is the only kind of writing you should do.

The key to participant observation as a fieldwork strategy is to take seriously the challenge it poses to participate more, and to play the role of the aloof observer less. Do not think of yourself as someone who needs to wear a white lab coat and carry a clipboard to learn about how humans go about their everyday lives. If you find you are comfortable only by remaining distant and aloof, why do you insist on describing yourself as a participant observer? Perhaps a more formal approach will get you what you want to know, far more efficiently. Fieldwork entails more than data gathering. If you just want "data," turn your emphasis to activities that get you data. Semistructured interviewing might be a good compromise. If that doesn't do it, turn to more structured forms of interviewing (to be discussed next) that lead to questionnaires and surveys. Consider also the possibility that you may not have a natural affinity for fieldwork, especially if you begin to feel that it is getting in your way rather than helping you *make* your way.

At the time this manuscript was undergoing its major revisions (academic year 1994–95), I had the good fortune to be corresponding with Peter Demerath who, with his wife Ellen, was conducting fieldwork in Papua New Guinea. The Demeraths were more dramatically situated than any other beginning fieldworkers I knew at the time, and I was anxious to solicit their thoughts on the essence of fieldwork while they were deeply immersed in it. Peter's response gives a sense of the fieldworker's participation as performance, making oneself "believable."

When I think of the "art" in fieldwork, and ways in which the artist rather than the scientist is called for, I think primarily of how much of what we are trying to do here is to present, or compose, both personas and projects that are appealing and attractive (or at least comprehensible) enough, so that people will talk with us and ultimately participate in our research. In this sense, perhaps much of the art of fieldwork lies in effective public relations.

We find that we do many things—housework, pumping water, chewing betelnut, playing soccer and volleyball, chatting, greeting, poling a canoe, eating sea turtle stew after having just seen the animal slowly and painfully butchered—with an eye on how these things are perceived by the people here. We hope they will regard us and our actions as attractive (or non-threatening) to the extent that they will regard us as fellow human beings. It seems to us that the anthropologist must constantly attend to the "composition" of this public persona, and perhaps this is one of the areas where the art of fieldwork is visible. (Peter Demerath, personal communication, February 1995)

The Demeraths did not go halfway around the world to chat, play volleyball, or pump water, and ordinarily they would have had no opportunity at all to pole canoes or eat sea turtle stew. They were doing whatever intuition and common sense guided them to do as "fellow human beings," participating in the activities of others in the hope that those others would participate in their research. Their strategy addresses the concerns reviewed at the beginning of the chapter: gaining entrée and maintaining rapport, reciprocity, a tolerance for ambiguity, and personal determination coupled with faith in themselves. There are no guarantees. But any experienced fieldworker will recognize that this is what genuine *participant* observation entails.

Getting Nosy

A ready topic for debate among experienced fieldworkers is whether interviewing or participant observation is the key dimension in the work; which is "more important"; and which logically should precede the other when initiating a new inquiry. Again, the best answer seems to be "It depends." Interviewing, the other major fieldwork activity to be discussed, includes a broad spectrum of activities, but it is easier to define. Participant observation remains as the residual fieldwork category that includes anything that is not some kind of interviewing.

I distinguish between the two in recognition of the profound difference in what fieldworkers do when engaging in participant observation—used here in the sense of experiencing—and interviewing. It is the difference between passively accepting what comes along, information that is virtually handed to us, and aggressively seeking information by "getting nosy."

In the simple act of *asking*, the fieldworker makes a 180-degree shift from observer to interlocutor, intruding into the scene by imposing onto the agenda what he or she wants to know. That does not make questioning a sinister business, but there is a quantum difference between taking whatever happens to come along and taking charge of the agenda. The difference might be likened to the contrast between being served an institutional or hosted meal and ordering from the à la carte menu of a restaurant. In the first case, one takes what is offered; in the second, one makes personal preferences known.

There are artful ways to conduct interviews, artful ways to ask questions, artful ways to make informants more comfortable when using a tape recorder, artful ways to check the accuracy of informant responses. Decisions about how much to record from informal conversations, how much to transcribe from formally recorded ones, or how long to conduct interviews in the course of an inquiry, all require judgment calls. One needs to develop a "sixth sense" about which data may ultimately prove most useful, toward the objective of accumulating less data rather than more. I will highlight a few points deserving of special mention, but I offer no magic formula for turning a poor interviewer into a better one. We all can improve our interview style by attending as carefully to our own words recorded in transcribed interviews as we attend to the words of our interviewee.

Longtime fieldwork allows a researcher to develop a keen sense of what, when, and under what circumstances it is appropriate to ask something, and when it is better to remain quiet. That requires distinguishing between what you would like to know and how to go about making that interest known. Sometimes that means holding questions for later; sometimes it means holding them forever; as often, it means recognizing the moment to raise a question because circumstances open a window of opportunity on a normally taboo or sensitive issue.

I recognize a cultural norm that guides my own behavior in this regard, one that makes *all* fieldwork a dilemma for me and rears itself on every occasion when I want to interrupt with a question, even in ordinary conversation: Do not intrude. In *Halfway Home*, novelist Paul Monette describes the reluctance to intrude as "the first WASP commandment." This is why the most thorough and inquisitive of researchers might be aghast at the suggestion that they ought to seek the same level of intimate information about their own colleagues or students at home that they feel professionally obliged to achieve in the field. Anthropologist Fred Gearing reveals the uneasiness he felt from the first moments of his introduction to fieldwork:

> During the next several days I sought out certain Indians, and we talked. Our conversations were typically low-keyed, filled with long silences. I never quite felt that I was intruding, but was never fully confident that I was not. (Gearing 1970:9)

Asking does more than merely intrude, however—at least when it goes beyond exchanging pleasantries of the day. And even exchanging pleasantries can lead to unexpected awkwardness, as when a friendly Thai asks, "Where are you going?" in the custom of a people for whom this, rather than our innocuous "How are you?" is the proper greeting in passing. Our questions as fieldworkers become increasingly intrusive as we seek to understand what is going on. Too easily we may put informants on the defensive by insisting or implying that they should be able to explain not only *what* is going on but *why*. In framing our questions we also tip our hands in ways that subtly influence the future course of our work. While we almost routinely insist that we are interested in "everything" about the lives of our informants, our questions belie that claim by revealing that some "everythings" are of more consequence than others.

Years ago, writing what turned out to be a spectacular chapter on interviewing in general but was intended only as a methodological preface to their pioneer study of male sexual behavior, Alfred Kinsey and his colleagues pointed out that although their questions were on sensitive topics, the very act of questioning can make *any* topic sensitive. (Kinsey, Pomeroy, and Martin 1948:Chapter 2). Through interviewing, we risk turning any topic about which we express interest into a sensitive one, inadvertently alerting informants to issues of our special concern. At the same time, local issues of purely academic concern to us may be fraught with political or economic overtones for respondents. We cannot naively assume, for example, that informants are delighted to be asked about the value of their personal possessions, the size of their livestock herds, or the amount they pay in taxes (Christensen 1993).

Let me offer an illustration of the difficulties in obtaining sensitive information. I was invited to comment on a redrafted proposal for researching condom use in AIDS prevention among minority populations. Indicative of the influence qualitative approaches now exert—even among agencies that insist on final reports with totally quantifiable results— researchers in the process of applying for a grant had been directed to augment their essentially quantitative approach by including semistructured interviewing among their data gathering strategies. I noted that the way the interview schedule had been designed required the researchers to introduce the topic of condoms early in the interviews. Thus interviewers were likely to lead respondents to answer along socially acceptable lines that did not necessarily square with actual behavior.

The underlying question is one of the most difficult in nondirective interview strategies: how to find out what you want to know without framing questions in a way that you, rather than your informants, introduce and pursue topics? How can the context remain theirs, rather than your own? In this case, with one-time interviews, some possibilities presented themselves. Interviewers might ask respondents to name (free list) all the "safe sex" practices they could think of, returning to those of special interest to the project only later in the interview, and perhaps prompting with other practices not mentioned. Or they might provide a comprehensive list of their own, "burying" items of concern to the researchers, as, for example, a list that included but did not specifically highlight condom use. In addition, specific questions on that topic could be introduced near the end of each interview, so that interviewers (and coders) would be able to track when, where, and how in the course of an interview the topic was formally introduced.

It has taken years for me to become so bold that I risk the disapproval of dental hygienists by looking them directly in the eye and stating flatly that I do not now and never intend to floss! Why would a minority respondent, answering intimate personal questions about sexual practices, want to disappoint a researcher by claiming to be socially irresponsible about the risk of transmitting a disease as devastating as AIDS? Further, if you tell interviewers what you think they want to hear, maybe they will go away sooner. Interviewing is not all that difficult, but interviewing in which people tell you how they really think about things you are interested in learning, or how they think about the things that are important to them, is a delicate art. My working resolution to the dilemma of assessing what informants say is to recognize that they are always telling me *something*. My task is to figure out what that *something* might be.

What interviewing can do, of course, is introduce efficiency into fieldwork. That "efficiency" can reach a point in which fieldwork itself—the participating kind that is the focus of this discussion—may be eliminated altogether. If the questions to be asked can be tightened up enough, perhaps the principal investigator need not enter the field at all. Research assistants, even contract pollsters, can get the needed information.

One cannot do participant observation without "being there," although, as pointed out in the previous chapter, fieldwork consists of more than "just" being in the field. On the other hand, one can conduct fieldwork through extensive interviews that do not assume or require residency on the part of the fieldworker, if sufficient time is allowed for research in depth, as with the collection of life history data. I think most qualitative researchers consider participant observation and interviewing to be complementary, but that does not require drawing on them equally or necessarily even drawing on both of them at all in every study. Fieldworkers invest more heavily in whichever of the two better accommodates their research style and their research question.

Some fieldworkers do little or no *formal* interviewing, maintaining instead a casual, conversational approach in the manner of Gearing's "low-keyed conversations." Mike Agar takes a strong position that underscores his ethnographic concern with meanings: "Ethnographic question-asking is a special blend of art and science. . . . Ethnography without questions would be impossible" (1980:45). If his statement is too strong to apply to all fieldwork, we must at least recognize that fieldworkers who ask no questions are sorely tempted to become their own informants.

105

I take interviewing to include any situation in which a fieldworker is in a position to, and does, attempt to obtain information on a specific topic through even so casual a comment or inducement as, "What you were telling me the other day was really interesting. . . ." or "I didn't have a chance to ask you about this before, but can you tell me a bit more about . . . ." To categorize the major types of "asking" in which fieldworkers engage, I offer the following list. Descriptive titles make the categories seem obvious, yet each is worthy of the scholarly attention it has received in the extensive literature devoted specifically to aspects of interviewing:

- Casual or conversational interviewing

- Life history/life cycle interviewing

- Semistructured (i.e., open-ended) interviewing

- Structured interviewing, including formal eliciting techniques
  - Survey
  - Household census, ethnogenealogy
  - Questionnaire (written or oral)

- Projective techniques

- Standardized tests and other measurement techniques

The list could easily be expanded or collapsed, depending on one's purposes. My bias toward ethnographic research shows through with the inclusion of two categories. One is the category for household census and ethnogenealogy, once a mainstay in initiating community studies and still a good starting place when conducting them. Another is the category for projective techniques. That category accommodates the once-fashionable fieldwork practice of collecting Rorschach or Thematic Apperception Test protocols (see, for example, Henry and Spiro 1953), as well as more recent interests in projective interviewing such as the Spindlers' Instrumental Activities Inventory (1965) or Robert Textor's work in Ethnographic Futures research. There has been a longtime practice of asking informants straightforward but nonetheless projectively aimed questions about the foreseeable future: "Ten years from now, what do you think things will be like?"

Work in educational research leads me to include as a separate category the kind of tests associated with schooling, and thus my inclusion of the category "Standardized tests and other measurement techniques." For the fieldworker, however, such measurement techniques should be regarded as *a special type of interview*. What makes standardized tests different from other forms of interviewing is that the interviewee supplies an answer already known to the person administering the test. As a general rule, fieldworkers ask questions to find out what informants know and know about, not to "test" their knowledge. The questions we ask, the manner in which we ask them, and what we do with the information given are intended to signal our interest in and regard for what people know. In spite of experiencing too many years under the tyranny of testing in their own lives, practitioners of the *art* of fieldwork never, *never* "put down" those among whom they study. Fieldworkers as attuned to the art of teaching as to the art of fieldwork are able to follow that practice in their classrooms as well. It is critical to keep in mind that testing is a very special kind of interviewing, designed for assessment in terms of normative standards. Although fieldwork cannot help but have evaluative overtones, formal testing arises out of a quite different tradition, and one hopes that fieldworkers make nontraditional use of whatever test data they collect.

One way we show appreciation for what informants tell us is the serious respect accorded to the information they provide. I felt I had conveyed that idea to two African field assistants assigned to help me conduct a questionnaire survey in my study of the beer gardens of Bulawayo (HFW 1974). As soon as we started interviewing, however, I heard each of them roaring with laughter at responses to the questions they posed, in marked contrast to the studied reactions they had displayed during an earlier practice session. Out in the real world—we were conducting our interviews in urban, municipally operated beer gardens—their better judgment took over. It was risky to ask anything of total strangers, they explained, and if you wanted to keep respondents talking, you had better make sure they understood how appreciative you were of their responses. They weren't laughing *at* their respondents, they wanted me to understand, they were laughing *with* them. And how were *my* somber interviews going, they inquired tactfully?

The convenience of gathering any type of systematic interview data is always undertaken at the risk of losing rapport, although we can never anticipate exactly what anyone's reaction will be. For every individual too busy to talk, someone else may be reluctant to bring the interview to a close. For someone annoyed with questions too personal, another may insist on volunteering far more, and far more personal, information than that requested. Adherents of particular approaches have their stories to offer as testimonial. Chances are that approaches and questions that make the researcher uncomfortable will have a similar effect on respondents.

I know that fieldworkers have sometimes gone out of their way not to appear too inquisitive, too "pushy," too calculating in their approach, too like teachers giving examinations, journalists tracking down a story, or government agents ready to impose more taxes or exert more control. Most people are uncomfortable with the notion of a "file" being kept on them, a universal and growing discomfort as we realize how commonplace this has become in an age of information processing. The experienced longtime fieldworker is not likely to make his or her first appearance at the door with a questionnaire to be answered. The researcher who does show up at the door with a questionnaire is not likely to stick around to learn any more than what is asked on the questionnaire form.

Do I seem to be advocating a fieldwork approach, particularly in regard to interviewing, in which "slow is beautiful" and therefore "fast is bad"? Frankly, when thinking about what fieldwork can and cannot accomplish, that *is* my position. Issues surrounding the topic of interviewing help me to clarify it. There are things one can learn quickly by asking direct questions revealing of what one wants to know. There are things one can ask directly without much assurance about the answer. There are things about which we do not ask, guided by our own standards, or about which interviewees do not offer answers, guided by theirs. And there are underlying questions, often the kind of question that undergirds social research, that can neither be asked nor answered directly (for example, "Please tell me your world view," or "Why do we have schools at all?" or "When everyone seems so dissatisfied, why do you continue with your form of government?").

In a hurry-up world, with technologies that devour information byte by byte, there is constant pressure to get the facts and get on with it. Fieldworkers are in an excellent position not only to get facts but to be able to put facts in context. But fieldwork is a grossly inefficient way simply to gather factual data. When time is of the essence—as it is so often perceived to be—then fieldwork as represented here is out of the question, even when field-based research for collecting necessary data is essential. It is only the integrity of the label *fieldwork* that I seek to protect, however. There is no mandate that says if you can't devote at least a year, you shouldn't bother to go into the field at all. I agree with Russ Bernard, who *insists* on participant observation in the conduct of all scientific research about cultural groups and who argues more generally that "it is possible to do useful participant observation in just a few days" (1994b:140).

Contemporary fieldworkers have responded to the need for speed by incorporating survey-type techniques into their standard repertory, although there is nothing new about having to compress a heavy dose of fieldwork into a short period of time. As with any human activity, there are times when everything seems to be happening at once, or a brief foray is all that time or resources allow. Robert Redfield was so pleased with a 3-day field survey he conducted in 1941 with his then student and field assistant Sol Tax that he coined the term Rapid Guided Survey. However, the document that resulted from the work retained "Report of a 3-Day Survey" in its title, and the researchers had a clear idea of the information they sought, for their fieldwork was then in its seventh year (see Rubinstein 1991:297, 304). At that, they attributed their success at least in part to sheer luck.

Rapid Appraisal or Rapid Rural Appraisal became more commonplace in development projects in the Third World during the 1970s and 1980s when Appropriate Technology was the buzzword; Rapid Rural Appraisal itself has been recognized as a form of appropriate technology. Today there are numerous variations on "R.R.A." in both name and application, including Rapid Anthropological Assessment, Rapid Ethnographic Assessment, and Ethnographic Reconnaissance. Practicing anthropologists have their own handbook, *Soundings* (van Willigen and Finan 1991; see also Beebe 1995), that outlines and illustrates a number of "rapid and reliable" research methods. These procedures can retain something of a fieldwork flavor through what is described—or rationalized—as an iterative and exploratory team approach. In this approach, the research begins with (but moves rapidly beyond) preliminary observations and semistructured interviews with key informants. These preliminary data are used to guide the construction of appropriate survey or questionnaire instruments, the entire process to be completed in a limited time.

To an old-time and old-fashioned ethnographer like me, terms like *ethnography* or *fieldwork* join uneasily with a qualifier like *rapid.* Then again, I've never been in a hurry to do things. My motto, to "Do less, more thoroughly," may be nothing more than rationalization for my preferred and accustomed pace. Perhaps I envision a fieldwork entirely of my own making, having mistakenly accepted pronouncements about its duration (such as "one year at the least, and preferably two") as minimum standards when today's fieldworkers regard them as impractical and unnecessary. Russ Bernard now proclaims *three months* as the minimum time "to achieve reasonable intellectualized competence in another culture and be accepted as a participant observer" (Bernard 1994b:151). I heartily agree that *any* amount of time a researcher in our "rushy culture" (Dianne Ferguson's phrase) can devote to participant observation should prove useful for gaining a sense of context. But I am concerned whenever participant observation is simultaneously portrayed and faulted as a quickie exercise. Similar efforts have been directed at determining how *few* informants one really needs in gathering technically reliable information about a cultural domain (e.g., Bernard 1994b:Chapter 8; Romney, Weller, and Batchelder 1986). It is hardly surprising that these researchers are strong advocates for the efficiency of formal procedures and structured interview schedules. I hope Bernard has not inadvertently foreshortened the acceptable period for fieldwork for those who will carefully misread his statement to reassure themselves that the three months he says is adequate to *establish* oneself in the field is all the time one needs to devote to a study.

Although I am not an advocate for finding faster ways to do fieldwork, neither am I committed to making fieldwork more time-consuming simply for its own sake. Time in the field is no guarantee of the quality of the ensuing reports. Nor need efforts to speed things up and find ways to get better data in less time be seen as detracting from efforts to make interviewing a better art as well. With that in mind, I offer some suggestions about interviewing, accompanied by a reminder that this topic has been well served in the vast "methods" literature, including early statements still brimming with cautions and insights (e.g., Paul 1953) and more recent how-to-do-it monographs (e.g., Seidman 1991; Spradley 1979). My comments relate especially to semistructured interviewing of the sort that virtually all field researchers employ, whether constructing a rapid survey or embarking on a long-term inquiry into world view.

Doing Better Interviewing; Using Interviews Better

- *Recognize listening as an active and creative role.* I once heard the late educational historian Lawrence Cremin eulogized for his capacity as a "creative listener," a phrase that lingered in my mind as both an unusual compliment and a wonderful insight into the art of interviewing. Creative listener. Certainly that includes being an attentive listener. But it seems to imply more, a listener able to play an interactive role, thereby making a more effective speaker out of the person talking. An interview ought to be a satisfactory experience for listener and speaker alike.

  I regard myself as a listener, but that is not the same as being a creative listener. I confess that I frequently tire of listening, although surely Cremin must have experienced some of those same feelings, especially after assuming the role of college president. There are a few individuals for whom I seem to play the role of creative listener, and there are a few individuals who play that role for me; on either end of such conversations, I find the interaction not only satisfying but intensely stimulating. To consciously strive to become a creative listener seems a wonderful talent for any fieldworker to develop, especially anyone who depends on semistructured interviewing as a major field technique.

- *Talk less, listen more.* If the idea of creative listening seems too elusive, try simply talking less and listening more during any interview. As an easy first step, practice waiting one thousandth of a second longer before intruding on a momentary pause to introduce a comment or new question. Interviewers are reminded to distinguish between a "pregnant" silence and a dead one. A lengthened pause on the researcher's part may be enough to prompt the interviewee to pick up the conversation again. Our own conversational patterns display a certain inertia: A

111

conversation in motion tends to remain in motion. Silence poses a threat. We can become our own worst enemies during the interview process by rushing to fill in the pauses. If the researcher does not immediately plug the gap, the interviewee is likely to do it instead, without even realizing why.

- *Make questions short and to the point.* If necessary to repeat, do exactly that. Do not expand or elaborate, for in doing so you are likely either to start an answer or to change the question. This is usually done inadvertently, in the spirit of helping both the respondent and the dialogue. If you study interview protocols—and I particularly urge you to study your own—you are likely to discover that one simple question usually becomes two or three competing and increasingly complex ones through the course of the solicitous prompting that follows.

- *Plan interviews around a few big issues.* Successful interviewers return again and again to develop dimensions of an issue, rather than detailing myriad little questions to ask. For initial interviewing, anthropologist James Spradley recommended what he termed Grand Tour questions (Spradley 1979) of the sort, "So, tell me something about yourself" or "How did you happen to get here?" The interviewer might then have several major topics in mind to which attention can be turned repeatedly in minor variation. For example, family and kin might be the central topic in the interviewer's mind, to be translated into more detailed questions about each family member, sometimes with a simple prompt such as, "Can you tell me anything more about that?"

- *As soon as possible after an interview, write it up.* Transcribe the interview, if it was taped, or index its contents (topics discussed and their location on the tape) if you do not intend to make full typescripts from each interview. If it was not taped, all the more reason for fleshing out your brief notes while your informant's words remain fresh in your mind. Then "study" the transcript, or listen to the tape, both to see how you are doing as an interviewer and to immerse yourself in what you are learning from and about your informant. If time allows (as it should), do not proceed with the next interview until the previous one has been processed. Always be thinking about how you intend to use the information, both for the immediate purpose of guiding future interviews, and for your eventual incorporation of the material into your final account.

• *Anticipate and discuss the level of formality you plan for the interview.* If you intend semistructured interviews to be more formal than earlier dialogues—to be more than casual conversations that happen to be recorded—explain any shifting ground rules so your informant understands what may otherwise appear as a personality change that has suddenly come over you. Formal taped sessions can provide opportunity for a different kind of exchange, one in which the person being interviewed is clearly "in the know," and the researcher is the person who wants to find out. Michael Agar calls this the "one down" position, with the fieldworker assuming a subordinate role as learner rather than the one-up role assumed by the scientifically oriented hypotheses tester (Agar 1980:69).

Recognize nonetheless that the person with the tape recorder ought to remain in charge of the setting. You may need to think through whether you can live with that. Perhaps you will have to give way to egalitarian urges to make the exchange more evenly reciprocal. Be advised that when you listen to the tape you may discover that *you* were the one being interviewed.

I have always felt that a formal interview is and ought to be a special, asymmetrical form of conversation, one party seeking information, the other providing it. Work toward achieving that format if it suits your style and purposes. Explain that in your formal interviews you want your interviewee's words and explanations recorded, even if your informant wants it understood that some comments may be declared "off the record." Offer to turn off the tape recorder any time your interviewee prefers to speak off the record, desires a break, or wishes to discuss the interview process with you. You might also suggest that if your questions

113

prompt similar questions your informant might like to ask of you, they can be noted for discussion later.

Conversational approaches in tape-recorded interviewing are less efficient, and may not be necessary if your informant understands how you distinguish between ordinary conversation and a formal interview in which you will take special care to record the interviewee's exact words. You may have to overcome an urge to be more casual, but both you and your informant probably need to remember that your association, while friendly, is essentially professional. Someday you will go away, and you intend to take the interview with you.

Make informants aware of the importance of their interviews to your work by your actions as well as your expressions of appreciation. Better to err on the side of being too formal than to create the impression of being too casual. Try to use a tape recorder, if possible. Augment that with brief notes, if possible. Conduct the interview in private, if possible. Formalize the occasion with a formally arranged appointment that you yourself (rather than an assistant or secretary) have arranged, if possible, perhaps even suggesting in advance the major topics you would like to discuss. And leave the tape recorder running after the formal interview ends, if possible, in the likelihood that although the interview is finished, your informant may not be.

If such formality seems the very antithesis of the kind of interpersonal exchange you want to foster, then follow your intuition to find a style more suitable. There is no rule against being more interactive, no rule insisting that somewhere in your report you must include the words of your informants. Perhaps the idea of "capturing" someone else's words precisely is precisely the kind of fieldworker you did not want to become. As integral as formal interviewing is to fieldwork in general, you must always consider the possibility that it is not for you.

• If you are not under the gun to work through your interview data as rapidly as possible, see how long you can hold off before you develop a questionnaire or a tightly structured interview schedule. The question of when and how interview schedules are developed reveals a major difference between fieldworkers and survey researchers. The survey researcher typically enters the field with a prepared schedule. Fieldworkers are more likely to administer such an instrument near the conclusion of the field research, when they know the questions that have yet to be asked and have a clearer idea of how best to ask them. The exception might be a household census or similar inventory through which the researcher also introduces the research project, gathers relevant basic demographic data, and looks for knowledgeable informants willing to be interviewed in depth. Even under those circumstances, try to keep the interview open. Ask as few specific questions as necessary, and include an open-ended question or two to invite respondents to say what is on their mind or to help provide context for the research topic.

A maxim directed at quantitative researchers (although too seldom heeded) holds in our work as well: Behind every question asked, there ought to be a hypothesis. We don't have to be that sticky about formalizing hypotheses, but data should never be gathered simply for the sake of gathering them or because it is so easy to add another question or two. If it doesn't really matter whether respondents own their own home, graduated from high school, or have ever been arrested, don't ask. If it does matter, give ample opportunity for them to explain, and include their explanations in the information you record. That's the difference between hit-and-run surveys and the fieldworker who intends to stick around to try to figure out how things fit together.

• Invite informants to help you become a better researcher. Agar's notion of the interviewer in the one-down position can be extended to the research process itself. Keep in mind that your interviewees have "views" about your interview techniques as well as about the scope of your questions. Don't fish for compliments, but a direct question such as "Do you have any suggestions about these interviews?" may prove immediately helpful as well as lend insight into how the interviewee is feeling as a participant in the research process. A further question can get directly at content: "Are there topics we might explore that I haven't asked about?" Should you get no response at first, you nonetheless are emphasizing the extent of your interest and effort at thoroughness and your respect for the intelligence of your informant; suggestions may follow later.

• Search for patterns in responses, not only for what is there but for cutoff points in discussion, or topics consistently skirted or avoided—on your part as well as on the part of your informants. Don't forget to go back through *all* your interviews if you work with an informant over a period of time. I have often discovered that informants gave important information, and important clues to what they felt was important, in early interviews. Everything was new, coming at me so fast that I failed to pick up on much of the information and clues the first time around.

In studying interview protocols, I find it useful to distinguish between what informants are telling me and what else, if anything, they may be *trying* to tell me. In one sense, everything an informant tells you can be taken as a fact—a linguistic fact, if no other kind. But informants make choices, sometimes leading us, sometimes leading us astray. Occasionally I find myself anticipating what they will say next, as a way to assess whether my informant and I are on the same wavelength. I believe it important to be able to quote back to informants, in their exact words, topics mentioned or alluded to in earlier conversations. There may also be times, however, when an ambiguous reference to an earlier topic is a more appropriate way to reintroduce it. That approach keeps you from leading the discussion or from phrasing questions in such a way that the only response needed is a yes or no.

• Finally, do not become so committed to the qualitative dimensions of responses that you fail to count and measure those aspects that warrant being counted and measured. Keep your research purposes clearly in mind in deciding what and how much to analyze. Carefully recorded language, for example, lends itself to rigorous analysis, but the rigor can set up an illusive smoke screen of carefully conducted but totally inappropriate analyses, lending an aura of science but indicative of a poor artistic choice. Behind every decision intended to advance science lies an opportunity for exercising sound human judgment.

Looking Over Others' Shoulders

Data gathering is not limited to information that fieldworkers gather through participant observation and interviewing while actively on site. There are additional, often critical, sources of information, especially but not limited to personal documents and other written records. This third category, archival research, concludes this review of the basic arts in the fieldwork part of fieldwork.

I used to think there was a degree of art involved in searching out information in a library; today I am willing to concede that task to science. I watch in dismay as students run enormous computer searches on unfamiliar topics, perhaps hoping that if they can press the right combination of keys at their terminal, information will spew forth like coins from a slot machine. Given the exponential increase in recorded information, we can be thankful that the technologies that helped create problems are also available to help resolve them.

There is still some art required in using archives, however. The most obvious art clearly parallels the problem one faces in the field: How wide a swath to cut, how deep to burrow; in short, "What counts"? "No depth of commitment and sense of responsibility will ever be enough to permit any individual to do what is there to be done," Margaret Mead cautioned fieldworkers a quarter of a century ago (1970:258), and today it is quite thinkable that a fieldworker determined to get a thorough grounding in library research might, in Mead's words, be so "attracted by the inexhaustibility of the task" (p. 258) as to never leave the library at all. As with everything else about fieldwork, one needs to recognize how to focus and when to stop.

Libraries and the proliferation of information are everybody's problem, but those attracted to fieldwork probably are not going to get stuck in the library. We still hear arguments about whether we should go into the field

LIVERPOOL JOHN MOORES UNIVERSITY
LEARNING SERVICES

well informed or should consult what others have said only after forming our own impressions. I believe the better argument can be made for being well informed, as long as being informed is accompanied with the same healthy skepticism befitting all scholarly research. That is the first of the three suggestions discussed below for making the most artful use of secondary sources.

Making the Best Use of the Work of Others

- *Be as skeptical of anything you read as you are of anything you are told.* A lesson we learn too well as schoolchildren must be cast aside in scholarly pursuit, that printed texts are sacred texts. Most certainly, what earlier fieldworkers have reported may no longer be true, even if it was accurate at one time. Skepticism is absolutely essential to all aspects of fieldwork, including any use made of printed sources.

A skeptical stance does not give license to demean all prior efforts, however; academics sometimes get carried away in their truth-seeking zeal. It is tempting, for younger scholars especially, to find fault with earlier reports and "bring down the elders." I think it far more constructive, and more consistent with a spirit of inquiry, to take the position that earlier researchers did not quite get it right, just as future researchers will probably show that we did not quite get it right, either. If it is any comfort, know that fieldwork's "greats" continue to take their licking, as in this passage from Clifford Geertz, "Firth, not Malinowski, is probably our best Malinowskian. Fortes so far eclipses Radcliffe-Brown as to make us wonder how he could have taken him for his master. Kroeber did what Boas but promised" (1988:20).

A healthy skepticism must always be maintained, even when everything seems to be checking out perfectly, past with present, established landmark studies with your own embryonic inquiries. While Ron Rohner and I were doing our fieldwork on the Northwest Coast, Ron discovered an excellent informant in Bill Scow and was sometimes surprised at how consistently Bill's accounts validated the early work of Franz Boas. But one of Ron's questions stumped Bill one day, and he explained, "I can't answer that one, Ron. I'll have to look it up." Only then did Ron realize that the old informant and the young anthropologist were using the same references; an earlier descriptive ethnography had now become a prescriptive one!

• *Look far afield for all you might include as "the work of others."* Sometimes anthropologists join the "stack rats" to do their work entirely through library scholarship, but fieldworkers are more likely to be sensitive to any suggestion that they never, or hardly ever, go to the library. Whether they spend much time in the library or not, most fieldworkers make use of a vast array of materials in addition to the customary library resources. (See Hill's useful guide for conducting original archival research "with quality and dispatch," 1993.)

Personal documents are especially high on the list of non-library sources: correspondence, diaries, travelers' journals, any sort of written account that might never find its way into a formal collection but can be invaluable to understanding everyday life or special events. Government records, newspaper accounts, surveyor reports—there is no end to the possible resources to be considered. Similarly, fieldworkers examine, and frequently collect, artifacts of all sorts, things in addition to words.

Fieldworkers need to think creatively about available sources of information that are not ordinarily regarded as data, to avoid falling victim to habits that find us invariably gathering the same limited information in the same limited ways. In my study of a school principal, for example, I was interested in getting some sense of how the principal's professional relationships with other teachers and administrators overlapped with his personal relationships among family and friends (HFW 1973). An opportunity to get some "hard data" on the topic occurred when his oldest daughter announced her forthcoming wedding. I asked the principal if he would be willing to review the wedding list and say something about everyone invited, paying particular attention to invitations extended by the parents of the bride rather than to the young couple's own social network. I might

119

have obtained similar information by going over the list of people to whom the principal and his wife regularly sent Christmas cards. Personal documents such as these are not likely to end up at the Smithsonian, yet they are a ready source of data about social networks. Wouldn't a list of the telephone numbers frequently dialed, or a directory of e-mail correspondents for anyone who keeps such a record, provide similar insight into professional and/or personal networks?

- *Think about new ways to use data easily at hand.* The previous point emphasized looking at sources of data easily overlooked, so that we do not take too constricted a view of what constitutes data. The complement to that is to be equally creative about using readily available data in unusual ways.

    It may, for example, be easier to document, and even to discern, patterns or trends by looking at the frequency or space devoted to certain kinds of events in the local newspaper over a period of years than by having to rely solely on the impressions of older informants. Margaret Mead was able to give a historical perspective to her interest in child training by comparing the range and detail of topics discussed in government manuals throughout a period of several decades. The changing tables of contents in introductory texts in fields like anthropology or sociology provide an excellent basis for watching the evolution of those disciplines. Old catalogues or photographs offer evidence of changing fashions in clothing, hair style, and the like. That such sources of data exist is hardly a revelation, but it doesn't hurt to remind fieldworkers to remind themselves that participant observation and interviewing are not the only ways to get information. Such extraneous sources also invite researchers to compare what they are being told with sources less susceptible to being reinterpreted with a knowing backward look.

This chapter has reviewed some basic arts in fieldwork, as perceived by a fieldworker committed to a personal investment of sufficient duration that data gathering is subordinated to insight born of, or informed by, direct experience. Potential problems were recast as challenges to be recognized and reckoned with. I turn next to examining some related problems from what might be called the dark side of fieldwork. Given the focus of the book, I refer to them as the Darker Arts.●

CHAPTER SIX
FIELDWORK: THE DARKER ARTS

It is necessary to be relentless in ferreting out the dark side of fieldwork, for only then can the other side, the rebirth of the anthropologist, be fully comprehended and understood in a rigorous manner.

—John L. Wengle
Ethnographers in the Field, 169

Cultural analysis is intrinsically incomplete. And, worse than that, the
more deeply it goes the less complete it is. It is a strange science whose
most telling assertions are its most tremulously based, in which to get
somewhere with the matter at hand is to intensify the suspicion, both
your own and that of others, that you are not quite getting it right.

—Clifford Geertz
"Thick Description," in *The Interpretation of Cultures,* 29

It took me a long time to discover that the key to acting is honesty.
Once you know how to fake that, you've got it made.

—John Leonard
quoted in J. Douglas, *Investigative Social Research,* 55

Definitions of art reviewed in Chapter 1 included reference to
trickery, cunning, or artificiality in behavior. Among the definitions of artist, we recognize the trickster, clever at deceit, or the
"con artist," who abuses confidence. The last thing any fieldworker wants

to be is a con artist. Yet it is virtually impossible to do and report fieldwork without risking someone's integrity, either theirs or your own. Taking a cue from John Leonard in the epigraph immediately above, what do we have to be prepared to "fake" in order to succeed at fieldwork? I won't take refuge this time in my customary caveat, "It depends." I'll say straight out: In fieldwork one must be prepared to fake everything.

The dilemma is inherent, given the openness of our approach and the subject matter of our concern—the social behavior of our fellow human beings (and ourselves). We are honest enough when we declare that we cannot state *exactly* what we are looking for, but we ordinarily have more in mind than we let on, and we are not adverse to discovering—or *uncovering*—information we did not anticipate. Nor are we able to anticipate how we ourselves will use whatever information we get. In its darkest sense, fieldwork's much-lauded openness to inquiry is also an invitation to moral disaster. I will attempt to identify some major predicaments. As with a parallel discussion of some major *conceptual* dilemmas to follow in Chapter 7, one needs to be prepared to meet the *moral* dilemmas to be discussed here. A first step is to realize that one is not alone in confronting them. Better, I think, to face them boldly than ignore them in the hope they will go away, because they won't. Should you want to insist that you have no talent for such things, maybe other, safer approaches to research are more your style.

The categories of darker arts identified here, and the sequence for discussing them, are necessarily arbitrary. I have pulled them together under six major topics and presented them starkly. I offer whatever insight I can for addressing them, but my major concern is simply to get them "on the table" so that we can acknowledge and talk about them forthrightly. The categories are presented as problems, a set of potential accusations directed at fieldwork that we might prefer to deny: superficiality, obviousness, being self-serving, lack of independence, deception and betrayal, and clandestine observation. The categories may seem to be self-contradictory—for example, if fieldwork can be faulted for being superficial, how can it also be equated with spying? That is, how can it be both obvious and clandestine at the same time? The fact is that, as a human activity, it is suspect on every dimension. And contradictory or not, we are uncomfortable when certain questions are raised about what we are up to, or when what we are up to raises other uncomfortable questions among those whom we study.

Superficiality

Good actors are not the only performers who learn how to fake it. Field researchers usually try to convey a sense of commitment consistent with in-depth study. That does not guarantee the sense is genuine; it may simply be part of a fieldwork pose. When it is real, as it usually is, it carries no guarantee that the fieldwork will be completed competently or carried through to the critical step, the completion of a final account. Fieldworker types, willing to make research commitments on such a grand scale, are likely to be overcommitted in other aspects of their lives. They too easily extend themselves beyond what can reasonably be accomplished, or accomplished within restricted timelines.

There is a temptation to make too many promises while "selling" the idea of a research project. Researchers fail to recognize that overzealous promises may eventually work against them. It is particularly easy to overestimate the time one will actually spend on site in the "fieldwork" part of fieldwork. I served as a consultant to one generously funded project during the early 1970s that initially promised to maintain resident fieldworkers on site for as long as five years! That level of sustained research had broad appeal for studying change, but it proved to be unrealistic. Five years was not enough to study the long-term effects of planned change, while it was way too long to ask of young researchers setting out on new careers. At the other extreme, one of my own doctoral students aborted a deeply held commitment to overseas fieldwork after being on site less than one week, a decision that resulted in a traumatic career change for him and left an overseas research director forever at odds with me. Perhaps commitment to fieldwork is like commitment in marriage vows: at the time, the words are what everyone wants to hear; their strength and intent must be measured in other ways.

Fieldworkers have an understandable but perhaps unfortunate tendency to represent themselves not only as different from those who do "quick-and-dirty" studies but somehow as more sensitive and caring humans as well. That tendency can invite comparisons in which they portray themselves as a breed apart, more committed, more deeply interested, more determined to hear the whole story. They want everyone to know they are there to grasp what Malinowski referred to as "the *native's* point of view" (1922:25), a view we have learned to refer to more respectfully as the *emic* or insider one.

Ideally, of course, such claims ought to be warranted, but that does not warrant making them publicly. Claims about commitment are difficult to substantiate. How can we ever demonstrate in advance that we can be trusted, have only our subject's interest at heart, conduct our studies "in depth," and so forth? Only with the passing of time can we demonstrate that we "stick around longer," that if we aren't going to stay forever, at least we intend to stay longer than most. We intend, as some anthropologists put it, to "live our way into the community." Sooner or later, however, we too must leave. My hunch is that fieldwork often gets foreshortened due to "unforeseeable circumstances." We end up being pretty much like the others after all—not really different, just a bit slower.

Leave-taking is itself something of an unrecognized art. It has been pointed out that with sexual liaisons, getting *out* of bed gracefully requires more art than getting in it. I think there is an apt parallel with getting out of the field, especially after we work energetically to create the image of researchers so deeply interested and sympathetic.

I advise underplaying the intended depth of involvement we hope to achieve or the extended period we propose to spend. Those circumstances must speak for themselves, and that can only happen through time. Practical considerations arise in addition to the ethical ones of not making false promises. Fieldworkers are admonished not to leave the field any worse than they found it. Certainly that includes not creating a basis for ill will toward future fieldworkers, based on unfulfilled expectations about the duration of one's stay. And one never knows when it might be necessary, or highly advantageous, to be able to visit or otherwise contact one's informants after fieldwork ends, or to invite members in a researched setting to read and critique preliminary drafts of a developing report. (For further discussion, see Maines, Shaffir, and Turowetz 1980.)

I think our commitment to "in-depth" study should be treated more like a professional secret than a public boast. Whatever depth we do actually achieve is better left for others to acknowledge. I always *hope* that my work will give evidence of its depth through the understanding I achieve. To whatever extent I succeed in that, however, I should not be the one to boast of it. I rather doubt that we ever understand *anything* all that well, including ourselves. If we never fully understand ourselves, how well do we understand those among whom we conduct our studies? Our efforts to study in depth are destined always to exceed our accomplishments.

In the last decade, that realization has come to haunt me not only figuratively but literally. My awareness evolved out of an anthropological life history I published in 1983 that, with additional articles published subsequently (1987a, 1990a), became what I refer to as the "Brad Trilogy." (The three pieces appeared together in HFW 1994b.) As readers familiar with the trilogy are aware, that account addresses personal issues in a manner that I describe as "heady candor," the effort to lay bare relevant details and to be as frank about what I do not understand as what I do understand of the case. Such candor has drawn unexpected support from some quarters (certainly not all), but to a large extent I believe it is an artifact of reaching the twilight years of a long career during an era that allows even social scientists to be "who they are." Issues of candor are familiar to any seasoned fieldworker. If I seem finally to have achieved some admirable level in my reporting, let me note that I have struggled with such issues since beginning fieldwork more than three decades ago: How and how much do we report of what we have seen and understood?

And how much do we see and understand? We should be the first to recognize that we never do, never could, and wouldn't even want to "get it all." Our boast of working in depth is countered by the realization that we never quite get to the bottom of things, never are able to inquire fully enough into every relevant aspect of human behavior no matter how carefully we define the limits of a study. We can never get all the possible detail into the figurative canvases we set out to paint, and of what we do get, as Clifford Geertz reminds us, we can never escape the suspicion that we are not quite getting it right. As well, we are also put on the defensive about those aspects of a setting to which we failed to attend, given the inordinate amounts of time we dedicate to the descriptive task: "You mean to tell me you spent all that time and yet never heard anyone mention such-and-such?"

Time itself does not guarantee quality fieldwork. Full time participant observation that includes residing in a strange community and coping successfully with the strangeness can be so demanding and draining that it

126

sometimes works against data gathering rather than on its behalf. But for all those fieldworkers able more or less to "get their act together"—and fieldwork success, like successful living itself, is all relative—one is faced with impossible decisions about what and how much to record, and what is enough.

What is enough? I have consoled myself and others with another of Geertz's observations, that it is "not necessary to know everything in order to understand something" (Geertz 1973:20), but the nagging doubt remains that we neither are nor could ever possibly be "thorough enough." How do we communicate to our audiences—especially to our more skeptical ones—that what we have reported is what we have seen and understood, and that we recognize, as must they, that it is partial knowledge at best. And how do we reassure them, and ourselves, that what we have seen and understood is what warrants reporting, or that we have quite gotten it right? As Charles Bosk observes (1979:193), "All field work done by a single field-worker invites the question, Why should we believe it?" Why, indeed?

My resolution to such concerns is subsumed under the phrase introduced above, "heady candor," a serious recommendation conveyed in a lighthearted play on the name Eddy Cantor, an old-time vaudeville and radio comedian. Heady candor requires being open and "up front" about both the research process and the persona of the researcher, in addition to customary attention to what has been researched. If that seems an obvious thing to do, keep in mind that until recently fieldworkers have been in the habit of disappearing from their own accounts, as though they themselves had never exerted a presence.

Today's qualitative researchers are strongly advised to leave a "paper trail" tracing the route along which they have collected data critical to the final reporting. The same guideline can be used to depict the fieldwork experience itself—of what duration, under what circumstances, with what limitations? That seems preferable to trying to establish a minimum number of hours of interviewing, days at the site, or months away from home. I recognize that aspiring fieldworkers would welcome firm pronouncements in this regard, just as survey researchers seek in vain for firm guidelines about the minimum number of respondents or minimum acceptable rates of return. But to those questions I retreat once again to my catch-all response, "It depends."

One of the first students to take my graduate seminar "Ethnographic Research in Education" telephoned the year following completion of his doctoral studies to report excitedly on a research project he had proposed. He planned to do an ethnographic study of a school superintendent, comparable to the study I was then writing of a school principal, albeit he was quick to mention that his study would not be on such a grand scale. (My fieldwork extended through 24 months, the write-up about the same again, all sandwiched in among other faculty responsibilities.) I offered congratulatory and encouraging remarks before I thought to ask exactly how long he *did* intend to spend with his apparently willing informant. "All day!" came an enthusiastic response. "From first thing in the morning right through a meeting he has scheduled for that evening." His enthusiasm, I must confess, was not matched by a comparable enthusiasm of my own. A one-day study proposed as *ethnography* by one of my former seminar students!

What went racing through my mind was whether to inform him, in no uncertain terms, that a one-day study could never warrant being called an ethnography. I could anticipate his next question, "Then how many days would I have to spend before it *would* be an ethnography?" Whether or not that is the proper question, it did seem reasonable that if one day was not enough, I must have in mind some minimum number of days that would be. Twenty-five years ago, however, few educational researchers were doing any descriptive work at all; a full day devoted to carefully documenting the activities of one school superintendent was a gigantic leap for research in educational administration. And if his *single* day of research was too short, had it really been necessary for me to tag along with an educational administrator for *two years?*

The best answers are not in response to questions of "how long," measured in time, but to questions of purpose. Tighter conceptualization, cautious labeling, and a careful paper trail still seem the best protection against the inevitable charge that certain aspects of our work are superficial. A bit more attention to parameters in this case might have set the idea on a manageable course with a more carefully chosen title such as "A Day in the Life of a School Superintendent." Although a comparable study might not receive enthusiastic review from an educational journal now, it would have been groundbreaking then. Actually, it would have been well ahead of its time. In those days, survey research provided the basis for virtually all reporting in educational administration except for a few corny "experiments" in leadership style that invariably showed a democratic approach to be superior to an authoritarian or laissez-faire one.

I do not recall whether the observation was conducted. It probably was, since the superintendent had already agreed to it. I do not believe it was published. I have a vague feeling that the chap who so enthusiastically proposed the study felt uncomfortable about whether a day spent observing really qualified as "research." Here is where the art of conceptualization might have helped in thinking through what could be accomplished with the opportunity at hand: a single day of intense observation, an energetic and ambitious observer, and a "subject" willing to have a researcher tag along. Some recognition of recurring cycles might also have helped him see a way to contextualize his initial observations and to project a more substantial inquiry conducted over time.

To anyone who has not actually tried to conduct observation for a sustained period, let me also caution that the proposed 15-hour stint would have proved quite taxing for the observer. Most of us who have tried this kind of "shadow" study recognize that it is difficult to sustain rapt attention for even a couple of hours of uninterrupted observation. Our own powers of observation prove a major contributor to the superficiality we seek so assiduously to overcome. The seeming ease of descriptive research—just following another human around in the course of a "typical" day—is itself a deception, a darker art.

It is not all that clear exactly what anyone does look at, should look at, or should record to adequately fulfill the role of observer. Clearly what one can observe and record for five minutes will be more intense, and far more detailed, than what one might observe and record during two consecutive hours. Observation itself, cloaked as it is in mystery, may be the darkest of fieldwork's arts from the point of view of those who conduct it, yet it leaves us subject to the related accusation of obviousness, the next problem to be reviewed.

Obviousness

The "obviousness" of our approach is not lost on some. It is easy to turn the tables on fieldwork approaches by suggesting that the obviousness of

129

how we go about our research is matched by the obviousness of our results:
The end product of our painstaking efforts at description does no more than
recount what everyone already knows.

How does one respond to the charge that we only succeed in making
the obvious obvious? One response is to argue that "making the obvious
obvious" is itself an art form. Clyde Kluckhohn captured that idea in the
title and message of his well-received introduction to anthropology, *Mirror
for Man* (1949), a book still worth reading for anyone willing to overlook
language of the 1940s with its masculine pronouns and references to
studying *primitives* or *insignificant* nonliterate peoples. Kluckhohn
described the cultural anthropologist as the "silverer" of that mirror:
"Anthropology holds up a great mirror to man and lets him look at himself
in his infinite variety" (p. 11).

Another approach is to question whether what appears to be obvious is
in fact so obvious after all. Kluckhohn raised that question, reminding us
about taking our surroundings for granted: "Ordinarily we are unaware of
the special lens through which we look at life. It would hardly be fish who
discovered the existence of water" (p. 11).

In both these points, however, Kluckhohn was building the case for
anthropologists who studied not just "others" but others *dramatically different from themselves:*

> The preoccupation with insignificant nonliterate peoples that is an
> outstanding feature of anthropological work is the key to its significance
> today. Anthropology grew out of experience with primitives and the tools
> of the trade are unusual because they were forged in this peculiar work-
> shop. (Pp. 10–11)

Collectively those "tools of the trade" made up the ethnographer's kit
bag and were intended to help ethnographers describe the "cultures" of
other groups, initially those "insignificant nonliterate peoples" of Kluckhohn's account but always people whose customs differed sufficiently to
provide an explicit cross-cultural and comparative basis for description.
Comparison is, of course, implicit in all observation, but questions about
the role of strangeness came to be ever more vexing as anthropologists began
studying closer to home under such rubrics as urban anthropology or
microethnography. One caveat was that ethnographers whose credentials

had been validated through initial cross-cultural fieldwork were sub-sequently regarded as qualified to conduct genuinely ethnographic research in their own society, a position that conveniently accommodated the work American anthropologists like Lloyd Warner had been doing for years. As a professional concern, this problem is of anthropology's own making as anthropologists have sought to redefine their turf. Sociologists have never been overly concerned with a cross-cultural perspective, and most of the qualitative research currently being conducted addresses applied problems in the researcher's own professional field. Nevertheless, the question of the comparative basis of our accounts remains, turning today on the issue of whether insiders can do adequate research in groups in which they hold membership or to which they owe allegiance. I think the answer lies in recognizing what the insider perspective can and cannot offer. We can temper the position popular in some quarters—that only an insider can get the inside view—by noting that an inside view is not the only view and that there is no single inside view, anymore than there can be a single outside one.

The fact remains, however, that we may stretch the point, even do ourselves a disservice, by making too much either of what we have to report or of how we have come to report it. As to method, I have already raised the issue of whether we might be better off to insist that fieldwork is fieldwork, rather than allow others to drive us into a corner insisting that it is "research." As to accomplishments, Howard Becker suggests that the work of his colleagues in sociology only gives us "a deeper understanding of what people are already pretty much aware of" (1982:x), while the parallel claim for traditional anthropology might be that its comparative perspective offers a deeper understanding by pointing to what people are already pretty much *unaware* of. This is often characterized as "making the familiar strange," a phrase either coined or reaffirmed by T. S. Eliot (1950:29; see also Spiro 1990) and frequently mentioned in anthropological explanations of what fieldwork is all about. Schlechty and Noblit put another spin on the idea by suggesting that what we are up to is "making the obvious dubious" (1982:290).

As for the newness of qualitative approaches—that today we are witnessing groundbreaking efforts—I think modesty is warranted in boast-ing about that aspect, as well. What strikes us as new may be nothing more than our own sudden consciousness of the approaches or a sudden interest in some particular field not previously so receptive (such as business, journalism, nursing, music, physical education, even computer scientists with their quarterly journal *Human-Computer Interaction*).

As a latecomer among the social sciences, anthropology is not the best place to look for origins; but terms like *ethnography* and *fieldwork* have been around for decades. No discipline or century claims observation as its own, a point Kluckhohn underscored with a reminder that the Greek historian Herodotus, who "described at length the physique and customs of the Scythians, Egyptians, and other 'barbarians,' " is "sometimes called the 'father of anthropology' as well as the 'father of history' " (1949:2).

The phrase "participant observation" appears at least as early as the 1920s in a rather casual use by E. C. Lindeman (1924:191). However, I believe Kluckhohn's wife and co-researcher, sociologist Florence Kluckhohn, first wrote formally about participant observation as a fieldwork technique, based on research in a Spanish-American village conducted with her husband and begun in 1936 (F. Kluckhohn 1940). Prior to her legitimating it, the idea may, as James Clifford suggests, have been regarded more as a predicament than a technique (see Clifford 1988:93). Good (i.e., "scientific") observers of social settings in an earlier day only observed. They neither identified with nor tried to become part of what they studied; rather, they tended to write themselves out of the script, as though no outsider had been present at all. Boas, for example, directed his attention to a past "from which one hundred years of Western contact was filtered out" (Sanjek 1990:196). I need not reach back so far for illustration. I felt no hesitation in placing myself in the Kwakiutl village as teacher, but no other "white guys" are introduced unless they were official visitors to the school. It just seemed to make a more dramatic account with me as the only outsider. Today we do not have to try so hard to re-create a romantic past. Not all that much to crow about, other than keeping science itself in perspective.

Another element in obviousness is the very nature of our inquiries. Our intent is to render studies on meaningful topics, presented in depth. Our risk in this regard is a double one: rendering studies that lack depth, or conducting studies in depth on "obvious" topics that do not seem to warrant it. When we do address problems that command respect, we cannot escape the nagging question of generalization.

The cards are stacked against us on this. I do not think we must all become "artful dodgers," but any time the argument against qualitative approaches hinges on the obvious fact that our cases typically examine very ordinary circumstances, and only instances at that, we are probably better off to accede the point than to try to argue it. We ordinarily study the ordinary, and we only study instances.

Given our concern for and attention to the individual case, it seems reasonable to inquire as to how attentive we are to selecting the cases we study, not only in choosing among sites or informants—matters over which we may be able to exercise little control once we are in the field—but in choosing the problems to which we devote that attention. Qualitative researchers have rightly been cautioned about this issue, although it is not unique to their work alone.

Novices intent on gaining formal approval for their studies may inadvertently get the idea that "anything goes as long as you can get it approved." Their more senior mentors, besieged with students competing for the precious little time mentors have for their own scholarship, may offer little by way of guidance or honest assessment. The "publish or perish" ethos that pervades the university community pushes faculty into the same boat with their students: Find some study that will lead to a publication or two; forget trying to pursue topics of significance. The result, at least in those fields where research proliferates but does not aggregate, is that countless research projects are undertaken that are destined to become little more than practice exercises. Nothing will ever come of them. That is not dark art, but it does seem a darkly kept secret. It is a dark secret because we ourselves do not attend to it as a collective problem of scholarship. My new analogy is that the accumulated effect of the myriad qualitative studies undertaken can be likened to trying to fill the Grand Canyon with popcorn.

And how does that affect you, if you are just setting out to do research? Only in this profoundly disturbing way: The research you undertake is not likely to matter. Obviousness is a major distracter, and the modest scope of our studies raises doubts whenever our inquiries suggest that things are not as obvious as they seem. We lack any capacity for, or commitment to, aggregating countless little studies into something bigger, something that collectively can transcend the limits within which most fieldwork studies are carried out. Lacking such capacity means that if anything is to come of your research effort, it will be entirely up to you to make it happen. To say that fieldwork itself was just the beginning is a colossal understatement. You will have to figure out what to do with your research, how to bring it to the attention of others. They need to know why you needed to know, and how your work moves things forward, regardless of whether your efforts have made the obvious obvious or dubious.

Self-Serving

Whom does research best serve? The inescapable conclusion is that it best serves those of us who conduct it. It serves even better those who present it—whether their own work or that of others—in papers and publications dealing either with process or product.

This self-serving aspect is especially evident in graduate programs in professional fields where research is added to careers originally set in another direction. Experienced teachers, for example, "go back to school" ostensibly to become better at what they are doing (classroom teaching) but actually to obtain a license to do something quite different (e.g., administer a school, pursue scholarship or research at the university level). There is a decided emphasis on research in graduate study; the doctorate is touted as a *research* degree. Candidates for advanced degrees must become students of research to reach their new goal.

The kinds of topics so often selected by masters and doctoral level students in fields where the degree itself, rather than the achievement of any particular level of competence, is what truly matters, suggest the extent to which the research exercise is blatantly self-serving. Rather than engender a deep commitment to learning new skills or making a significant contribution to theory or practice, research often proves little more than one more hurdle along the route to an advanced degree. This churning of topics and churning out of uninteresting and unimportant studies in fulfillment of a research "ritual" has always struck me as a great waste of energy and talent. I join with others who wonder whether, at the master's level— and perhaps in some cases at the doctoral level as well (especially with the doctorate awarded in applied fields like Education or Public Administration, in contrast to a Ph.D. awarded as an academic research degree)—a satisfactory effort at synthesis and critique might be a more appropriate way to demonstrate research acumen. Paul Bohannan goes so far as to identify the need for a good program of synthesis as the "gravest need in social science" (1995:ix). Such an alternative might prove attractive to a majority of advanced students who recognize a need to become highly informed consumers of research but are unlikely to become producers of it. I propose this alternative as an exercise demanding of tough-minded critique, the sort usually reserved for the conscientious members of dissertation committees and conscientious reviewers for professional journals. Another alternative might be in demonstration itself, making critical application and appraisal of the research of others, a literal effort to translate theory into practice.

One consequence of such alternatives would be to reduce the pressure for and emphasis on *new and original* research, to place emphasis instead on making research better and making better use of research reported. It ought as well to improve research quality and significance. The anticipation of intense subsequent scrutiny by one's peers should exert a healthy influence on the quality of reported research, since novice researchers would realize that their efforts are more likely to be read and critiqued than has previously been the case. Attending to synthesis, critique, and theory building also suggests a way to promote efforts at aggregating individual studies of the sort that fieldwork produces, to assess where we are making headway or only spinning our wheels, and to identify areas of neglect. At present, too many students producing theses and dissertations the world over go through the motions to accomplish no more than research "exercises" on topics of virtually no consequence, with yesterday's inconsequential experiments and field trials replaced today by quickie descriptive studies endlessly inventorying inconsequential similarities and differences. Surely there are other ways to demonstrate a capacity for independent scholarship that can harness the energy now spent in trivial pursuit meeting program requirements.

For those who *do* find satisfaction and fulfillment in research, another of the darker secrets is that, for the most part, research continues to be self-serving throughout one's career. If there is a call for art in this aspect of our work, it is the art of self-deception in perceiving ourselves as working in service to humanity. I have no evidence that my own research ever helped anyone I thought it might help or intended it to help, except for testimonials from a few who graciously insisted that something I reported helped them to gain a fresh perspective. Although I have realized little royalty income

135

from my fieldwork publications (as sponsored research, my university kept the royalties on two of my studies; another university kept the royalties on a third), the prime beneficiary in every instance has been myself as I worked my way up the academic ladder.

Altruism and research make strange bedfellows. The dark art is to get others to think that your research is for their good, and perhaps to try to convince yourself of it as well, all the while looking for anything you might do to make this really happen. The call today is for collaborative or participatory research; in an earlier day we talked of "action research" involving participants, or applied research intended to bring about desired results. Best intentions notwithstanding, I think we must concede that the person who stands to gain the most from any research is the researcher. This does not reflect greed or selfishness as much as the fact that research carries with it a host of potential rewards and payoffs for the researcher that cannot accrue to the researched, even if—on rare occasions?—they stand to gain something. It is the researcher whose career is benefited, it is the researcher who gets the recognition, and it is the researcher who draws the salary and related "perks." Researchers may redistribute some of their material benefits—it is not unknown for American anthropologists to dedicate royalties from a study to a tribal fund, for example—but the researcher reaps the rewards of research on several dimensions, while the subjects of the study are limited because they are not in a league where research itself is likely to gain them anything except possible notoriety.

An assigned orator may someday be moved to state on my behalf, "He dedicated his life to his teaching, research, and writing." (Oh, yes, "And he will be sorely missed.") The implication will be that I gave unstintingly of myself, taking little in return. Collectively my research might be heralded in that brief moment as a "major contribution." Had I not conducted those studies and made that "major contribution," however, I do not think the world would be a different place. My place in it would have reflected the difference.

We do what we can to dispel the idea that our work is self-serving. We tout the good already accomplished (see, for example, *Making Our Research Useful, Case Studies in the Utilization of Anthropological Knowledge*, edited by van Willigen, Rylko-Bauer, and McElroy 1989) and, pressed for more, expound on the potential that *should* or *might* result from whatever new inquiry we are proposing. It is definitely an advantage in gaining access to a research setting and enlisting cooperation if one can claim that those in the setting will be among the beneficiaries of the research. These days that claim usually receives close scrutiny.

"Scientific research" has an aura of respectability about it, tending to be associated in the public mind with outcomes so unquestioningly beneficial that medical practitioners now warn an unwary public against the prevailing bias toward intervention and treatment that such faith has engendered. Social research tends to slip in under the same tent; whatever is being examined is charitably assumed to be in need of being examined. (The idea of a Golden Fleece Award, which recognizes large sums of federal money spent researching topics of questionable merit, may amuse us but seems not to precipitate any concerted effort to stop the "fleecing." The Government Accounting Office is responsible for seeing that contracted research services are performed, but it does not monitor the quality of ideas funded by Congress.) A related assumption is that problems targeted for research will subsequently be treated and fixed (for instance, that "research" on home-lessness, abuse, or gang violence will eventually rid us of those problems). In the public mind, "good" research implies both of these conditions: topics of importance leading directly to remedial action. "Bad" research suggests something altogether different: research poorly designed or poorly exe-cuted, not research devoted to inconsequential or unworthy ends.

Expectations regarding the "helpfulness" of social research vary among the disciplines and professions and the prevailing norms of the day. The mood at present favors applied, practical social research, typically under the broad umbrella of some politically correct cause. The prevailing mood of an earlier day demanded less researcher involvement or social consciousness. Results were reported as basic research. Practitioners were expected to make the necessary applications.

There have always been well-intentioned projects at "directed change." Looking again at the field of anthropology, one can see interests generated in the 1940s and '50s in applied or action anthropology giving way to more theoretical interests in the '60s and '70s. Somewhere in the 1980s those applied interests reappeared, and so did applied anthropologists. Today we expect anthropologists proposing fieldwork to be able to assure us not only how they plan to protect their subjects but *how* (not whether) the research will benefit those being studied. We expect the same of qualitative researchers everywhere. "First, do no harm" is no longer enough, although the criterion "no harm" is not all that easily met.

I have mentioned anthropologist Fred Gearing, and since his career spans this era, let me quote from his earliest fieldwork to illustrate a then-current mood that has returned to guide our work—or at least what we say about our work—again today. Although Gearing's account was not completed until 1970, his fieldwork with the Fox Indians actually began in 1952, under the guidance of his mentor, Sol Tax. Gearing explains, "I was in the Fox community to do something called 'action anthropology,' to help while learning and to learn while helping" (1970:26). (In today's cost-conscious research arena, Gearing's definition seems to have had the "l" kicked out of it; applied social research "helps while earning and earns while helping.")

By the time I began fieldwork of my own in 1962, some ten years after Gearing, it was no longer necessary to underscore the immediate benefits of research. A case study examining why Kwakiutl Indian children did poorly in school might lead to some modification in programs designed to educate them, but I was not duty-bound to promise that it would. At the same time, I *hoped* it would, and there were times when I wanted to shout over the rooftops of the village (as reservation schools often are, this one was located on a rise above it), "I'm doing this for your own good." It was a sustaining thought, if not a completely accurate one.

It is the sustaining thought that assuages us. If a teacher affects eternity, then fieldworkers ought to affect eternity too, although we dare not ask just how. I did not have to search far for an example of the opposite case, where a rapidly changing sociopolitical scene ultimately rendered a research pro-ject ineffective:

> The intervention that was designed, however, was never implemented. While the research was commissioned by the state health department with the full cooperation of the local health department, was "good" grounded research that focused heavily on the problem from the viewpoint of the affected persons, and was specifically designed to develop an intervention that would be tested and evaluated, the project ended when the final report was submitted. (Eisenberg 1994:36)

I would like to *believe* that somewhere along the line my studies have helped, but if they did, it had to be through my efforts to help others understand things as they are, not through any intent on my part to improve them. Although I work in "Anthropology and Education," generally regarded as an applied field, I do not regard myself as an applied anthropologist. I was pleased to see *A Kwakiutl Village and School* (1967) used in teacher training, particularly for teachers planning to teach in the Alaskan bush, but that was not the audience I had in mind either in writing the dissertation or revising it for publication. Similarly, I was pleased to see educator reception to *The Man in the Principal's Office* (1973), but was surprised to realize that the monograph served far more widely as a model for qualitative research than for insight into the principalship itself (see HFW 1982). None of my other studies seems to have fared any better: too little, too late (e.g., HFW 1977, 1983a), ignored by those I thought might be informed (e.g., 1983b), or simply filed away and forgotten. The original report prompting the Brad trilogy was actually commissioned after the fact: A Congress that had already become history had commissioned a report never completed; the file was waiting to be *shut* as soon as our reports were submitted. ("Your government dollars at work," political satirists like to remind us.)

For all the questions that they *do* ask, fieldworkers are often faulted for failing to ask those in the research setting how the research or researcher might be of help to them, at least in any ways other than securing funds. I think the criticism valid. It suggests a way for those who wish to be of service by inviting fieldworkers to take the issue of "helping" into the field with them—thus making it a topic for investigation—rather than initiating projects with the question "How can we help?" already answered, as we are obliged to do at present.

It is unusual to inquire deeply into the life of nearly anyone—certainly the lives of the kinds of people most often studied by fieldworkers—and not develop a sense of empathy or concern. Not infrequently that concern is joined by rage, even outrage, at the conditions under which so many humans live; as poet Robert Burns reflected, "Man's inhumanity to man makes countless thousands mourn." The very nature of fieldwork finds us often among the downtrodden or oppressed or, as often, finding oppression in social systems generally regarded as benign. We are moved to want to

139

help them tell their stories or to tell their stories for them, to "let the world know" of the (needless?) suffering that takes place.

One cannot help but assume an air of self-righteousness in getting the word out. It is immensely satisfying to uncover wrongdoing and to make pronouncements as to what ought to be done about it. One owes one's informants at least that! Perhaps I have become jaded after attending so many national and international meetings and hearing so many fieldworkers describe the plight of so many peoples for so many years—and I must admit to having indulged in such efforts myself—but I have begun to regard my own efforts as essentially self-serving and self-satisfying as well.

Engaging so wholeheartedly as we do in this "rhetoric of reform" helps us feel we have addressed critical issues and courageously spoken our piece. We make it *appear* that if we cannot always make a difference in the case at hand, at least we do not dodge responsibility in bringing underlying issues before a wider audience. Pretty safe work, perhaps all the more satisfying for that: decrying the world's injustices from the safety of a podium to an audience of our (not their) peers in Grand Ballroom A of some major hotel in some major city, a pitcher of ice water comfortingly nearby, heads nodding with compassion at the circumstances we can but briefly outline in 900-second allotted time slots. It is nice to seem to be at the cutting edge without having to do any cutting and without being noticeably near the edge. "Give 'em hell, Harry," one of my reviewers once commented in commendation. I felt I had. Nothing changed. I was applauded for my spunk in being so outspoken; I wasn't really expected to do anything about it.

Where we derive satisfaction from believing that we are making the world a better place, we ignore the better place we make for ourselves in it. In that regard we prove to be all-too-human ourselves. Nothing particularly wrong with that. It's just a bit awkward to have to own up to being our own beneficiaries.

If fieldwork efforts will continue to be largely self-serving—and I do not see how they could ever be anything else—should researchers themselves, collectively, have a larger hand in identifying what is to be researched? Burgeoning interest in qualitative research has probably made a bad situation worse, with more individuals going off in more directions under the banner of research than ever before. Qualitative studies tend to be smaller in scope, typically conducted by a principal investigator working alone, with little or no supervision, guidance, or assistance.

Perhaps here is one way research-oriented faculty might exert more influence than they have, toward the goal of improving the quality of research even if it does not change its self-serving nature. Too little attention, individual or collective, is being devoted to discerning what *needs* to be researched from all that *might* be researched. As an unintended consequence of the graduate school experience, when finding *any* topic to call one's own was enough, too little attention is given to establishing priorities as a collective responsibility of a community of scholars. That dialogue is not likely to come out of research units scrambling for grant money, but it is a dialogue for individuals willing to take on the role of the connoisseur/critic so well established in art worlds.

This suggestion is not intended to interfere with the independence of researchers, to be discussed next. What we might do is join together to become more acute critics of the processes by which problems are identified. We have been remiss in efforts to educate our own patrons; we patronize them when we could be politicizing them. Research itself is highly political. I doubt that we are ever fully cognizant of the extent to which our research options are bound up by local and national politics, one more aspect that art worlds and fieldwork worlds share. As long as academics are able to sustain the comfortable institution of tenure, those of us blessed with it have an opportunity to perform a valuable service to all qualitative (and quantitative) researchers by functioning individually or collectively as critical reviewers of what is and is not being attended to under the broad rubric of research. That is a question of research agenda.

Lack of Independence

Freedom newly won from the academy with the completion of the dissertation may prove ephemeral, especially for newly minted fieldworkers who discover they like doing this kind of research. The "performance" element of fieldwork occurs in the field, but the discerning audience is back home among those who train for, sponsor, or constitute the limited market for this type of inquiry. That audience consists not of those laundry lists of individuals whom we try to inveigle into reading our completed studies— those legislators and other policy makers, administrators, civil servants,

141

practitioners, community leaders, chief executive officers, board members, teachers, funding agencies, and on and on—but of a relatively small group of others like ourselves who do similar studies or who tell others how to do them by offering courses or writing texts. That is not an insignificant audience, but neither is it exactly the one we like to imagine. As editor Mitch Allen has observed in a telling comment, "The writers of qualitative research are also the buyers of qualitative research. It is a closed system."

You may celebrate feeling free as a bird during the fieldwork stage, but unless you are really going to "fly the coop," you will probably have to return to academia, and thus to academic scrutiny, to gain an audience for your efforts. That cannot help but exert a heavy, even deadening, influence on the way you subsequently organize and present your account. You do not buy freedom *out* of academia by becoming competent at qualitative research; if anything, your newly acquired competence may envelop you further in it. Ironically, if you were able to support yourself through part-time employment as a field assistant in a university-based research project, you may find that completing your studies, thus "earning your freedom," has cut your ties to the research arena rather than secured you a place in it. To pursue a professional career that includes opportunity to further pursue qualitative inquiry, you may have to demonstrate some art at getting into—or getting back into—academia in the new role of a faculty member. And if you succeed at that, you must master whatever art it takes to remain there. In some professional settings, that may even require you to deny your qualitative leanings, at least until you feel your reputation as a quantitative researcher is firmly established.

There is some opportunity for continuing employment in which research plays an important, but not exclusive, role. Usually this involves working under university auspices or conducting fieldwork for private contractors or agencies underwriting specific projects. Unless you are able to write your own ticket by securing funds for a project entirely of your design—a distinction implied in differentiating grants from contract research—you will undoubtedly find yourself subjected to as great or greater restraints than exist in academic research. In part this is simple economics as you take time out from research to do the things necessary to support it—report writing, grant writing, lecturing, and so forth. I have heard independent scholar-researchers lament that they must devote as much as one-third of their time to garnering financial support, in order to devote another third of their time to field research, leaving the final third for organizing and reporting. Paradoxically, then, the more one enjoys research and wants to devote major time to it, the more likely others will call the shots as to what gets studied.

For the most part, the research that gets attended to is research on topics where the money and status are—two political factors beyond the control of researchers themselves. As pointed out in Chapter 3, the constraints are not entirely economic, but whoever controls the purse strings has a major voice in determining what is to be researched. In the real world, researchers are a powerless lot; within their own world, it is the administrators of research who wield what little power there is.

What researchers have to do if they wish to keep research as a central activity in their careers is to follow the money around, to make (force?) a fit between their interests and talents and the funded problems of the day. In the protective language of grantsmanship, that is called "responding" to proposals, but those responses are as conditioned as was the salivating of Pavlov's dogs! Grant and proposal writing are now taught as skill areas in the social sciences. Dollars received through research grants and awards provide a convenient bottom line by which some academic departments assess the relative "value" of individual faculty.

I am not sure what advice grows out of these dour observations other than to help the prospective fieldworker realize that the opportunities in qualitative research are likely to be narrow or adjunct to a career focused elsewhere (such as teaching) rather than devoted exclusively to research itself. That would seem to call for making the most of whatever fieldwork opportunities come your way, if you find that the doing of fieldwork in and of itself proves satisfying.

One additional art you may have to develop, at least in the early part of a research career, is the art of extricating yourself from pressure toward joint authorship from what probably began as independent research while you were in the field. This is not a problem in genuine *team* research, but not all research touted as team research proves to be quite so collegial. Although I tend to think of fieldwork as a solitary enterprise (I work essentially as a loner, and thus tend to think that is how *all* fieldwork is best accomplished), there is a long tradition in ethnographic work, especially in community

143

study, for research conducted and reported by two-person teams. Most notably among anthropologists these have been husband and wife teams; in allied disciplines, the teams seem to get bigger, usually involving a principal investigator and numerous field assistants. In such cases it is usually decided in advance whether field assistants will have any responsibility (or opportunity) for the final reporting.

My recommendation is that field assistants be given the opportunity to report their own fieldwork separately, under their own names, in addition to whatever they are expected to contribute to the data pool or to drafting a collective report. The important thing is to make expectations clear from the beginning if fieldworkers will not retain full access to their own data.

A different situation arises when independently conducted fieldwork presented in dissertation format goes on to reappear in joint publication coauthored by professor and student. There may have been justification for this practice in ongoing quantitative research projects in which graduate students took responsibility for tiny segments of a large project and thus became coinvestigators. I have also been told that in times past it was the prerogative of The Professor, as head and chair of a department organized along the lines of British universities, to have his (a male, most likely) name included on *any* research conducted and reported by a member of the department.

I hesitate to examine such traditions out of context, but I do not think they are appropriate models for the reporting of qualitative research today. I encourage professors to find ways to circulate and celebrate the qualitative studies performed by their students. Joint authorship is not the only way—and certainly seems to me not the best way—to accomplish it. A synthesis of the work of others, reported with careful crediting in our own writing, is a commendable way to make our students' efforts better known. Coauthorship based on fieldwork conducted by subordinates is not. Whoever does the fieldwork ought to report the fieldwork; someone else can take it from there.

Another factor that contributes to lack of independence in the fieldworker role is the (obvious?) circumstance that it *is* a role. As a role, it has its own built-in constraints. We all like to step out of role at times, often with a self-conscious effort to transcend role and simply "be ourselves." There is a curious paradox here for the social scientist. Role is a convenient way to generalize about virtually everyone (else) with whom we have contact, while we perceive ourselves essentially in terms of personality. We experience discomfort when others press role conformity (and thus *their* role expectations) upon us; somehow they fail to recognize how marvelously we have transcended them.

The role of the participant observer fieldworker has this seductive quality about it, that we somehow expect it to lift us above the role of researcher to become its antithesis, the nonresearcher researcher, the person who acts (acts?) naturally, in order that those studied will act naturally as well. In fact, the role can both consume and sustain you as a researcher but it does not free you from *being* a researcher. It gives purpose to your presence, but in return you can expect to be expected to act like a researcher, even when you yourself are responsible for creating those expectatons. While trying to be yourself, you may be tested for your ability to observe more intently, reflect more thoughtfully, and literally to make something different of the experience from what anyone else in the setting is obliged to do. Those are, after all, the qualities you have attributed to researchers in presenting yourself in that role. If you are beset by a strong work ethic—and people who are attracted to research are not the world's great hedonists—then you will be besieged by your own morality pressing you to work harder, see more, record better.

An argument put forward on behalf of long-term fieldwork—and I trust you are keeping in mind throughout this discussion that I take genuine fieldwork to be of no other kind—is that the researcher remains in the field long enough that those present cannot maintain a pose. Sooner or later, and probably sooner, you should begin to learn how things *really* are. But that works both ways; you will not be able to maintain the pose of your own "best self" for long, either. You undoubtedly will want to be seen as neutral, objective, equally fair to and interested in all alike. But you will be put upon, and you have your own appetites to contend with. In time, you may feel that in your role as researcher you are always "on duty." Occasionally you might want to go "off duty" to catch your breath, gain a bit of perspective, perhaps simply enjoy some privacy. If you are really immersed in the field, you probably will find no easy escape, trapped in the very role that once seemed so natural, so inviting, so unencumbered.

What to do? Well, don't torture yourself with feelings that you are the first ever to find the role more difficult to sustain than you realized. Try to discern your own coping strategies. Rosalie Wax confessed to a noticeable weight gain during her first fieldwork as she literally ate her way into compensating for the stress and loneliness eating away at her (Wax 1971:72). If you can pass up the bonbons, or equally tantalizing options such as unusually long hours devoted to sleeping or escapist reading, and you really are as work-oriented as I suspect you are, you might try writing. Writing and writing. Sooner or later that is what you must do anyway.

For many individuals, researchers included, writing has therapeutic as well as professional value. Clifford argues us that "One of the ways Malinowski pulled himself together was by writing ethnography" (Clifford 1988:104). That is a fairly candid assessment, the kind one makes years after the fact and after we are sure that the researcher did actually pull himself or herself together and pulled together a significant research account as well. (Clifford is less generous on the latter score, noting that "Malinowski never did pull together Trobriand culture; he produced no synthetic portrait, only densely contextualized monographs on important institutions" [p. 104].) In whatever ways writing helped Malinowski—and it did give us, among others, both *Argonauts of the Western Pacific* (1922) and *A Diary in the Strict Sense of the Term*, published posthumously in 1967—consider the possibility that it might also work for you. An important part of the discussion to follow (Part Three) will emphasize writing, especially the idea of beginning one's writing early in the fieldwork.

Fieldwork itself is unquestionably that aspect of qualitative inquiry in which one can assert the least control. One can be *prepared*, but that does not necessarily entail formal "training" of any kind. How one has learned to cope with all the other exigencies to be confronted in the course of everyday life surely has more predictive power for fieldwork success than how many courses one has taken, manuals one has read, or ethnographers one has known. In the two major aspects of the fieldwork process to be discussed in the next chapters—conceptualizing what one is doing, and getting on with the writing—one can probably be better prepared than for the doing of fieldwork itself. Some measure of confidence should spill over to the field encounter simply because you have a good idea of where the work is leading. You are more apt to get there if you have an idea of where you are going, even if you are unsure of the way. But never delude yourself into thinking that your choices along the way will be yours alone to make. All you may really be free to do is to make a whole new set of mistakes and then decide how candid you intend to be about reporting your efforts to deal with them.

Deception and Betrayal

Of all the risks inherent in fieldwork, none is more personally disturbing to me than the suggestion, and sometimes the outright accusation, that those whom we have studied feel betrayed by what we have said or written. I know no more disturbing sentence addressing this topic than the one Miles and Huberman included in the first edition of their widely acclaimed *Qualitative Data Analysis* and stoutly reaffirmed in the expanded second edition a decade later:

> It is probably true that, fundamentally, field research is an act of betrayal, no matter how well intentioned or well integrated the researcher. One makes public the private and leaves the locals to take the consequences. (Miles and Huberman 1984:233; see also 1994:265)

In further support of their point, they add by way of footnote a quote attributed to writer Joan Didion, "I am so small, so neurotic, and so inoffensive that people invariably forget an important point: the writer will *do you in*" (quoted in Miles and Huberman 1984:248n, my source for the epigraph attributed to John Leonard as well).

Sociologist Maurice Punch goes a step further to suggest that if a latent aim of fieldwork is to create trust in the researcher, then the relationship actually involves "a double betrayal: first by them of you but then by you of them." As he puts it, "Often in fieldwork the subjects are conning you until you can gain their trust and then, once you have their confidence, you begin conning them" (Punch 1986:72–73).

Discomforting as it is, we must face the charge of betrayal head on. I do not subscribe to the idea that field research is *always* an act of betrayal, but the possibility is ever present. There is no way we can do this work without uncovering additional information, complexity, and linkages; no way we can claim to be in the business of finding things out without finding things out; no way we can report what we have understood without the risk

147

of being misunderstood. The whole purpose of the enterprise is *revelation*. Our quest may be ennobled by our seeking for understanding, but it aims at revelation, nonetheless. There is always the likelihood that in what is revealed some party or parties will feel betrayed, always a matter of individual perception. That is not to suggest that betrayal itself is one of our darker arts; rather, our obligation is to attend responsibly to the art of revelation. That can be, but need not be, sinister business.

Closely related is another charge that we must learn to live with rather than deny. Our efforts to live our way into the groups we wish to study, and particularly our efforts to win over informants for extended and close collaboration, can be viewed not only as establishing rapport but also as seductions, and "massive seductions" at that. This phrase, suggested by cross-cultural psychologist David Gutmann, is quoted in Langness and Frank's introduction to anthropological life history, *Lives* (1981):

> We are too apt to play at being democratic "good guys" at the expense of our often very hungry and vulnerable informants. We think that we are being cool, and unconcerned with status; but they too often experience our transient gestures toward equality as *massive* seductions . . . Thus, it is not enough that we develop sensitivity to our informants' motives; we should also be very sensitive toward and corrective of our own. (Langness and Frank 1981:131)

Gutmann's recommendation was that "all fieldworkers in training should be supervised not only by experts in their particular discipline, but also by clinical psychologists or psychiatrists" (p. 131). Langness and Frank pared that to a need for life historians to "learn the rudiments of personality theory and clinical practice," a seemingly worthy objective although an unlikely one. But the phrase "massive seductions" continues to ring in my ears. Like Blanche DuBois in *A Streetcar Named Desire*, fieldworkers must rely on the kindness of strangers to help get where they want to go. On some of those strangers a fieldworker may press inordinately.

Is seduction one of our darker arts? As craftspeople, are we so crafty that others don't know when they are being seduced? Is there some ethically acceptable approach to, or level of, seduction appropriate for fieldworkers? Is seduction necessarily so one-sided, the powerful always overwhelming the helpless? When we ourselves are not doing the conning, are our informants conning us?

Many such interpersonal dilemmas are associated with fieldwork. There are situations in which the better the artistry in confronting them, the less rather than the more we might admire the guile of the fieldworker. Maybe we are better off to recognize and confront the fact that, however well intended, our work cannot, and need not, transcend being a human endeavor, with attendant costs as well as benefits. We may as well acknowledge those costs and be alert to ways to minimize them, rather than deny them or be too quick to point an accusing finger at others.

No fieldworker ever has a license to tell all. Is there an art to recognizing how much to tell? That is where trust comes back, haunting us about discretion that one might assume to be an implicit part of the bargain. The consequence for fieldworkers is that we cannot avoid a certain amount of deception. David Nyberg has defined deception as the artful deployment of the varnished truth (Nyberg 1993:7), reminding us of a Caucasus proverb that a man who tells the truth should keep his horse saddled. Since the write-up may not be completed until long after fieldwork is concluded, fieldworkers who do not prematurely divulge the nature and extent of their proposed reporting do not have to keep their horses saddled. Not all of them ride off in the same direction twice, however.

Along with not knowing enough about the subject of an inquiry, as described above under the heading "Superficiality," as a fieldworker you are also likely to discover that you know too much. The seriousness of the problem will probably be proportional to the quality of your fieldwork: the more successful you are as a fieldworker, the more you will learn things that you did not intend—and possibly did not want—to learn. You will experience concern about what you should disclose, at what cost, for what audiences.

To a large extent, this becomes a problem of reporting, for that is when you make decisions about what needs to be made public and, of that, how much you take responsibility to report. Anticipating the problem will influence your thinking from the outset as you make choices about what to study, and to what depth to pursue your inquiries. The same people who may try to put you off may also unburden themselves once they discover that you are a good listener, particularly if you are perceived to be a nonjudgmental or sympathetic one. Qualitative researchers inadvertently may find out too much of the wrong stuff while trying to learn more of the stuff that fills their own definition of how the inquiry is supposed to proceed. What to do?

I think fieldworkers should always have in mind clear boundaries for their inquiries. At the same time, they need to keep those boundaries flexible, allowing themselves room to refine or redirect the focus of the study, should that become necessary, as well as to accommodate personalities and circumstances on a moment-to-moment basis during the interpersonal processes of being in the field. You have to respect people's efforts to convey what *they* want you to hear, just as you hope they will talk candidly about what *you* want to hear. Your sense of courtesy will guide the extent to which you allow them just to "go on." The limits set for the inquiry should guide the extent of extraneous material to record.

Whether and how often to caution those in the research setting about your presence and purposes is, of course, a judgment call, but I think people need not only to know but periodically to be reminded why you are there. To whatever extent possible, you should also help informants maintain some sense of the scope of what you intend to report. When appropriate, you can achieve the former simply by keeping your notebook or other recording devices visible at all times, even though the contents of what you record are for your eyes alone. You can achieve the latter—foreshadowing the direction you plan to take in reporting—by commending information that is particularly helpful, or remarking on topics clearly beyond the boundaries of your intended study. Such signals from you may help to allay second thoughts among those who realize too late that they have talked too freely or divulged information they do not wish to see in print. Those signals also provide some hint about the kind of information most likely to make it into your final reporting.

Fieldworkers often discover to their surprise that informants try to use them as conduits for communicating problems and concerns to a wider audience. Those in the research setting cannot later claim to be disappointed in your work if, from the outset, you have made clear the limits of what you expect to do and to acknowledge concerns they may have that you know you will not address. I could assure my Kwakiutl friends that no matter what I put in my "memory book," no Royal Commission subsequently was going to be appointed to investigate their concerns about fishing rights. For that problem, I simply was not their man.

An artful sense of discretion, plus a close reading of the social scene and research climate, will guide much of your decision-making about what you report. You may feel torn between the extremes of daily news coverage and television fare on the one hand and gun-shy colleagues and administrators warning you about possible lawsuits on the other. The personal guideline I draw from others is both a Confucian proverb and a restatement of the Golden Rule, to *not* do unto others anything you would not want them to do to you.

My counsel is to be candid but discreet. Whatever you do divulge, reveal accurately, but always stay within the limits of the research focus rather than fostering a reputation for "selling diaries" or telling tales out of school. Important points tangential to a particular inquiry can be flagged for reader attention by noting issues raised but not resolved in your research or by footnoting topics worthy of future study. Similarly, sticky issues can often be alluded to in such a way that insiders recognize whether you were being discreet, rather than simply naive, while outsiders need be no more the wiser.

Clandestine Observation

Exactly what is it that motivates those of us who commit ourselves so wholeheartedly to be the self-appointed watchers of others? Do we engage in some special, socially approved form of voyeurism in which, through our insistence that we are attentive to all aspects of human life, we can also insist that no aspects of it are to be denied us?

Few fieldworkers (Van Maanen 1978:346, is one exception) have been so bold as to use the term *voyeur* in looking at our roles in research, but not even the least hint that we derive scintillation from our observations and inquiries rests lightly. Nonetheless, exclusion is the enemy: We want to see it all. We search for arguments in support of claims about seeking knowledge "for the common good" to counteract the concerns of others about rights of privacy. We rankle at demands of full disclosure of our research purposes among those whom we study, yet express surprise and most certainly express dismay to discover that they are rankled at something we have observed too closely or disclosed too fully.

151

We may vigorously deny that we are voyeurs, but we must be able to face that accusation head-on and to acknowledge whatever influence it may exert on our work itself and others' perceptions of what we are up to. Perhaps we are better off to admit to both personal and professional leanings in this regard—as fellow humans and as social researchers—but to make sure they are seen in context. Our interest in what others do certainly extends beyond a strictly prurient one—virtually *everything* that humans do is of potential interest to us. Whatever it is, we want to see "how they do it," especially if it is something that we also do, would like to do, or perhaps would like to help them not to do.

A fundamental curiosity about what others think and do, how they live out their lives similarly to, and different from, my own, drew me to the study of cultural anthropology. I can live with being identified as a kind of licensed social voyeur, someone who wants to, and to some extent gets to, look at life in all (or much) of its intimacy. Maybe by simply bringing these aspects of fieldwork into the open we can keep them from seeming to be one of our darker preoccupations.

But I can, and do, draw the line between being a voyeur and being what is known as a Peeping Tom. A key word associated with the latter may help distinguish the darker dimensions from our everyday actions as fieldworkers. Although we sometimes use the expression *Peeping Tom* to refer to (or subtly reprimand) those prying into something not legitimately their business, specifically the label is directed at anyone who obtains sexual gratification by observing others surreptitiously, a glimpse of Lady Godiva replaced today with the caricature of an individual peeping through a bedroom window while someone unaware inside is disrobing.

The catch word is "surreptitious." And that points to a darker, clandestine element in our work. It is not surreptitious observation itself that presents the problem but a recognition of when such observations are appropriate or acceptable and when they are not. We humans are not above making surreptitious observations, but we most certainly hate to get caught making them. If fieldworkers are sometimes like detectives, and perhaps too often likened to spies, then a certain degree of stealth may be warranted. When those in the setting are observed and described "naturally," we commend the stealth of the fieldworker.

In the name of ever-escalating national defense expenditures, huge sums have been directed toward the development of Stealth bombers and stealthy submarines difficult to detect. On the international scale, then, the art lies in knowing which side to get caught on! In our own fieldwork literature, it is not that many years since something as sinister-sounding as "lurking" was presented as an appropriate fieldwork technique (see Strickland and Schlesinger 1969). Issues related to disguised observation, both in general (e.g., Erickson 1967; Hilbert 1980; Roth 1962) and to Laud Humphreys' investigations into *Tearoom Trade* in particular (e.g., Humphreys 1989), have been part of the research dialogue for years. A realistic review and appraisal of the problems can be found in Richard Mitchell's *Secrecy and Fieldwork* (1993). He recognizes secrecy as "a pervasive feature of contemporary social life" (p. 1) and secrecy in research as "risky but necessary business" (p. 54). "If the social sciences are to continue to provide substantive, enduring insights in human experience," he continues, "timid inquiry will not do." Mitchell also cautions against confusing secretive research methods with harmful research results. He is neither an advocate of nor an apologist for deception; it is a fact of life and a fact of fieldwork life. The moral obligation of acting responsibly remains on the shoulders of the individual fieldworker.

Proceed with Caution

Of course there are counterpoints to be offered for each problem I have raised, just as it is tempting to insist, "Not me!" to each accusation. Conversely, one might draw longer lists (see, for example, Gary Fine's "Ten Lies of Ethnography," 1993), or more damning ones. My purpose is achieved in emphasizing that our high calling has its own dark underside, especially as seen by outsiders put at risk because of our inquiries and sometimes amazed at both our self-righteousness and our audacity about pursuing them.

I think we had best soft-pedal the self-righteousness: We do what we do, create what we create. We should take pride in doing it as well as we can. But it's not a bad idea now and then to take a look in that mirror we are so anxious to turn on others and to face some of the tensions in a role that we often need to explain and sometimes need to defend. Our collective ambivalence on this score can show up in the labels we apply or deny, as, for example, when anthropologists in the field refer to themselves as sociologists or linguists, and yet take umbrage at journalists or others who pose as anthropologists. We are all engaged with both the professional and personal dimensions of impression management.

In her monograph *Surviving Fieldwork*, Nancy Howell states that about 25 percent of her sample of cultural anthropologists report having been suspected of spying (1990:97), which, as she points out, is "a difficult charge to defend against when one is there in search of information." Far better, I think, to have a realistic picture of how others sometimes see us than a Pollyannaish one of the image we might like to think we have created. As with others, our works and our ways of working must speak for themselves.●

PART THREE
FIELDWORK
AS MINDWORK*

Without an ethnographer, there is no ethnography. . . .

—Paul Bohannan
How Culture Works, 157

Fieldwork is a state of mind. And something you put your mind to. Whatever goes on in your mind as you prepare for it, engage in it, reflect back on it, and report from it, constitutes its essence. In the previous chapters attention was directed toward the more interpersonal, physical, and mechanical aspects of fieldwork—social courtesies, gaining access, observing, asking, leave taking—moving your body through space to get to a suitable place at a suitable time. Careful attention to such details can get you properly located with a willing informant or in an appropriate setting, perhaps a camera or tape recorder at the ready, along with your trusty notebook. All very helpful, great for making you *look* like a field-worker.

---

* The chapters in Part Three are new. However, some of the ideas in Chapters 7 and 8, expressed in some of these very words, were first published in an essay contributed to *Schools and Society: Learning Content Through Culture*, a Festschrift edited by Henry Trueba and Concha Delgado-Gaitan honoring George and Louise Spindler and published in 1988 by Praeger. My chapter, " 'Problem Finding' in Qualitative Research," appeared on pages 11–35. Readers found that discussion helpful and encouraged me to make it more widely available. Although my writing is now informed by another decade of dialogue, the issues raised earlier remain central to the mindwork of fieldwork. Similarly, in *Writing Up Qualitative Research* (HFW 1990b), I dealt in greater detail on matters of presentation. Chapter 9 highlights several ideas from that monograph that seem especially relevant to preparing fieldwork accounts.

But what counts—the only thing that really counts in the long run—is what is going on in your mind, your sense of purpose among an infinite number of purposes that might be accomplished. I can't state it any better than the way I heard it on television in the fall of 1993 during the premier season of the award-winning series "NYPD Blue," when its red-headed protagonist Detective Kelly turned to another character and asked succinctly: "What do you want to accomplish?"

What do you want to accomplish? We have some slightly fancier terms—problem-finding, problem-posing, problem-seeking—but they all address the same concern. Problem-finding, rather than problem-seeking, is at the core of the creative process—for artist and scientist alike (see Freeman 1993; Getzels and Csikszentmihalyi 1976).

My mentor George Spindler once labeled this as "the problem problem." During a period when he and Louise Spindler assumed editorship of the *American Anthropologist*, they became acutely aware of what other anthropologists were investigating and, especially, how those others went about reporting to their peers. The Spindlers were intrigued that drafts submitted for review often lacked focus, taking on an air of "haphazard descriptiveness" that is an occupational hazard for anyone who engages in descriptive research. The Spindlers' writerly advice, included in the inevitable letter of rejection for such manuscripts, was for the author/researcher to go back to the original problem statement, or to refine or rework the problem statement that eventually evolved, so that it would bring the necessary focus to the process of revision. Their contributors needed to work through their "problem problem."

Possibly the most serious misconception about qualitative research—and for those who harbor it, the biggest disappointment as well—has to do with how our research questions arise in the first place. What is the genesis of the problems we study? Somewhere out there lurks a wrong-headed notion that problems rise up before our eyes in a sort of intellectual equivalent of spontaneous combustion. That is not how it happens.

The "problem problem" is not embedded within the lives of those whom we study, demurely waiting to be discovered. Quite the opposite: *We instigate the problems we investigate.* There is no point in simply sitting by, passively waiting to see what a setting is going to "tell" us or hoping a problem will "emerge." Yes, the Eskimo carver wonders aloud, "Who hides there?" but the answer is never "Ah! Giraffe" or "Ah! Missionary!" And there is no simple answer to the seemingly straightforward question, "Just tell me the steps one follows in qualitative inquiry. What does one do first, what next? No theory. Just the steps."

When such questions come to us, typically disguised as questions of fieldwork *technique*, they are usually answered with "It depends." The response is well-intended but not always well-received, for it is at once profound and exasperating. I have had occasion to use it often enough in these pages. The underlying point is that, except in the broadest of terms, fieldwork techniques cannot be distilled and described independently from the questions that guide the research. They are the tools of our trade. In the hands of an artist, tools of the trade produce art; in the hands of craftspeople, they produce craft. In the hands of the careless, they may also result in injury.

There are numerous fieldwork manuals, including those that outline explicit efforts to systematize fieldwork into neat sets of step-by-step sequences (see, for example, Fetterman 1989; Spradley 1979, 1980; Werner and Schoepfle 1987a,b). Such manuals present some seasoned veteran's attempt to demystify fieldwork procedures and to guide novices in using the tools and techniques of field research. Regardless of how systematic such efforts may appear, they never achieve the meticulous algorithms and elegant formulae that give quantitative researchers an edge over what are perceived as our too-casual, too-vague approaches.

Not surprisingly, aspiring fieldworkers and seasoned veterans alike sometimes appear self-conscious about issues of method and become defensive at any mention of a standard litany of conceptual issues such as reliability, generalizeability, or objectivity. Therefore, the first problems I address in this section devoted to "mindwork" are matters I have put under the topic for Chapter 7, "The Art of (Conceptual) Self-Defense." I deal with these problems to offer both perspective and encouragement, for they seem forever to get *in* the way without any likelihood that they will ever *go* away. I address them first, then proceed (in Chapters 8 and 9) to deal with the essential arts of conceptualization and write-up.●

CHAPTER SEVEN

THE ART OF
(CONCEPTUAL) SELF-DEFENSE

C ertain problems keep recurring not only in the dialogue between quantitative and qualitative researchers but also among qualitative researchers themselves. Fieldworkers need perspectives and coping strategies for dealing with them. They do not need definitive answers that resolve the issues for all times, for these are the debates that surround the inquiry process itself. They are critical issues in the research dialogue, yet they are potentially subverting of that process whenever turned full-force against any particular research effort, qualitative or quantitative.

My advice to beginning researchers is to be informed as to the substance of these debates rather than to be drawn prematurely into them. Leave them for others, or for yourself on another day when you are prepared to deal with issues on a grand scale rather than confronting a modest research task immediately at hand. Think of these issues as on a par with environmental protection, human rights, a world without war, or the ultimate answer to a question like, "What is art?" There are myriad issues, ethical, methodological, and philosophical, about which you may be asked or challenged to take a stand. If you are, you will be expected to have a thoughtful position, not expected to come up with "the answer." Any of the dilemmas identified in the previous chapter can be posed as a broad challenge to qualitative research in general, or a focused one addressed to how you propose to approach a particular topic. The issues identified in this chapter are methodological in nature, the sort likely to occur in dialogue (or, sometimes, interrogation) between qualitative and quantitative researchers. Do not get lured into believing that the entire rationale for qualitative approaches now rests on your shoulders alone, or that until you have satisfactorily resolved each of these methodological perplexities, you may not proceed with your own research.

The issues to be raised here concern the scientific method, objectivity and bias, neutrality, reliability, validity, and generalization. The closely related issue of theory introduces the chapter that follows.

Scientific Method

There is not such a thing as a Scientific Method.

—P. B. Medawar
The Art of the Soluble, 148

In Chapter 4, I inventoried some important techniques currently employed in the more scientific approaches to fieldwork. I did not inquire into the broader issue of "a" or "the" scientific method itself. What about the criticism one hears that fieldwork is the antithesis of scientific method, that quantitative approaches have all the method and fieldwork has none?

A method is a procedure, a technique, a way of doing something.

Fieldwork is a way of doing something.

As a way of doing something, fieldwork includes several rather standard techniques, all of which can be adapted for any particular setting as needed. All fieldwork techniques can be subsumed under one single heading, Participant Observation, or under two major headings if Participant Observation and Interviewing are paired off to become the dynamic duo of field research. The choice, as discussed in Chapter 5, depends on whether interviewing is taken to be the complement of participant observation or a major facet of it.

The approaches to fieldwork are, in their almost infinite variations, alternatives rather than sequenced steps, choices among strategies rather than selections of proper techniques. As George Homans observed years ago (1962), research is a matter of strategies, not of morals. Qualitative approaches avoid any semblance of the rigid step-by-step sequence generally associated with tight research designs. They are intended to allow researchers to follow a suitable course of inquiry rather than to dictate in advance what that course should be. The essence of qualitative research, as Becker puts it, is that it is *designed in the doing* (Becker 1993:219). Although that makes fieldwork difficult to explain in the abstract, anyone who has engaged in it recognizes that in practice it can proceed no other way. We should rejoice that we are not encumbered by the Scientific Method in pursuing our work, even while we may feel a bit of envy in recognizing how convenient and self-validating such recipes might be when trying to teach (or having to convince) others about how we proceed. It is easy for us to forget that "scientists" themselves are not particularly encumbered by the scientific method. As observers have pointed out, there is no particular incentive for those assumed to work under its aegis to tarnish their idealized reputation for systematic work, since it does not get in the way of actual practice. Paradoxically, the very idea that "real" scientists relentlessly follow the scientific method provides the cover that permits them to be more imaginative (or at times just plain bumbling), while the complementary idea that qualitative research is not guided by rigorous methodological doctrine is held up as one of our major shortcomings.

On the wall of my office hangs a sign gleaned from words attributed by anthropologist Roger Keesing to biologist Paul Weiss: "Nobody who followed the scientific method ever discovered anything interesting" (Keesing and Keesing 1971:10). It is hardly surprising that a biologist's comment about the scientific method is offered as solace for cultural anthropologists torn between wanting their discipline to be, as Eric Wolf stated years ago (1964:88), the most scientific of the humanities, the most humanist of the sciences. Except perhaps when lecturing or conversing with colleagues outside their discipline, cultural anthropologists have emphasized the *results* of their studies, whether "findings" or "interpretations," rather than their methods. In recent years, however, "method" has come to assume a more prominent role in their dialogue, a preoccupation that has tended to divide them into two camps, those concerned with methods and those concerned with those so concerned with them.

Such methodological preoccupation has also found many anthropologists going farther afield, deeper into modes of analysis rather than deeper into fieldwork to achieve methodological sophistication. In the days when "participant observation" was explanation enough, advice as to how to go about it tended to be offhand. "Hang around." "Talk to folks." "Try to get a sense of what is going on." It was always pragmatic, sometimes too much so, as reflected in what Jean Jackson calls the Take-a-big-stick-for-the-dogs-and-lots-of-marmalade jokes (1990:24), sometimes humorously profound, as with Radcliffe-Brown's purported advice, "Get a large notebook and start in the middle because you never know which way things will develop" (quoted in Rubinstein 1991:14). Any such advice was intended to bolster confidence in the fieldworker. It was not intended to reassure fieldworkers or their critics that they were going about their work The Right Way.

Nonetheless, fieldworkers do become self-conscious whenever method is at issue. Scientific methods in general, and the essentially mythical Scientific Method in particular, continue to hang as specter over our efforts. What is our equivalent? Unscientific or Nonscientific Method? Humanistic Method? The Rejection-of-Method or Absence-of-Method Method?

It may be comforting to keep in mind that even the most scientific of research procedures, regardless of how systematic and objective, can be neither perfectly systematic nor ultimately objective. Descriptive studies of how laboratory science proceeds remind us that on close inspection the investigative process is (of necessity) totally susceptible to human judgment, a product of social construction subject even to plain old down-and-dirty politics (see, for example, studies by Fleck 1979; Latour 1987; Latour and Woolgar 1986; Woolgar 1983). It is the insistent demand of outsiders for the guided tour of the laboratory and a proven formula for discovery ("Just tell me the steps you follow . . .") that traps researchers of all persuasions into portraying as a neat, linear, logical sequence what is, in fact, a dialectical process in which all critical judgments are made by humans. "All worldly truth rests ultimately on direct individual experience," Jack Douglas states boldly (Douglas 1976:6).

So exactly what are we being defensive about? Insight, intuition, imagination, luck—yes, even serendipity—each is critical to *all* discovery processes, ours no more than theirs. The phrase "scientific breakthrough" nicely credits scientists for maintaining control, always knowing where they are going, although I recall Aubrey Haan suggesting years ago that "scientific fall-through" might be the more appropriate phrase in most cases. The critical art in all observation is achieved not in the act of observing but in recognizing when something of significance has been observed.

Fieldwork proceeds that way, too, not simply through observation but in recognizing when something of significance—of *potential* significance—

has been observed. The difference is that we try to exert as little interference as possible. We typically deny any suggestion of our own power and authority even when made uncomfortably aware of our advantaged status in the settings we study.

Tight research designs strike me as a good strategy for researchers who need to exert control over what they study, both control *of* and control *for*. Qualitative approaches represent a different way to achieve a different kind of understanding, one that appeals to those who find satisfaction in partial or tentative explanations of what is going on without the hope of ever quite achieving the authority of cause-and-effect studies. Every way of knowing has its place. Science cannot proceed without controlled experimentation, but neither science nor controlled experimentation can reveal all we seek to understand about ourselves and our fellow humans.

Objectivity and Bias

"Objectivity" is perhaps best seen as a label to hide problems in the social sciences.

—Michael H. Agar
The Professional Stranger, 41

The process of forming links between ideas in the observer's mind and what one has observed is dialectical: Ideas inform observations and observations inform ideas. The prime mover in the process is the researcher. Whatever constitutes the elusive quality called "objectivity," mindlessness is not part of it.

Observation cannot proceed without an idea in the observer's mind of what one is to look at and look for in qualitative research any more than in quantitative. This runs counter to claims made on behalf of objectivity (and, by extension, to warnings about the evil influences of bias), stated in strong terms such as this declaration by ethologist Konrad Lorenz, writing on behalf of an outdated position but writing not all that long ago:

> It is an inviolable law of inductive natural science that it has to *begin* with pure observation, totally devoid of any preconceived theory and even working hypotheses. (Lorenz 1950:232)

163

Another ethologist, C. G. Beer, my source for the above quotation (1973:49), cogently presents the counter view to that of Lorenz, whose position he dismisses lightheartedly as the "doctrine of immaculate perception." Beer cites philosophers of science like Karl Popper who argue that "preconceived theories or working hypotheses must always be involved in scientific observation to enable the scientist to decide what is to count as a fact of relevance to his investigation" (p. 49).

Malinowski tried to put preconceived ideas to rest some 50 years earlier, dismissing them as "pernicious," in contrast to "foreshadowed problems," which he endorsed as "the main endowment of a scientific thinker" (1922:9). For a while the distinction caught the attention of other field-workers, but it proved too facile. Beer and other observers of a later day were more instructive in equating preconceived ideas with the working hypotheses essential to scientific observation. Scientists like that word *hypothesis*, but I take impish delight in substituting a different label, *bias*.

Rather than dismiss bias as something we should guard against, I have come to think of it not only as something we must live with but as something we cannot do without. Bias might be likened to our human need for "air." Air is an undifferentiated substance to which we give little notice in ordinary circumstances. Air can be subject to great variability as to composition and quality. It is absolutely necessary in some amount, regardless of quality, but as its quality deteriorates, it can exacerbate, if not directly cause, problems for those lacking an optimum amount of the best of it.

Like air, bias can be good or bad, energizing or polluting. It can freshen or be stale, nurture good health or aggravate bad. And as with air quality, we can exert some minimal control over some aspects of bias, checking its quality, regulating contaminants. For the most part we take it for granted, becoming conscious of it only when some aspect becomes so conspicuous as to call attention to itself. Bias that does not simply call attention but dominates one's view might be likened to the odor of mothballs permeating a roomful of guests at the first autumn wearing of wool clothing stored away all summer, or to rising concern of airline passengers over air quality on today's crowded jets. (I can think of no fate worse than being a traffic policeman in a congested city like Bangkok, virtually assured that constant exposure to deadly exhaust fumes will prove ruinous to your health.)

Good bias not only helps us get our work done; by lending focus, it is essential to the performance of any research. In the total absence of bias, a researcher would be unable even to leave the office to set off in the direction of a potential research site. Bad bias, then, is a matter of excess, like bad air crowding out good. In the case of qualitative research, bias becomes excessive to whatever extent it exerts undue influence on the consequences of inquiry. In the extreme, conclusions may be foreordained without investigation of any kind. The way to guard against this is not to deny bias or pretend to suppress it, but to recognize and harness it. Bias should stimulate inquiry without interfering in the investigation. That surely requires art. The critical step is to understand that *bias itself is not the problem*. One's purposes and assumptions need to be made explicit and used judiciously to give meaning and focus to a study.

I doubt that, as long as it is fully explicated, bias ever really gets in the way. It offers an answer to the criticism heard by insiders who claim that only they can understand their own group. Bias requires us to identify the perspective we bring to our studies as insiders and/or outsiders and to anticipate how that may affect what we report. Its counterpart, "prejudice," is our true foe, judgment formed without that explicit basis. If you can distinguish your prejudices from your biases, let the former guide you away from topics on which your opinions are likely to interfere with research. But covet your biases, display them openly, and ponder how they help you formulate both the purposes of your investigation and how you can proceed with your inquiries. With biases firmly in place, you won't have to pretend to complete objectivity, either. Try instead for what Frederick Erickson has labeled "disciplined subjectivity" (1984:61). No artist could wish for more!

Neutrality

Whereas traditional researchers cling to the guard rail of neutrality, critical researchers frequently announce their partisanship in the struggle for a better world.

—Joe Kincheloe and Peter McLaren
"Rethinking Critical Theory and Qualitative Research," 140

At one time I harbored the misconception that neutrality was another essential element in descriptive research—that, to be "fair," one had to regard all humans with equal esteem—the anthropological proclivity for "deferred judgment" run amok. An experienced fieldworker—John Connolly, in this case—raised for me the question of whether one really needs to be neutral in order to be objective. I've never completely sorted out what being objective means, especially in the subjective and sensitive business of humans observing and interpreting the behavior of other humans. I admit to being relieved to realize that having likes or dislikes—a rather human quality in which I have been known to overindulge—did not exclude me from doing fieldwork.

I recall my initial dismay that Jules Henry had allowed himself what seemed too free a rein in presenting his "passionate ethnography" of American society, *Culture Against Man* (Henry 1963). A decade later, Colin Turnbull was roundly criticized not only for his negative portrayal of the Ik (Turnbull 1972) but also for revealing his disaffection for them, violating the anthropological preference for deferred judgment. In the interim since those works were published we have seen innumerable instances in which personal preferences have provided anthropologists the impetus for writing their accounts. A wave of postmodernists insisted that the only understanding a fieldworker could gain in the course of research was of himself or herself. For a while, it seemed that anthropologists might become so taken with describing their own feelings that fieldwork would be nothing more than a vehicle for self-understanding. Perhaps that time of self-reflection (bordering on self-absorption) was inevitable after so long a period in which fieldworkers were not expected to demonstrate any feelings at all. In that earlier day anything recorded privately in diaries or personal correspondence was assumed to remain privileged information forever.

I take deep and genuine interest in the people and settings I have written about. I have learned to recognize and to appreciate in those feelings a source of energy for conducting and completing my studies. My feelings have not always been positive, and I have never known any group of people that did not have its share of rogues and rascals, most certainly including my associates in academia. Nevertheless, I cannot imagine initiating a study in which I had no personal feelings, felt no interest or concern for the humans whose lives touched mine, or failed to find in those concerns a vital source of inspiration and energy. Neutrality is another of those topics we must be able to address without having to embrace.

Reliability

Reliability preoccupies those who hold anthropology to be a behavioral science, and who thus place severe limits on what the ethnographic method should include. It is a valuable quality in laboratory, medical and product safety research, and in some social research operations.

—Roger Sanjek
"The Ethnographic Present," 620

Reliability remains beyond the pale for research based on observation in natural settings.

That is unfortunate, for it is hard to escape the connotation that if our work is not reliable, then it must be unreliable. That is not its technical meaning in the lexicon of researchers, however, where reliability refers to what might better have been termed *replicability* or *consistency*, "the extent to which a measurement procedure yields the same answer however and whenever it is carried out" (Kirk and Miller 1986:19). In order to achieve reliability in that technical sense, a researcher has to manipulate conditions so that replicability can be assessed. Ordinarily, fieldworkers do not try to make things happen at all, but whatever the circumstances, we cannot *make* them happen twice. When something does happen more than once, we do not for a minute insist that the repetition is exact. As James Fernandez observes, "We anthropologists have long had the Heraclitean understanding that we cannot step into the same stream twice" (1994:136).

Reliability—along with its partner validity, to be discussed next—is frequently raised as a critical component of research, the pair sometimes described as two complementary aspects of objectivity (Kirk and Miller 1986:19). It is awkward to have to admit to those following strict adherence to a quantitative tradition that fieldwork does not lend itself to what reliability is all about. I have never been all that convinced that reliability necessarily serves *quantitative* researchers well, either. The problem with reliability is that the rigor associated with it redirects attention to research processes rather than to research results. *Similarity* of responses is taken to be the same as *accuracy* of responses. The problem with equating them is that one might obtain consistent temperature findings consistently in error due to a faulty thermometer, obtain consistent responses to survey questions that make no sense to respondents, or obtain consistent ratings among raters trained to look for the same things in the same way, in each instance achieving a high degree of reliability on unreliable data. The strain for *identifying* consistency in findings thus yields to *establishing* consistency through procedures. Reliability is, therefore, an artifact.

We do need to recognize the circumstances that render reliability essentially irrelevant as a central concern in fieldwork; we do not need to apologize for it. Kirk and Miller recommend that we handle the problem through carefully documented ethnographic decision-making (1986:73). I heartily concur as to the value of documentation, but I am not convinced that it solves the issue of reliability. Nor am I am convinced that we need to address reliability at all except to make sure that our audiences understand why it is not an appropriate measure for evaluating fieldwork. That is not to say that reliability in this technical sense is out of the question. Certainly some of the systematic data we gather are amenable to statistical treatment. For anyone concerned primarily with reliability, however, I think the more systematic methods for data gathering would have greater appeal than the kind of fieldwork I am advocating here in which we try to be right but do not turn to statistical manipulations to validate our claims.

Validity

What the ethnographic method aims to achieve are accounts that support the claims they make. In terms of validity, there *are* better and worse ethnographic accounts.

—Roger Sanjek
"The Ethnographic Present," 621

Although fieldwork should yield highly valid results, I have argued elsewhere against the relevance of validity as a criterion measure in qualitative research (HFW 1990a). Nevertheless, I find validity to be a more robust concept than reliability, one to confront boldly if we must confront it at all. *Whether* to confront it brings us again to the issue of whether we are willing to accept the language of quantitative researchers as the language of all research, or whether different approaches, like different art forms, warrant different criteria for judging them. To me, a discussion of validity signals a retreat to that preexisting vocabulary originally designed to lend precision to one arena of dialogue and too casually assumed to be adequate for another.

As originally employed in its technical sense, validity looks at whether a researcher has measured what the research purports to measure. That issue is of vital significance, yet in practice validity is nowhere near as rigorous as reliability. Instead of generating coefficients that allow numerical comparisons, it is more akin to a property like neatness, where one thing may be recognized as neater than another but nothing achieves "absolute" neatness.

Validity has taken on wider meaning, today being associated more closely with truth value—the correspondence between research and the real world—rather than limited to measurement. To illustrate: The underlying question of the "validity" of an IQ test is related not to performance as revealed by an individual's test score, but to the issue of whether the test has tapped into something as complex as *intelligence* or has only measured how proficient someone has become at taking paper-and-pencil tests of a particular kind.

Clearly, our "I was there" approach to research positions us well in terms of the potential truth value or warranted assertability of our reports. They *should* be substantially accurate and substantially complete—in spite of the fact that sometimes they are not. We can, and often do, make the validity claim. Anthropologists Pertti and Gretel Pelto offer an argument on its behalf:

> "Validity" refers to the degree to which scientific observations actually measure or record what they purport to measure. . . . In their field research anthropologists have invested much effort to achieve validity, for we generally assume that a long-term stay in a community facilitates the differentiation of what is valid from what is not, and the assembling of contextual supporting information to buttress claims to validity. (Pelto and Pelto 1978:33)

A question that remains is whether we need such claims at all. Anthropologists like the Peltos have worked on behalf of a more scientific anthropology and thus a more systematic approach to fieldwork. They strive for validity. Fieldworkers as strongly committed to the *art* of fieldwork might instead be content to remind a reader that their stay in the field was long but never long enough. They would be less insistent about their ability

169

to differentiate between what is valid and what is not, holding instead that whatever information they provide offers illustration but in no way constitutes proof.

Validity can be dismissed, but it does not go away, although qualitative researchers may find comfort in Russ Bernard's observation that validity is never demonstrated, only made more likely (Bernard 1988:53). Fieldworkers need to be able to speak to the issue of what they do on behalf of making the truth value of their accounts "more likely" or—in Egon Guba's suggested alternative term for internal validity—more "credible" (Guba 1981). Similarly, they must be able to address issues of external validity and generalization; in Guba's suggested alternative, "transferability." Such issues can and should be addressed, but they are better regarded as an invitation to dialogue, not as a barrier to research. We can demonstrate our willingness to join the dialogue; we need not be distracted or intimidated by it. Pulling off such a feat while one is still discovering which terms must be addressed requires some artistry at game playing. One needs time to figure out how the game is played before deciding whether and how to participate in it.

Generalization

Whatever the approach, ethnography is always more than description. Ethnography is also a way of generalizing. This way differs from the standard scientific model, however, and in some ways is closer to the arts . . . As in good literature, so in good ethnography the message comes not through explicit statement of generalities but as concrete portrayal.

—James L. Peacock
The Anthropological Lens, 83

Although issues underlying the topics addressed here pose serious problems, debate about them often takes on a sophomoric quality, neither side really listening to the other or appearing to comprehend the existence of an alternative view. Objectivity, for example, is argued as attainable or unattainable; there is no middle ground. Qualitative researchers need to understand what the debate is about and to *have* a position; they do not have to resolve the issue itself. As Becker notes of all such epistemological issues underlying research, "if we haven't settled them definitively in two thousand years, more or less, we probably aren't ever going to settle them. These are simply the commonplaces, in the rhetorical sense, of scientific talk in the social sciences, the framework in which debate goes on" (1993:219).

Generalization is another of these epistemological issues, but I find it more generally worrisome than those already reviewed. It raises a fundamental issue in qualitative work where we invariably look at *one* of something or at a *single case* of something. Even when we are cajoled into increasing our Ns, perhaps to do three, four, or five little case studies instead of devoting rapt attention to one, we are always disadvantaged by our inability to generalize. That disadvantage raises the critical question, "What can we learn from studying only one of anything?"

My immediate and perhaps too-glib answer to that question bespeaks my strategy toward all such questions rooted so solidly in a positivist orientation. What can we learn from studying only one of anything? Why, all we can!

The quick counter-offensive is a good device, and "All we can" is enough to cut short a diatribe, although admittedly it is only the beginning of an adequate answer. Most certainly we need to demonstrate how our cases contribute to some larger picture. We are particularly in need of such explanation, given the paucity of effort at aggregating our myriad case studies into some bigger picture. Once again we find ourselves figuratively trying to fill the Grand Canyon with popcorn, one piece at a time.

Another, less comforting, answer to the question, posed in slightly different terms to ask "How do you generalize from a qualitative study?," is the candid and succinct response, "You don't." That is a safe and accurate answer. It is the basis on which American anthropology was founded under Franz Boas. With an empiricism directed toward rigorous historical particularism, Boas insisted that no generalizations were warranted from the study of any particular society.

As a discipline, anthropology was founded on the horns of a dilemma that committed it to the detailed *study of individual societies* while professing passionate *concern for all humankind*. The inevitable resolution was, and is, to maintain two camps, one more inclined toward postpositivist scientific practices that look at frequencies and distributions from which generalizations are deemed to be warranted, the other more attentive to interpretivist meanings and symbols played out in the course of individual cases and lives. Depending on purposes, the two can be reconciled to some extent, but a preoccupation with eclecticism obscures attention that should be directed toward purposes themselves.

I am inclined to treat generalization as something highly desirable yet always just beyond grasp. I have repeatedly emphasized that I have never studied more than one of anything, "one village and school, one school principal, one major aspect of urban African life in one community in one southern African nation, one sweeping effort at educational change, one sneaky kid" (HFW 1994b:181). Someone who recalled hearing me make that statement remarked, "Didn't I hear you say you have never studied more than one person at a time?" With a major effort devoted to the ethnography of one school principal (1973) and another devoted to what has become the Sneaky Kid Trilogy (1994b), that impression (generalization?) might have seemed warranted, but it is not correct.

What I meant to say, and here make a matter of record, is that the *unit* of study in my various efforts at field research has varied: one individual, one village, one institution (urban African beer drinking), the implementation of one educational innovation in one school system. Whatever can be learned from a well-contextualized study of a single case is the contribution that each of those studies has to offer. If you are interested in averages, frequencies, distributions, and the like, my accounts are not a good source. If you want to know about an instance of something I have studied, my reports should be a rich resource, and that suggests a reasonable criterion by which to judge them. In each of those studies I make a few generalizations, implicate a few more, and leave to readers the challenge of making further ones depending on their present concerns and prior experiences.

Years ago my attention was called to a statement about generalization that I have always kept as a guideline. It was penned by Clyde Kluckhohn and Henry Murray (1948:35) to introduce their coauthored chapter on personality formation and, except for now outmoded gender language, still represents an elegant way to think about the individual and society, the nexus between the one and the many.

Every man is in certain respects
  a. like all other men,
  b. like some other men,
  c. like no other man.

In any fieldwork I have conducted, I have substituted my unit of study into Kluckhohn and Murray's aphorism and thereby felt some freedom in offering whatever generalizations seem warranted. I regarded the Kwakiutl village and school of my first fieldwork to be a village and school *in certain respects* like all other villages and their schools, *in certain respects* like some other villages and their schools, and *in certain respects* like no other village and its school. There seemed little point in spending an entire year as village teacher and participant observer in village life, and then devoting another entire year to writing up an account, if nothing was to be learned that might be of relevance to other villages and their schools as well.

At the same time, I did not want to claim that the village was "typical" or truly "representative." There were many ways in which it did not seem typical even among other Kwakiutl villages, let alone villages in other North American Indian communities where the teacher was not regarded so hostilely. Nor had I been able to exert any influence over the location of my assignment, other than to put myself in the hands of Lyman Jampolsky, director of Indian education in British Columbia at the time, to request an appropriate village placement for me—a single male teacher (thus a one-teacher school) in a region under Anglican rather than Catholic jurisdiction. To an American raised under the strict separation of Church and State, it seemed shocking that my religious affiliation was a major criterion affecting my teaching assignment.

Like many qualitative researchers, I pretty much had to take potluck on the assignment, making the best of whatever opportunities it afforded rather than trying to find a site that I could defend as "typical." What I needed instead was to specify how the village and school to which I happened to be assigned fit within some broader spectrum. This idea, a sort of artful end run around the sampling problem, followed advice written by Margaret Mead in 1953 to explain how researchers in natural settings can address issues of "sampling" when sampling itself is neither practical nor possible. Her essay concerned the issue facing Kluckhohn and Murray quoted above: how we arrive at statements about groups of people when we meet them only individually, and thus how to deal with representativeness.

Anthropological sampling is not a poor and inadequate version of sociological or sociopsychological sampling, a version where n equals too few cases. *It is simply a different kind of sampling*, in which the validity of the sample depends not so much upon the number of cases as upon the proper specification of the informant, so that he or she can be accurately placed, in terms of a very large number of variables . . . Each informant is studied as a perfect example, an organic representation of his complete cultural experience. (1953:654-655; italics in original)

What Mead did was turn the sampling issue around, instructing us to contextualize the cases we sample. Unable to control the sampling process, the fieldworker redefines the problem to fit the circumstances under which we are likely to obtain not only our informants but also our research sites themselves. We do not presume to identify the "typical" informant or village or setting; instead, we ask how our informant or village or setting fits into a larger scheme of things. To what extent is the one in some *important* ways like the many?

This way of approaching generalization asks the researcher to make what seems an essentially artistic choice between emphasizing how the single case informs more generally or how its uniqueness must be cherished. In my Sneaky Kid account, I came down on the side of the former, emphasizing that Brad's story was unique but not an isolated case. I drew on Clifford Geertz for the authoritative footnote: "The important thing about the anthropologist's findings is their complex specificness, their circumstantiality" (Geertz 1973:23). That "complex specificness" remains the heart of the matter, the characteristic of a fieldwork approach. While the effective story should be "specific and circumstantial," its relevance in a broader context should also be apparent. The story must transcend its own modest origins: The case remains particular, its implications broad (HFW 1983a:28).

Some fieldworkers play a more cautious hand, underscoring that they have *not* tried to find the typical informant and do *not* want to detract from the uniqueness of the informant or the case. I know of no better example than the way anthropologist Sidney Mintz introduces his key informant

Taso in *Workers in the Cane*, a statement to which I refer students who get caught up in this question of "typicality":

> He is not an "average" anything—neither an average man, nor an average Puerto Rican, nor an average Puerto Rican lower-class sugar cane worker. He has lived just one life and not all of that. He doesn't think of himself as representative of anything, and he is right. His solutions to life's problems may not be the best ones, either, but he seems satisfied with his choices. I have tried to put down his story in the context of what I could understand about the circumstances under which he lived and lives. (Mintz 1974[1960]:11)

It is interesting to realize how persuasive a powerfully written statement can be. Mintz steered clear of seeming to write about "some other men" in his portrayal; the story was Taso's own. When invited to write a preface for a reissue of the account a number of years later, however, Mintz confounded the question, seeming to want to portray Taso as "average" but not "typical." (I think I might have wanted to have it the other way around, typical but not average.)

> In fact, except for his very unusual intelligence, Taso might be described as quite average in nearly every way. This, then, is the autobiography of an average man. But I tried to make clear when I first wrote the book that this emphatically does not mean that Taso is "typical," representative of others, or ordinary; and in these regards, the book—and Taso's own words—must stand on their own account. (Mintz 1974:ix)

In preparing our cases we want to have it both ways. Each case is unique, yet not so unique that we cannot learn from it and apply its lessons more generally. We are provided a way out of our seeming ambivalence if we resist the trap of an either/or position, keeping in mind Kluckhohn and Murray's interpretation, broadly restated, that every case is, in certain aspects, like all other cases, like some other cases, like no other case.

Self-Defense Vs. Getting Defensive

I have identified these topics—Scientific Method, Objectivity and Bias, Neutrality, Reliability, Validity, and Generalization—because they are problematic in field-oriented research. Individually and collectively we need to be thoughtfully aware of them, to have both a sense of the underlying problems they point to and a working resolution for them. My call is for fieldworkers to be well coached in the art of self-defense, intrigued with, rather than defensive about, epistemological issues.

Neophyte researchers also need to be attentive to the research climate in which they propose their inquiries. You are not likely to be lauded for your creativity in conceptualization if your "audience" is hammering away at you about objectivity and reliability. I have not meant to give false hope that methodological issues like these are easily brushed aside. When they are placed more like barriers than as challenges to help you achieve better clarity of purpose, then you should weigh the wisdom of pursuing a qualitative approach at that place or that moment. Artists and fieldworkers alike must find receptivity for their efforts in at least some quarters.

The issue of *theory* follows hard on the heels of topics discussed here. Issues concerning theory cannot be sidestepped by the individual field-worker, regardless of how basically descriptive or atheoretical he or she might claim to be. I turn to that topic to begin a new chapter dealing further with fieldwork as mindwork.●

CHAPTER EIGHT

THE ART OF CONCEPTUALIZING

In questions of art, learning is a sort of defeat; it illuminates what is by no means the most subtle, and penetrates to what is by no means the most significant. It substitutes theories for feelings and replaces a sense of marvel with a prodigious memory. It amounts to an endless library annexed to a vast museum: Venus transformed into a document.

—Paul Valéry
quoted in S. Price,
Primitive Art in Civilized Places, 12

I defend my compulsion to collect ethnographic data. I believe it is done less by anthropologists today than by those of my generation, which was not so much concerned with theory. . . . Except those of recent years, my publications are heavy in ethnography, and much of the theory is implied, covert, or shyly presented.

—Simon Ottenberg
"Thirty Years of Fieldnotes," 150–151

The original working title for this chapter included the words *conceptualization* and *design*. Both words point to what I want to discuss. Yet it seemed strange to be discussing design, for I associate that term with tight, formal experimental or "treatment" studies, the very antithesis of fieldwork. If, as Howard Becker suggests, a distinguishing feature of qualitative research is that our studies are designed "in the making," then design must have a special meaning among fieldworkers, referring to an ongoing process rather than a fait accompli.

John Creswell, a colleague equally receptive to qualitative and quantitative approaches (see Creswell 1994), tells me that when discussing aspects
of research design he asks his students to think of research as involving
choices and applications among *compositional techniques*. He sees the process
of composing a study as similar to composing a piece of music or a painting.
I like that analogy. Without in the least diminishing the importance of
assembling the necessary raw materials or having the requisite skills for
blending them together in the final composition, it underscores the critical
component for inquiry, the ability to conceive, or to generate, the ideas that
prompt and guide inquiry.

The analogy is also a subtle reminder that neither materials alone, nor
skills alone, nor technique alone, is sufficient. Everything must come
together under the genius of the composer. Or of the artist at the easel:
Stephen Sondheim's "Sunday in the Park with George" becomes Monday
at the Site with Mead or Malinowski. Order. Design. Tension. Balance.
Harmony. So many possibilities, true, but someone must be able to bring
them together to achieve a clear purpose.

"The Art of Conceptualizing" as used here refers to how fieldworkers
put together—how they "compose"—studies in the absence of tight formal
designs. Granted, no purposeful inquiry proceeds without conceptual
underpinnings of some sort. So what do fieldworkers do that is comparable
to what researchers of other persuasions refer to as "design?" We can begin
by looking at the role of theory.

Theories are always being contested, sometimes bitterly, in the social
sciences. In art worlds, by contrast, I have the impression that more often
it is theory itself—its role and significance—that is contested. Performance
or product is what matters, not how one gets there; in Paul Valéry's words,
one does not substitute theories for feelings. Artists whose work draws
inspiration solely from theory or "method" raise suspicion that creativity
itself may be in short supply.

The art metaphor invites that different perspective. At the least, the
role of theory appears less heavy-handed when analogies are drawn to art
rather than to science. The arts have their theories and their theorists, to be
sure, but they also have their movements, periods, eras, schools, and so
forth. There are many ways to categorize these styles and periods, and we
are more accustomed to hearing them identified with descriptive titles or

historical periods—The Romantic Period, Impressionists, the Dutch Masters, the _____ School—than with some latter-day scholar's efforts to impose a definitive theoretical label on them. Postmodernism itself, today more closely associated with music and literature, began as a style and movement in architecture, a rejection of an earlier "modernist" era with its "rules, geometric order, and austerity" (Kottak 1994:12n).

I find it refreshing to think of theory, or, more accurately, a *preoccupation with theory*, as a relative newcomer, a recent "era" in fieldwork rather than what every fieldworker has been doing all along without knowing it. That is not to insist that old-time fieldworkers did not think about what they were doing. Nor were they reticent about using terms like *theory*, *hypothesis*, or *proposition*. They simply were not so singularly preoccupied with explicit theory as we have become today.

I do not suggest that the current preoccupation is a passing fad, for theory provides a kind of clearinghouse and lingua franca for inquiry across disciplines as well as within them, and we are entering the era of the Great Interface. The pursuit of theory has a unifying effect even in the absence of unifying theory itself. Theory provides a focused way for us to talk to each other—and to ourselves—about what we are up to. It also provides a way of linking past and present, since we can attribute implicit *theory* to the lives and works of our forebears just as we can attribute implicit *culture* to them. But the self-conscious insistence on having and *using explicit theory* and *using theory explicitly*, is *a* way, not the only way, to pursue fieldwork. That insistence is another reminder of how wholeheartedly we have bought into the scientific paradigm. It is the task that theory addresses, not theory itself, that must be attended to!

We do not beat upon, or beat up on, composers or painters or sculptors to declare their theories before we allow them to proceed with their works. Indeed, artists who lean on theory to explain what they are up to may raise the suspicion that whatever artistic experience they are about to introduce is more likely to be *good for*, rather than *pleasing to*, an audience. Theory offers no magic or guarantee of quality in the art world.

Reflecting on his "Thirty Years of Fieldnotes," Simon Ottenberg's reference in the epigraph to theory "implied, covert, or shyly presented" in his work suggests how recently theory has come to occupy so central a role in fieldwork. The 30 years of Ottenberg's fieldnotes are roughly the 30 years of my fieldnotes as well, and I, too, have boasted of the same theoretical nonchalance with which Ottenberg describes all but his most recent work. The point of my foray into art worlds in Chapter 3 was to underscore how the art any individual produces is like the work of his or her fellow artists and is produced in a social milieu. In like manner, today's fieldworkers scurry about in search of appropriate theory because that is what they are expected to do and what everyone else seems to be doing. But it has not always been so. I remember being startled to learn of anthropologist David Bidney's book with a title that struck me as oxymoron: *Theoretical Anthropology*. Apparently that book, originally published in 1953 and reissued in paperback in 1967, never gained a wide audience among anthropologists, at least among the earlier fieldwork-oriented ones.

In those earlier days, Theory was not so imposing and was never a prerequisite. But *thinking* was! What I was expected to come up with in proposing a dissertation study in the early 1960s was not a theoretical orientation but a conceptual one. As a result, I have always been comfortable with the idea that conceptual frameworks are sufficient; I do not bully others about theory and am unswayed by those who would bully me. Acculturation studies were still in vogue in those days, and they provided sufficient link to a broad social problem and a body of ongoing work in cultural dynamics/ culture change. Today that same research effort and setting would—and easily could—be translated into some highfalutin' theoretical framework. But the essence is this: I did have an idea of what *in particular* I would be looking at, within the broader context of an ethnographic account of a contemporary Kwakiutl village and its school.

In the article already cited, Ottenberg goes on to make an interesting contrast between broad "ethnographic" inquiries and the more problem-focused ones that began to take explicit form in the work of Margaret Mead but have always been inherent in the ethnographic task itself. To explain why his own publications seem "heavy in ethnography," Ottenberg continues:

> This suggests a hypothesis: those who produce ethnographic, nontheoretically oriented notes will produce ethnographic writings; those who produce problem-oriented or theoretically directed notes will produce like writings. (Ottenberg 1990:151)

I don't know why Ottenberg felt he needed to present his you-are-what-you-write idea in the form of a hypothesis (unless it is because everybody's doing it), but I like the contrast he makes between broadly descriptive studies and "problem-oriented or theoretically directed" ones. I think a clear distinction is warranted between these latter two as well; problem-driven and theoretically driven studies should not be confused with each other. One certainly holds different expectations for a broadly descriptive approach (perhaps ethnographically oriented, perhaps not), a problem-oriented study, and a theoretically driven one. At the same time, we dare not lose sight of the overlap inherent in all field-oriented inquiry. A theoretically oriented or problem-oriented study must provide enough of the same context one expects from a broadly descriptive one, and a broadly descriptive study must provide an adequate description of its orienting concept or problem.

In the early "salvage ethnography" days, when anthropologists raced to record what they could of relatively intact, relatively isolated societies, the imminent extinction anticipated for such groups was deemed problem enough. Subsequently, writing at mid-century, John Bennett noted the tendency of American anthropologists to begin fieldwork with a particular problem, and then gradually broaden their scope, while British anthropologists began with broad concerns and narrowed the scope of work as fieldwork progressed (see Sanjek 1990:226). Today's fieldworkers, looking more often into microcultural aspects of complex societies, can consider themselves fortunate not to have to fill the broad charter of producing holistic ethnographies as well. The fieldworker intent on producing a standard ethnography works with a set of categories that impose structure sufficient to set one purposefully at work for a lifetime. Painting by the numbers is still painting, at least by some definitions.

The art metaphor invites an examination of whether we have alternatives to "theory" for positioning ourselves conceptually. I think we do employ other systems of categories, however informally or unconsciously. I noted earlier that we do not identify "Schools" with the names of Great Masters of Fieldwork, yet we are not so far from it. Anthropologists and sociologists in some major departments exert enough influence that we literally "tag" their graduates and presume a certain likeness in their work as, for example, in Columbia- or Chicago-trained scholars. If we do not exactly have a Malinowski "School" of fieldwork, virtually anyone whose work is discernibly Functionalist tends to be regarded as following in that tradition. Recounting his own career history, George Peter Murdock once stated, "I have been, at different times and in different combinations, a cultural anthropologist, a functionalist, a structuralist, a comparativist, and even a historical anthropologist" (1971:17).

I have never regarded myself as belonging to any such "school," not so much because of any conscious resistance to categories as because of my uncompulsive nature about theory itself. Nonetheless, my categorizing colleagues are able to fit me into whatever schemes they propose, sometimes graciously discerning shifts in my work that seem to keep me current but actually remind me that I, too, am moved about by subtle forces. "For over three decades," writes one reviewer, Wolcott has "charted an interpretive, postpositivist approach to the anthropology of educational practices . . . In this collection . . . he finally breaks from this tradition and openly embraces a fully post-foundational approach to validity and textual authority" (Denzin 1994b).

The approach I present below will, I hope, reflect my casual attitude toward recognizing the role of theory as a "driving force" in fieldwork. I am tempted to match Ottenberg with a hypothesis of my own: The more strongly a researcher is drawn to theoretical issues, the less likely that individual will seek opportunity for sustained fieldwork; conversely, the more strongly one is drawn to fieldwork, the less one will look to Theory for either orientation or explanation.

Theory

In theory, theory is as essential to the pursuit of qualitative research as it is to all research. Indeed, if we are to believe a pronouncement attributed to William James (in Agar 1980:23) that "you can't pick up rocks in a field without a theory," theory is precursor to any purposeful human activity.

In the abstract, the notion that theory underlies not only our activities as researchers but also our every act as humans presents an intriguing way to interpret how we go about our daily lives. But enthusiasm for theory can as quickly pale when a colleague, committee, or funding agency confronts you boldly with a suspicion posed as a question, "What is your theory?"

I see theory as another of the many issues that must be reckoned with by every fieldworker. There are several levels at which to address it. Theory is something like physical exercise or taking Vitamin C: Some people are hooked on it, even to excess; others give it as little conscious attention as possible; no one can do without it entirely. That prompts a redefinition that at once elevates *formal* theory to what I call "capital 'T' Theory," or Grand Theory, and leaves numerous other terms more modest in scope—*hypotheses, ideas, assumptions, hunches, notions*—that also capture the essence of the mindwork that is critical to fieldwork.

As an ideal, Grand Theory stands clearly at the pinnacle. Grand Theory offers the ultimate means to transcend the limits inherent in our modest individual efforts. It allows us to aggregate those efforts, play them off against each other, and precipitate out from our observations the essence of what is significant at some higher level of abstraction, perhaps embracing multiple cases by multiple observers over extended periods of time. It is the kind of activity for which we admire (and romanticize) people like Charles Darwin, whose contribution, Kluckhohn has noted, "was much less the accumulation of new knowledge than the creation of a theory which put in order data already known" (1949:23). Darwin was a careful observer, but mindwork was his genius: He reports that for his study *Coral Reefs*, his whole theory was "thought out" before he had ever seen a true one (Darwin 1969[1887]:98).

We must learn how to protect ourselves from being beaten down (or up) by insistence that every field study must be linked directly to theory. Theory is often employed as a sort of intellectual bludgeon, a killer term used to menace problem-focused neophytes and belittle efforts at applied or "practical" research. The "theory question" poses a dual challenge—on the one hand to come up with an original problem and a theoretically adequate approach to it, on the other hand to be able to demonstrate how a unique case is embedded in some larger concern related to a significant body of theory. For those not initially attracted to or comfortable with theory in the first place, nagging issues of what-to-do-about-theory never get answered to everyone's satisfaction and never go away. The essential thing is to learn how to deal with them in a professionally adequate manner to ensure either that theory serves to guide and clarify (rather than to intimidate), or that the orienting function that theory addresses is accomplished even in the absence of theory made explicit.

The fact that you are reading *The Art of Fieldwork* may suggest that theory is not your long suit. You'd rather be out there doing research, or wandering and pondering in a potential research site, not sitting in your office ruminating about it or grunting out some set of supposedly linked hypotheses that should subtly prove you right if they don't do you in by proving to be wrong. If so, strategies are indeed what you need. Let me propose some guiding questions, followed by reminders of how theory can inform without intimidating.

First, you need to assess the nature and extent of your concern for (and commitment to) theory. Does Theory embody the kind of contribution you want to make, as revealed perhaps in recognizing that you wouldn't mind having your name or work identified as So-and-so's (your name here) Theory? If this is how you would like to be remembered, then you probably need to embrace the more systematic approaches to fieldwork and to evaluate critically whether there is much point engaging in participant observation at all beyond its broadest orienting function.

As I have stated, however, a concern for and intrigue with *what theory is intended to do* is critical to all inquiry processes. The descriptive task that anchors fieldwork is itself endless. Theory addresses the issue of sense-making. It can keep us from getting caught up in rendering accounts dismissed as travelogues or personal diaries. As a fieldworker—a self-consciously self-appointed researcher—you are already in the business of sense-making. Malinowski not only identified sense-making as critical to the fieldwork task, he made what anthropologist Edmund Leach has identified as "the *theoretical* assumption that the total field of data under the observation of the field-worker must somehow fit together and make sense" (Leach 1957:120, quoted in Sanjek 1990:211). That is what his Functionalism was intended to do. Functionalism still functions as a useful guide for fieldworkers, as long as they recognize a critical distinction between asking how (and whether) things fit together, instead of taking Malinowski too literally and insisting that everything *does* fit together and *does* make sense.

My sense of anthropologists in the days of old is that those willing to struggle with concepts and theory had more of a legacy to pass on than did those who "got on splendidly with the natives." That is because they were struggling with the problem of sense-making in the course of writing up their fieldwork, not to any particular theoretical contribution itself. Some of anthropology's brilliant writers did rather little fieldwork of their own (e.g., Ruth Benedict) or are reported to have failed at it miserably (e.g., Alexander Goldenweiser). Claude Lévi-Strauss must have surprised some readers with his candid revelation:

> Finally, why not admit it? I realized early on that I was a library man, not a fieldworker. . . In the unforgiving landscape of central Brazil, there was many a time I had the feeling I was wasting my life! . . . I did enough to learn and to understand what fieldwork is, which is an essential prerequisite for making a sound evaluation and use of the work done by others. (Lévi-Strauss and Eribon 1991:44–45)

To whatever extent the reverse is true—successful in-the-field researchers who never published—there is, of course, little record, only apocryphal stories. Writers are still trying to correct a mistaken impression that Frank Cushing, an anthropologist often singled out to illustrate the dangers of "going native," never wrote anything about the Zuñi among whom he lived and studied for four and a half years (cf. Green 1979; Sanjek 1990:189–192), but Cushing is only one among many fieldworkers whose mostly unwritten accounts accompanied them to the grave.

In terms of personal careers, some field-oriented researchers have become more interested in applications of, and contributions to, theory with advancing seniority. That offers a nice balance as the youthful energy that drives sustained fieldwork gradually gives way to more contemplative activities carried on largely at one's desk. On the other hand, I take solace from a few elders who have challenged the preeminence given to theory, similar to efforts directed at the concept of culture: not to eliminate it, but to cut it down to size. "Pete" Murdock, quoted above, was the first to come to my attention with his observation that good descriptive ethnography—"by far the greatest achievement in anthropology"—has depended "remarkably little on the specific theoretical orientation of the observer" and manages to outlive whatever theory may have spawned it at the time (1971:17-18). Ottenberg asks, "Where are all the theories today that existed then (and some seemed quite exciting to me at the time)? They are gone, dead as a doornail" (1990:155).

A second question has to do with how one wants to play at the theory "game." At least one among my colleagues has made theory the driving force throughout an academic career, holding tenaciously not only to an evolving theory that has guided more than two decades of fieldwork but to a personal theory of careers as well, that one cannot make meaningful headway in a scientific career without a clearly conceived and carefully explicated theory. If such preoccupation with theory points to one extreme, my own seeming obliviousness to theory might be taken as the other. While my colleague has hammered away at Grand (or "Baby Grand"?) Theory, I have shied away even from what is known as Middle Range Theory, satisfied to work within conceptual frameworks like "culture" and, especially, cultural transmission and acquisition. I am always pressed by journal editors and reviewers who insist that my writing should display greater theoretical sophistication. But I have seen too much phony theory and phony posturing about theory to feel defensive. I feel theory is overrated in terms of what most of us actually accomplish through our research. In theory-driven descriptive accounts, theory is more apt to get in the way than to point the way, to tell rather than to ask what we have seen.

Watching a colleague wind up a career in which singular preoccupation with contributing a big theory may have misdirected more than it helped, I hardly advise others to follow that course. I remain fascinated with the *potential* of theory, but in my own work and the work of my students, I have been more than satisfied with, sometimes, a great *notion, hunch, idea*, or tentative *interpretation*. Maybe that is why I remain so respectful toward *bias*. I regard bias as entry-level theorizing, a thought-about position from which the researcher as inquirer feels drawn to an issue or problem and seeks to construct a firmer basis in both knowledge and understanding.

A third question addresses when and how you want theory to play a role in your work. The logic crystallized in the Scientific Method suggests that it must come first, that everything proceeds from there. Committed believers concur. I have to agree, at least in the sense that we cannot initiate an inquiry without *some* idea of what we are looking for. But I am inclined to place those ideas along a scale of formality that reserves terms like *theory* or *hypothesis* for ideas formally stated. That leads me to propose a working definition: *Theory is a way of asking that is accompanied by a reasonable answer.*

If the research problem you intend to pursue is accompanied by a reasonable answer, you can proceed more-or-less theoretically, more if your "answer" is linked to some larger body of thought and prior work, less if the answer is your own modest hunch or hypothesis. Recognize, however, that you can proceed with fieldwork without a reasonable answer to the question(s) you are asking, as long as you have a reasonable sense of how to proceed, how to focus your attention. Descriptive research is purposive; it need not be pedantic. Something as casual as "curiosity" or "uninformed bias" might be sufficient to set off purposive inquiry. At the other extreme, so might a problem posed by a client or funding agency. Purposelessness, of the questions-asked-on-a-tour-bus variety, is the enemy. Explicit theory can be joined with fieldwork anywhere in the research process, from driving the inquiry in its initial stages to positing how it might help in situating a single case within some broader arena of concern.

When and how theory makes its real entry into the research process is often masked by the canons of reporting. This is especially so in the constricted format of thesis and dissertation writing, in which the typically tedious review of the literature in a traditionally perfunctory second chapter includes an equally tedious recital of "relevant" theory.

An alternative to this approach, one I have pressed upon students and recommended to colleagues, is to introduce theory into the final account in whatever role it *actually* played during the field research and write-up. Because I have never badgered my students about theory, the issue of theory (and the review of related literature) often has been reserved for the closing chapters of a dissertation, where a self-conscious but genuine search for theoretical implications and links *begins* rather than ends. One unexpected dividend from paying more attention to how theory *is* used rather than to how others say it *should be* used has been the publication of a set of original papers in which qualitative researchers candidly review their personal struggles with theory in fieldwork (Flinders and Mills 1993).

I see this question of "when theory?" as a choice between the alternatives of "theory first" or "theory later." I state it that way to disabuse qualitative researchers of the notion that everything and everybody (else) begins with a full-blown and formally stated theory. Broadly conceived, little "t" theory, acknowledging the conceptual role underlying any purposive inquiry, *has to* be there somewhere, in some form. But that does not necessarily mean it can be, or needs to be, stated formally. When others, students especially, tell us they neither know nor would recognize the theories that relate most closely to their own research interests, we perform meritorious service when we point them in the direction we think their theoretical predilections lie. Or we can tease out—but only by way of example—where our own interests might lead. We should neither insist that students be able to orient themselves in theory—a creative intellectual endeavor in which we all continue to struggle, and with only limited success—nor impose our own pet theories. A student (or colleague) without a theory is in a far better position to discover (and eventually even appreciate) how theory serves than someone who has been "given" a theory by someone else, no matter how well intended the gift.

Fourth and last is whether theory is better regarded in the singular or the plural. I find Johan Galtung's plea on behalf of *theoretical pluralism* refreshing. Galtung holds that our work should be guided by a *family* of perspectives, rather than by commitment to a single theory to which we give sole allegiance (Galtung 1990:101). And Barth advises that theories are to be "explored and played with" (1994a:358), suggesting that even if we regard our theories as competing with each other, the competition need not be a somber one. Thinking of theory in multiples helps keep it off the pedestal that has made it so formidable for some researchers, beginners especially. It is tempting to offer the advice that if you are asked the killer question, "But what is your theory?" you respond with, "I assume you mean what are my theories?" Whether you actually utter those words will, of course, be a matter of protocol. If you aren't in a position to say them, even thinking them may offer some comfort.

And how does theory serve the individual researcher? It serves in several practical ways, some of which are implied in the preceding discussion, and all of which help to keep fieldwork and deskwork manageable in terms of focus and linkages. These objectives are also accomplished through citations to "the relevant literature" under circumstances when theory per se is not the issue as much as is the need for every researcher to be able to place his or her work within some broader context.

• Theory offers the convenience of labels that help researchers identify and link up with prior work, both their own and that of others, and to call their work to the attention of those who share common interests.

- Theory offers a way to gain a broader perspective or provide a broader application for single cases of modest scope, thus overcoming a major limitation of qualitative research that so often is carried out by one individual.

- Theory offers a way out of the dilemma of generalization by allowing researchers to join their work to some larger issue or accumulating body of data.

- Theory offers a critical perspective by calling up previous dialogues in which certain aspects of a problem may have been singled out because they have been inadequately attended to or have raised new doubts or concerns.

- Theory offers a useful way to harness the power of disproof. We can never "prove" anything through efforts at qualitative research. We can, however, disprove ideas by providing negative instances. Theory allows us to make better use of that power by inviting us to look at classes of events rather than only at single instances.

What theory does is call attention to, and offer strategies for coping with, the dual problems of purpose and generalization. It is also a reminder that we ourselves need to be thinking about the underlying issue tersely summarized in a two-word question always on the tip of some skeptic's tongue: So what?

Through drawing attention to the art of fieldwork, terrorizing questions like "So what?" or "What is your theory?" are somewhat disarmed: Theory is not so exalted in art worlds. We want to have it both ways, however, drawing now from science, now from art, and theory is part of the baggage that accompanies the role of the researcher as a scientific thinker. Theory is supposed to help researchers of any persuasion clarify what they are up to and to help them explain to others what they are up to. Whether or not we are all that explicit about our theoretical dimensions, as fieldworkers we, too, must know what we are up to and be able to explain to others what we are up to. When formal theory seems to offer no helpful answer, the search for theory at a more modest level can be turned into a provocative question: What would be needed by way of theory to help me better organize and present my data and to recognize relevant aspects of my fieldwork experience? To be able to ask that question other than rhetorically, a fieldworker must be able effectively to share something of that data and experience. So one way out of an analytical or theoretical dilemma is to begin talking and, especially, to begin writing, in order to enlist the help of others. When I take up that topic in the next chapter, I will suggest that such writing can take place not only during and after fieldwork, but before initiating it as well.

Mental Set

I hope the above was helpful, particularly for anyone inclined to put Theory on too high a pedestal rather than enlist "little t" theory as another tool, a conceptual one, for helping fieldworkers accomplish what they want to accomplish. I have now said about as much as I have to say about such *tools* and about fieldwork *techniques*. I have tried to keep them in their place as tools and techniques; fieldworkers themselves make the difference as to whether the tools and techniques are used imaginatively in the pursuit of a more interpretive account, more cautiously in the pursuit of a carefully analytical one, or in some appropriate combination of the two.

There is no formula for conducting unique and original studies, but there is more potential for realizing them if the tools and techniques remain just that. Mindwork is the essential element. I return to the working definition of art proposed in Chapter 1 to underscore the critical need for an idiosyncratic human touch in order fully to realize the artistic potential of fieldwork:

> *Art is achieved when the addition of an idiosyncratic human touch in any production, whether performance or artifact, is recognized by a discriminating audience as achieving an aesthetic quality exceeding what is expected by the exercise of craft skill alone.*

There are a number of other practical matters relating to conceptualizing, particularly the need for a realistic assessment of the match between what a fieldworker hopes to accomplish and the talent and resources necessary to pull it off. The assessment must be candid, although much of what is to be assessed comes under the heading of attitude, or belief, or . . . faith.

Let me suggest some dimensions for any prospective fieldworker to consider before embarking on a field study. Such an inventory should result in a thoughtful decision about the extent of one's commitment both to the topic and to pursuing it through fieldwork.

Being Receptive

I begin by repeating cautions already expressed about ideas of immaculate perception in the doing of all research. No one can take even the first step toward "pure" discovery. Nevertheless, a distinguishing feature of the fieldwork approach is the need for receptivity or openness to the research setting. Such openness is exercised particularly in attention to context and to the opportunity for the researcher to be intuitive, in contrast to the quantitative researcher's need to exert control.

There is a balance to be struck. A fieldworker must rely on his or her ability to surrender to what the field observations actually reveal rather than prematurely to superimpose structure upon them. In *Transforming Qualitative Data: Description, Analysis, and Interpretation* (HFW 1994b), I proposed resolving this tension by attending to whatever balance between analysis and interpretation best achieves the purposes of the research. There is no "ideal" ratio of description to analysis to interpretation. The relative emphasis devoted to each depends on what one wants to accomplish. But there is little point engaging in a fieldwork approach if one cannot derive a sense of excitement and anticipation about "finding out." This should be coupled with a willingness to alter one's focus, should it become evident that either the problem or an effective way to investigate it needs to be better defined.

My advice is to strive to be even more open-minded than you would ever dare reveal, both when engaging in fieldwork and when subsequently reflecting upon it. Become your own Devil's Advocate to argue with yourself about what is really going on, what you are really looking at, and whether you are really homing in on something significant in the fieldwork experience.

I realize that grant proposal and dissertation proposal writers may feel hampered by requirements to present a carefully plotted research sequence that will emphasize systematic analysis and allow only modest interpretation. A research proposal is only that, however: a proposal. It should not be regarded as a contract. Research that is designed in the making is research that can be *re*designed in the making.

At the same time, it is foolish for a "proposer" not to keep a client, a granting agency, or one's committee members informed and/or to negotiate changes as work progresses. The flexibility inherent in the approach may not be matched by institutional flexibility on the part of others of authority who probably have their own expectations about outcomes. Graduate students are especially cautioned not only to weigh their own capabilities for conducting and reporting relatively open-ended inquiries but also to gauge the receptivity of their committee members to support such approaches. Even veteran fieldworkers have occasionally found themselves constrained by prior commitments that leave them unable to pursue a research problem in the way they might have preferred to define it. The analogy to art worlds reminds us that receptivity functions to restrain what artists are "free" to do as well. There is always that discriminating audience to seek out and to satisfy.

Being Realistic

It seems reasonable to make a realistic assessment of one's strengths and weaknesses as a fieldworker in terms of the problem to be studied and, especially, the setting in which the work will be conducted. That may be difficult for the novice fieldworker anticipating work in a totally unfamiliar setting, but one ought to be able to project oneself into a setting with some idea about, and confidence in, being able to pull the whole thing off. Reportedly, Alfred Kroeber's assessment about doing fieldwork was that "Some can and some can't" (Wagley 1983:16). The good news is that, especially with the fieldwork part of fieldwork, most can. Essentially, fieldwork requires us to involve ourselves professionally in unfamiliar social situations, something we have certainly had to do before. The new twist is to become more aware of the doing and, particularly, to be able to sustain the effort for an extended period of time.

One of the most difficult tasks for neophytes is to capitalize on the opportunity inherent in the participant observer role to act naturally, rather than to assume a stiff pose as observer or evaluator. Fieldwork offers such latitude that one can work from one's own interpersonal strengths and natural style to make it successful. A bit of *resolve* doesn't hurt, either: you must *know* that you can carry it off.

Unfortunately, graduate programs in general, and sometimes courses taught specifically to prepare qualitative researchers in particular, often nurture apprehension rather than instill confidence. I am dismayed when I meet students who introduce themselves with ever-so-humble phrases such as, "I'm planning to do a qualitative study, but I don't have a clue of how to go about it." As kindly as I can, I try to assess whether their lament is prophecy or pose. It is usually the latter, as responses to some "silly" questions quickly attest: "Do you intend to go to a hospital, jail, church, or school to make your observations?" "Do you plan to go on a weekday or weekend?" "Do you plan to do a formal interview on your first visit, or will that come later?" "Will you conduct a survey?" "For how long do you intend to conduct the fieldwork?" Even unorthodox questions such as, "How many chapters do you expect to have in your study?" or "What would be your tentative chapter titles if you were to start writing today?" usually lead me to conclude such conversations on a high note: "Sounds to me like you have quite a few clues!"

Novices are inclined to believe that their more experienced colleagues have learned exactly how to go about conducting a study. I think that impression is false. Veteran researchers may indeed appreciate the challenge that a new study presents, but they do not have a *modus operandi* as much as they have confidence in their ability to find their way into a study as it progresses. That is what I mean by the term "resolve."

Resolve reveals itself through answers to questions such as those posed above, including anticipation of how the fieldwork will be initiated—thus "designing" it one step at a time—and anticipation of what is to result as end product. The latter includes not only the manner in which one expects to report but also a clear idea of the kind of information needed to complete that reporting.

Taken one step at a time, the whole project must seem imminently doable, including a realistic assessment that the time and resources available are adequate. In the realities of the research world, genuine participant observer fieldwork may be the first casualty in delimiting options, with a few cursory "site visits" substituted instead. Or the researcher's own commitments may preclude a level of sustained observation deemed "highly desirable" but, for practical purposes, quite out of the question.

The important thing is to ensure that the research will be completed, which also means that it will be reported. Recognize here the possibility of being superficial, of merely touching the surface on a topic deserving of, and perhaps demanding of, more thorough attention, or trying to take on too much and ending up with nothing. Those Darker Arts are never far away.

Being Committed

The greater the commitment to pursuing in-depth fieldwork on the part of the researcher, the greater the need for a realistic appraisal of the return expected for the time, energy, and resources to be invested. A first concern is an assessment of the significance of the setting or problem to be investigated. What potential does the intended research have for producing "significant" results, such significance assessed in terms of competing problems that might be investigated instead?

In a strict risk/benefit analysis, the *physical* risks inherent in fieldwork obviously depend on one's professional or disciplinary affiliations and on one's choice of problem and approach. The greatest physical dangers, vehicle accidents topping the list, are, as Howell reports in *Surviving Fieldwork*, "at once the most dramatic and probably the most easily preventable" (1990:101). Among my colleagues who have done research in exotic climates, some continue to do battle with medical problems contracted initially during fieldwork. There are fieldworkers whose research on drug addiction, cults, gangs, and so forth has put them at considerable risk—see, for example, discussions by Mitchell 1993, or Lee 1995. Lee's succinct advice in dangerous situations is straightforward: "proceed on the basis of a worst-case scenario" (p. 36). Working in dangerous situations is largely a matter of personal choice, sometimes, I suspect, reflecting a conscious decision on the part of the more adventurously inclined to escape their placid institutional environments.

There are also psychological and professional risks. These include broad concerns, such as finding and nurturing a supportive climate for one's endeavors while actually in the field. It is not uncommon for fieldworkers to overestimate the extent of enthusiasm toward both the research and the researcher when initiating a new project. This can come about when we hear what we want (need?) to hear about the extent of interest in our work, or when we have enlisted support from too few and/or nonrepresentative members of the community, or when our presence begins to look more intrusive than the gatekeepers originally anticipated. Should this happen, the next fieldwork miscalculation may be to overestimate the extent of *disaffection* for the work, to about the same extent that affection was overestimated initially. More likely, no one has been paying that much attention one way or the other.

In a psychological sense, fieldworkers can easily become their own worst enemy. One trap is referred to as the *paradox of intimacy*, when a high degree of trust achieved too quickly actually curtails rather than enhances subsequent fieldwork (see Mitchell 1993:21). Many a fieldworker also has walked unsuspectingly into a power struggle in which an initial façade of cooperation hides unexpected intrigue, inviting the researcher into alignments that may later threaten the success of the research. The too-sensitive researcher may be more at risk here, but, overly sensitive or not, you must prepare yourself for the awkwardness of overstaying your welcome.

Evaluating the potential return of a qualitative inquiry should include a frank assessment of outcomes not only for the research but for the researcher as well, including indirect benefits incidental to the research process but integral to one's career, such as pay, publication, and promotion. Here again we confront the issue of why we conduct research at all, who benefits by it, and whether our rewards for wanting to *find out* must come at a cost to those who are *found out*. More of the Darker Arts!

It is important always to keep in mind that there are other, faster ways to find out and to obtain "results" to announce; in fact, it is hard to imagine a more cumbersome way than conventional fieldwork to conduct research for anyone anxious to obtain quick "findings." Fieldwork lends itself neither to speedy findings nor to dramatic ones. By its very nature, it presupposes a commitment of both professional career and personal responsibility; an opportunity to demonstrate what the approach can accomplish, coupled with an implicit challenge to make whatever contribution might be made from attending to a particular set of circumstances.

Commitment to fieldwork is not any easier to demonstrate than commitment to one's research participants, especially in the early stages of a career. Perhaps that is just as well; fieldwork is not well suited to anyone in a hurry. Still, the fact that through the years so many researchers have been willing to commit to the approach provides a constant reaffirmation to the research community of the importance of having some of its members devoted to studying problems in broad time frames and broad social contexts.

A Capacity for Judgment

Pursuing the art metaphor and thinking of fieldworkers who, like artists, work in a community of scholar-researchers, one also recognizes the need for fieldworkers to develop a capacity for reflecting on and assessing their own performance at every stage, from initial conceptualization to final write-up. This is another aspect in which the art of fieldwork requires more than technical elements of craftsmanship, the coordinating of materials and techniques. My colleague Tom Schram picked up on this idea so eloquently in correspondence on the topic that I quote him here verbatim:

> Becoming a skillful fieldworker goes beyond the acquisition of skills and extends to one's ability to *judge* his or her performance in concert with a *collective judgment* about what constitutes good fieldwork. So it takes a capacity for self-evaluation and a sense of appreciation that is developed and sustained in a community of other fieldworkers.
>
> Acquiring proficiency in the craft does require instruction and practice—as does art—and perhaps, as Werner and Schoepfle argue, "great art" is dependent on talent. For both art and craft, nonetheless, I think we need to attend as well to a capacity for judgment and a sense of appreciation that is sustained and defined at some collective level. (Tom Schram, personal communication, March 1995)

We come full circle, the lone fieldworker grappling with theory (or, better still, *playing* with *theories*), vowing to stay the course, mindful of the difference between being open-minded and being mindless, addressing an infinite task with the most finite of resources, working desperately to maintain an independence of thought, and, in the end, surrendering to judgment reflective of the community of others similarly engaged. Art worlds. Science worlds. Fieldwork worlds. Worlds of human judgment, every one.●

CHAPTER NINE

THE ART OF
SELF-EXPRESSION

Writing has emerged as central to what anthropologists do both in
the field and thereafter.

—James Clifford
"Introduction," in *Writing Culture*, 2

What the ethnographer is in fact faced with—except when (as of
course he must do) he is pursuing the more automatized routines of
data collection—is a multiplicity of complex conceptual structures,
many of them superimposed upon or knotted into one another, which
are at once strange, irregular, and inexplicit, and which he must con-
trive somehow first to grasp and then to render.

—Clifford Geertz
"Thick Description," in
The Interpretation of Cultures, 10

Reporting is the visible and outward sign of one's accomplishments
in fieldwork, revealing what the field researcher-cum-conceptual-
izer has made of it all. Clifford Geertz captures this nicely in the
phrase quoted above, "first to grasp and then to render."

Rendering is a particularly appropriate word choice, since it implicates
a broad range of activities. In addition to writing academic reports, articles,
and monographs, or to making lecture and seminar presentations, one can
render through slide, film, and video presentations; storytelling; photography and museum exhibits; stories and poems; ethnographic fiction;
accounts prepared for newspapers and popular journals; maybe even an

appearance on a TV talk show. All these options are, to borrow a badly overworked term, viable. Some of the discussion in this chapter is relevant to the full range of options. However, for at least two reasons, personal as well as practical, my focus will be on written accounts intended for professional journals and monographs, reflecting the print orientation pervasive in academia and government agencies.

One reason for a focus on writing is that my graduate training came at a time when writing was the only thinkable way to present the results of field research. Films and photographs were valued, but they augmented the standard ethnography; they were never intended to serve in lieu of it. A picture may be worth a thousand words, but words came first; pictures were optional. Franz Boas's 1897 account, *The Social Organization and the Secret Societies of the Kwakiutl Indians*, is augmented with 51 "plates" and 215 additional "text figures," but the text stands alone. Audiences were assumed to consist essentially of peers, and one wrote in scholarly fashion to and for them, with an emphasis on detailed description. Margaret Mead's colleagues were having a difficult time understanding how she could contribute a regular column to *Redbook Magazine*, drawing on her professional experience as a perspective for giving advice to American women, when most anthropologists were still preparing accounts in which fieldworkers themselves disappeared entirely from their texts.

For all their efforts at situated listening while conducting fieldwork, anthropologists did little to develop a listening audience beyond the lecture hall. In the early 1950s, Walter Goldschmidt was involved in the production of a series of half-hour radio programs to bring anthropology into the home by examining facets of culture (see Goldschmidt 1954). These recorded programs were sponsored by the National Association of Educational Broadcasters and produced by the Canadian Broadcasting Corporation. The programs were directed at the listening public. Anyone who replayed them for a class had the same worrisome feeling associated with showing classroom films—that they were more entertaining than instructive, yet dubious entertainment at that, setting students at a listening task without an accompanying picture to watch on film or, eventually, TV.

There were also heroic efforts beginning about the mid-1960s to bring anthropology into the classroom either as an identifiable subject area or as a major source of information for "discovery approaches" to learning (for example, the MACOS, Man, A Course of Study project). And there has always been a vast repository of sometimes wonderful ethnographic films prepared essentially for use in instructional settings, although their didactic quality seems more conspicuous today with the invasion such films have made into our homes via public service television.

In spite of efforts to bring anthropology before the public or to experiment with alternative forms of presentation, the old ways die hard. For most ethnographers, and for virtually all others reporting fieldwork except documentary filmmakers and the new video ethnographers, writing is still "where it's at." Reporting in print continues to be the dominant format, especially among aspiring academics. Whatever technological changes may occur in how we go about placing our words before others, tenure-seeking aspirants are sure to find the writing of books and articles pivotal in their careers. Contract-seeking researchers make their plans for dissemination part of their proposals for funding.

Writing with the intent of publication is the form of presentation with which I have struggled, happily as well as unhappily, for more than three decades. Writing has become more than just a habit; it is part of my definition of who I am and what I do. As I noted, I do not consider myself to be an author—an individual clever enough to make his living by writing—but there is no question that I am a person who writes. More accurately, I can be described as a person who "writes some and edits lots." An extended editing process allows for two other critical dimensions— ample time both for reflecting and reworking ideas, and for making judicious use of outside reviewers at critical stages along the way.

An equally important personal reason to focus on writing up qualitative research is that, thanks to the inspiration of and an invitation from editor Mitch Allen, I was given the opportunity to say whatever I could about that topic. Those are the very words I chose, *Writing Up Qualitative Research*, for the title of the monograph I prepared for the Sage series on Qualitative Research Methods (HFW 1990b). That monograph is widely available, and I need not reiterate its message here. However, I do want to review three major ideas emphasized in it: (1) Begin Writing Early, (2) Anticipate How You Will Parcel Out the Study, and (3) Work "Start to Finish" but Think "Finish to Start." I will also make a plea on behalf of style or panache.

Above all, let me emphasize the idea expressed by James Clifford that "writing has emerged as central to what anthropologists do both in the field and thereafter" (Clifford and Marcus 1986:2). Make that central to what *every fieldworker* does, both in the field and thereafter.

Begin Writing Early

My first suggestion, to begin early, is echoed by virtually everyone who has something to say about writing. You cannot begin writing too soon! I now go so far as to suggest that one consider writing before even *beginning* a field study. I recommend giving serious thought to this idea, which might be called *prewriting*. Allow me to present a brief on its behalf.

We never go into a study totally devoid of an idea of what we are about. Early writing invites us to make what we already know—or think we know—a matter of record. It also helps us recognize areas of inquiry in which our information is scant or nonexistent, and thus helps give focus and purpose to fieldwork still in progress.

Of course, the argument can be made that early writing might unduly influence the subsequent course of the investigation. I think a more powerful argument can be offered in rebuttal: Early writing should help ferret out biases and prejudices in such a way that we deal with them *explicitly*, and from the outset of an inquiry, rather than have to fight them off as we go along. Through prewriting, you might even recognize whenever your proposed fieldwork is intended only to validate a personally held position. If you are looking for a soapbox from which to declare your convictions, why not just skip the research pose. Cut immediately to the chase: Write your essay as the essay you should be writing, not as reported research that "happens" to prove you right.

Anticipate How You Will Parcel Out the Study

A second, related point is that early writing helps to keep the research focused on outcomes, on what is to result as a consequence of fieldwork. An essential step in achieving one's purposes is to develop a proposed outline or table of contents for the final report, including an estimated number of pages to be assigned to each of its component parts. It is critical to recognize from the outset that in all descriptively based research our bigger problem is not to try to get all the data we can but *to try to get rid of as much extraneous data as possible*, so that the corpus of data we actually deal with is manageable. Premature as it may seem, the rationing of pages among proposed subtopics can be an invaluable step in thinking about how to proportion the account.

In even the most descriptively oriented accounts, the space available for description is necessarily limited, and requisite attention to method, theory, literature review, analysis, interpretation, recommendations, or implications all crowd that space further. I hope I have not left the impression that topics such as "theory" or "literature review" need not be addressed in field-based studies. I have suggested that they be drawn into the account to whatever extent, at whatever place, and in whatever fashion seem most relevant and vital to the account itself. They are not routine matters to be dealt with ritually and dismissed with dispatch. They need to be addressed in such a way that they are integrated into the account. And it is important to recognize that each of these topics takes up precious space.

In the absence of real data at hand, it is difficult to offer suggestions about organizing material for presentation. *Transforming Qualitative Data: Description, Analysis, and Interpretation* (HFW 1994b) was born out of my own efforts to deal with the critical problem of "transforming" data from observation to final account. The three aspects that constitute my subtitle— description, analysis, interpretation—present a way to distinguish among what I see as the major options we exercise in organizing and presenting qualitative data. To ground my discussion in "real data," I drew on several of my earlier studies for example and illustration. For more technical aspects of analyzing qualitative data, an ever-expanding shelf of resources is available (e.g., Denzin and Lincoln 1994; Miles and Huberman 1994; Silverman 1993).

What I propose by way of an overall strategy is to move the question of narrative and data management, including the question of whether to emphasize analysis or interpretation, to the early phases of a qualitative inquiry—rather than waiting until you are buried in fieldnotes and data to begin to dig your way out. From the outset, a researcher needs to have in mind some broad categories, however tentative, that provide sufficient structure to guide both fieldwork and deskwork. Do not chastise yourself for imposing structure on what you are about to report. If you can't bear to impose structure, you will never be able to compose the account.

In selecting broad categories, try not to be tempted by all the categories that the text management programs can handle. Look instead for as few *major* categories as possible, categories that subsume numerous minor categories, yet keep important distinctions visible. A proliferation of minor categories or subcategories is not as worrisome; the more the merrier if you like to have a place for everything. As your work progresses, you should discover categories that can be collapsed or eliminated as you begin to distinguish recurring patterns from one-time events. Just keep a tight rein on the number of major categories, a number that ought intuitively to "feel right" as you continue your sorting. Recognize also the direction in which you tend most naturally to work, building up like the potter, in whose hands something new is formed, or carving away like the sculptor, to reveal in fine detail what was there all along.

In one major field study (reported in HFW 1977) I used an analogy to the two-part moiety form of social organization studied by anthropologists. Describing each of two moieties gave me two obvious categories, and subsequently describing them in interaction provided the third. First I described the "target" group. Then I described the innovating organization or "donors." Next I turned attention to the interaction between them. That proved a satisfactory way to present a basically descriptive ethnographic account, accompanied by an anthropologically oriented analysis derived from the perspective of social organization. The "target group-donor group-interaction setting" sequence was prompted by George Foster's *Applied Anthropology* (1969).

Software programs now developed for qualitative researchers are designed to utilize the remarkable capabilities of microprocessors rather than being well suited to the more limited capabilities of the human mind. My proclivity for dividing things into sets of threes serves me far better in this than a computer program capable of handling many categories at one time. In striving to keep the number of major categories as small as possible, I usually begin my sorting by trying to work with two categories, keeping an eye out for what I am missing that might necessitate a third (or, more reluctantly, a fourth, fifth, and so on).

Work "Start to Finish" but Think "Finish to Start"

My third suggestion extends the second, urging not only that you propose a tentative table of contents early on but that you "think through" your entire study in the reverse order of the way you intend to carry it out. Begin with a careful consideration of where you want to end up, what you want to have when you finish. I take this to be what John Creswell wishes his students to do in thinking of their task as "composing" rather than simply "doing" their studies, as discussed in the previous chapter. Try to anticipate as specifically as you can the outcomes you want to achieve. Then back up a step to identify the kinds of data and range of personal experience you will need to support or illustrate those outcomes. Then back up one more step to ascertain how to get that information.

Thinking "finish to start" invites a critical appraisal of whether your intended approach is really the best way to obtain whatever information you actually expect to *use*. One of the temptations of fieldwork is that it presents the unsuspecting researcher with so much potential data that might *possibly* be of use, data often *so easy* to attend to and record, that newcomers risk losing sight of what they are getting data for. In practice, it isn't a bad idea to maintain a running dialogue with yourself to ask, "Why am I recording this? What use am I likely to make of it?" My experience has been that the more clearly one can specify the data needed, the less likely a fieldwork "broadside" is an efficient way to proceed. If data are what you are after, just get them. If data alone cannot provide what you need, then your investment in a fieldwork approach is more likely to be warranted.

While you are stepping back, you might as well back up one step further. Reflect on how you have posed your problem or "purpose" statement and whether fieldwork offers a reasonable approach to it. As posed, the problem ought to invite the broad scope of inquiry that fieldwork allows, permitting you to develop, test, and modify ideas as necessary rather than binding you, right or wrong, to your original charter.

Alas, you may not enjoy ideal circumstances that will allow you to alter your course and redefine your problem or approach. Like the artist constrained by an art world, you need to recognize what you can accomplish under whatever terms are guiding your work, especially if you are conducting research in which the problem and parameters have been established by others. Since tension is more likely to arise over what you eventually report and how you report it than how you go about your inquiry, attention to early writing can help you anticipate your reporting problems and look for ways to resolve them.

None of this is intended to have you complete a study before you start; it is intended to keep you finely—and finally—tuned to what your study is intended to accomplish, as well as to help you assess your research objective itself. The more you are able to flesh out your ideas, the better, even to the point of writing a draft of the entire study. Just for yourself. Should you feel too constrained by circumstances beyond your control, you might want to prepare two early drafts, one presenting the study as you feel it ought to be told, the other presenting the study as it will have to be. That leaves you with a documented record of what you were thinking and feeling, an account to which you may want to return sometime in the future.

The quality of that earliest writing need be of no concern. Five paragraphs into the Preface of his book *Style*, Joseph Williams notes reassuringly that "We write a first draft for ourselves; the drafts thereafter increasingly for the reader" (1990:x). That you *are* writing demonstrates from the outset that you are already thinking beyond the fieldwork *experience* to how you will render that experience before an audience. Perhaps Geertz dismisses such experience a bit too casually with his reference to "pursuing the more automatized routines of data collection" (1973:10 and quoted in the epigraph), but it is hard to take issue with his insistence that ultimately the work turns on the ability of the fieldworker to render an account. There's neither help nor solace in his observation, but it is an accurate statement of the task that "renders" all previous steps worth the effort.

Writing with Panache

The remainder of this discussion turns on the term *panache*, drawing attention not so much to flair, the grand and flamboyant manner some actors evoke on stage, but to verve, as used in reference to literary vigor, and, especially, literary *style*. Style is not totally lacking in our work; descriptive accounts often provide at least a "dash of panache." When they do, however, it is not so much a consequence of our latent talents as a consequence of the fact that our accounts themselves often include poignant elements related through anecdotes, vignettes, or expressive language of those whose lives we examine. "The subjects of ethnographies, it should never be forgotten," writes Robert J. Smith, "are always more interesting than their authors" (1990:369).

Although it often fails to impress, and may fail to show at all, I think most academic writers would like to season their work with more than a mere dash of panache, and would prefer not to depend solely on informants to supply the light touch. Sometimes this is realized in unexpectedly revealing footnotes, an opening descriptive paragraph that deludes the reader into believing that what follows will be a delight to read, or intimate dedications, acknowledgments, or postscripts that speak in an altogether different voice from the body of the manuscript.

I do not suggest that everyone has or necessarily ought to strive for a light touch, giving each paragraph a sprinkle of humor or wit. I assume that writing with such a touch either comes easily or is best left to others. What I do encourage, however, is for academic writers to "lighten up" in general, especially through editing stilted academic prose written under the ill-conceived idea that we have to be boring to be believed.

I don't know exactly how to help anyone "lighten up." A new self-consciousness about representation, especially about *voice*, has allowed (and even encouraged) authors to put more of themselves in fieldwork-based accounts, but little was gained for those who bogged down in the jargon of postmodernism itself. Writing in the first person often helps. It leaves authors no place to hide, while inviting them to become part of their own manuscripts. Sure, it can be overdone; I am aware of my excesses in this regard, an unbecoming number of "I's" in almost every paragraph. On at least two occasions in my experience, however, I have had editors override my first-person style with a turgid third-person style of their own, sending a "corrected" manuscript on to the printer without the courtesy of consulting with me. How anyone could look at what they did to those manuscripts and call it an improvement beats the hell out of me!

See for yourself. The following is an abridged excerpt from the introduction to an article I wrote titled "On Ethnographic Intent." Here is the *edited* version as it appeared in an academic journal:

> In May of 1981, the author was invited to participate in a graduate student seminar hosted on the campus of a major North American

university. The collective mission of the seminar was to address issues of descriptive research, and his assignment was to discuss ethnography. Another agency co-sponsored the seminar, and a summary of the sessions subsequently appeared in its newsletter. In reading that summary, this writer was reminded of an uneasy feeling that had been experienced before and was at a conscious level during the seminar: Here was another well-intentioned effort—on the author's part to inform educator colleagues about ethnographic research and on their part to become informed about it—that was going awry. (HFW 1985:187)

I was later invited to reprint the article in a volume being compiled by the Spindlers. The invitation afforded an opportunity to see the account published as written. What follows shows how the original article began (abridged as above). Note that even my paragraphing had been changed in the edited version quoted above.

> In May, 1981, I was invited to participate in a graduate student seminar hosted on the campus of a major North American university. Our collective mission was to address issues of descriptive research. My assignment was to discuss ethnography.
>
> Another agency co-sponsored the seminar, and a summary of the sessions subsequently appeared in its newsletter. In reading that summary, I was reminded of an uneasy feeling I had experienced before and was conscious of during the seminar: here was another well-intentioned effort—on my part to inform educator colleagues about ethnographic research, on their part to become informed about it—that was going awry. (HFW 1987b:37)

I was mighty annoyed by what happened to that manuscript in the hands of an editor. Although there was no malevolent scheme at work, there was an unexamined and, to that time, an apparently unchallenged editorial policy of that journal of which neither I nor the guest editor invited to compile a special issue was aware. Too late to save my manuscript, I was at least able to insist on an accompanying footnote of explanation about such heavy-handed editing. (Subsequently we were successful in having the policy changed.) In any circumstances when authors are instructed to submit manuscripts written in the third person, I suggest one not "submit" at all if a first-person narrative is integral to the account. In field-based research it is hard to imagine how or why the author-researcher ever can totally disappear. There are enough editors who understand this; they are the ones to whom we should submit.

However, for any question related to style, I suggest carefully checking whether rigid prescriptions for academic writing really exist or are simply part of a lingering and often unexamined lore passed along in the halls of academe. We all observe and transmit "rules" that are not rules at all. Be suspicious of anyone who informs you knowingly that "Journal editors don't like . . ." or "The Graduate School requires . . ." Maybe they do, maybe they don't (do not?). Maybe the previous editor or provost was an old fogy but the present one isn't. Check for yourself.

There is no point in trying to inventory all the ways one can add a dash of panache. Such efforts are like selecting the right seasonings from a kitchen shelf—we all have our favorites, know what works best for us, and occasionally reach out for something different to add zest to a meal, just as we try to add zest to a manuscript. Natural storytellers introduce excitement, intrigue, surprise, even mystery. The more cynical work wonders seasoning their accounts with paradox or irony. Compassion seems particularly suited to our efforts as human observers, allowing us to temper our sometimes too analytical, too dispassionate observations with something from inside ourselves to remind the reader that researchers are human, too. Compassion is a powerful ingredient, best used with discretion so that it evokes empathy without tempting an author to become a bleeding heart. It might be likened to using just the right amount of cayenne pepper, curry, nutmeg, or any seasoning for which more is not necessarily better and the slightest excess can spoil the whole effect.

Another approach, seen perhaps too seldom in academic writing, is to make oneself—rather than one's "subjects," one's readers, or the rest of the world—the fall guy. As researchers turned authors, we often can better afford to be the naive one, the individual who completely missed the point or needed to be "taught a lesson." Better to point the finger at ourselves than for us always to be pointing the finger at the world. Yet how infrequently do we read accounts from fieldworkers who admit to foibles of their own or seem able to remain aware that, ultimately, it is ourselves we seek to understand?

Writing as Central to the Art of Fieldwork

Murray Wax was the first fieldworker of my acquaintance to insist that writing is not simply an adjunct to fieldwork but is a critical component of it. Prior to hearing the importance he bestowed on writing, I was content with the more cautious observation that readers were twice-blessed when a fieldwork account proved to be not only of substance but also well written. Writing was so little associated with fieldwork—and with the social sciences in general—that to have a work cited for being especially well written raised doubts as to whether that was another of its attributes or its only one.

Those doubts linger on, for there is nothing that raises more uncertainty for me than to have something I have published commended for being "well written." Such doubts did not spring full-blown by themselves. When I first encountered anthropology some twenty years after the initial publication of Ruth Benedict's *Patterns of Culture* (1934), her book was still one of the anthropological accounts most widely read among lay audiences. The book was touted for its elegant style but was often explained away by peers anxious to point out that Benedict was also a poet. By implication, as a poet she could be forgiven for writing well; conversely, as a poet she might not be the most authoritative source for a rigorous anthropology. Benedict herself was quick to point out by the book's second paragraph, "It may be that I have carried some interpretations further than one or another of the field-workers would have done" (p. vii). Oscar Lewis's *Children of Sanchez* (1961) was greeted similarly, its literary style so highly regarded as to cause concern among the peers about the extent to which the account was "authentic."

The ability to write well is now recognized as an essential element in fieldwork. Our accounts are meant to be read. We do not have neat findings, conclusions that can be summarized or reduced to tables and charts, or tidy hypotheses instantly e-mailed to colleagues around the world breathlessly awaiting reports of our results. If nobody reads our studies—virtually in their entirety—our efforts are doomed to obscurity. We need not apologize for efforts to make our work "interesting."

Anthropologist Gerald Berreman expressed concern years ago that ethnographers were likely to diverge into a majority who would "take refuge in scientism," seeking rigor at the expense of "content, insight, and

209

understanding," while a minority, with no pretense at being scientific, would become "essentially creative writers on anthropological topics" (1968:369, quoted in Sanjek 1990:242–243). One could do worse than being an essentially creative writer on anthropological topics. For openers, how about being an essentially uncreative one? None of us has been drawn to this work because of a demonstrated capacity for writing. Many people aspire to become writers, some of them do write, and some of what some of them write makes its way into the public arena. But I have never met anyone who turned to fieldwork because of the opportunity it presents for writing, and I have spoken with numerous individuals who cannot imagine doing fieldwork because of the writing that must be joined to it.

One does not ordinarily think of researchers of any type as "authors," and there are certainly more efficient ways to go about getting a story than spending the time or trying to reach the depths ordinarily devoted to fieldwork. Fieldworkers become writers out of necessity, drawing on personal resources never tapped except perhaps for preparing class assignments. They may not have been required to do enough writing to become proficient even in that. Only as a doctoral student did I have the "opportunity" (that is the word I use now; I may have used other words at the time) to write major term papers. I had no idea how one went about writing a "book" (i.e., dissertation). By the time I was ready to write the dissertation, however, I did have two things going for me. One was time itself. I gave dissertation writing top priority in my life and I devoted myself exclusively to the task. The other was that I felt I had *something worthwhile to say*.

Opinions vary as to which stage is the most difficult in the writing process. The initial hurdle is to overcome inertia and get *something* written without becoming discouraged by the quality of the product that ensues. I have both struggled with and delighted in the problems of organizing and finding my way into each fieldwork account. The art is to present material in an engaging yet coherent manner sufficient to hold the interest of a reader who may not expect to be entertained but hopes not to be bored. In most cases, we have just one chance to capture the interest of a reader. (We might borrow an aphorism from people who sell Christmas trees: "Never let a customer leave the lot without one." Neither a customer nor a reader is likely to come back.)

Choosing how to get *into* the account, in a manner intended to draw the reader along with me, provides the toehold I need to get the writing started. Of course, I sometimes get off on the wrong foot and find myself on a tangent instead of on target. That produces a second problem: "throwing out" material once written, which I am always reluctant to do, or becoming locked into a particular way of conceptualizing an account and being unable to shake loose from it. Sometimes we simply have to take a fresh start. It may take an outside reader to tell us to do just that. Among your invited early readers, you ought to have one or more whom you can count on to tell *you* like it is, *before* you get to the stage where rejections start to close out options.

It is the final product that must be written well, not the earlier drafts. It matters not how many drafts it takes to arrive at an acceptable final one. Therein lies hope, for what an experienced old hand or gifted newcomer may achieve in a single draft, the rest of us ought to be able to achieve through the processes of minor editing and major revision. It may take iteration upon iteration before we get a version that satisfies not only critical colleagues—reviewers, journal referees, editors, dissertation committee— but also ourselves. If we have chosen our problem well, conducted our fieldwork well, and organized our data in a form suitable for analysis and interpretation, then we owe it as much to ourselves as to our readers to come up with a well-written account to present it.

Once I have a draft in hand—the completed draft of the entire manuscript, so that I know where it is (or was) going—I begin editing and revising. Editing and revising with a passion! From then on, both figuratively and literally, things have to get better, and they do. I cannot stress too heavily that my manuscripts improve through sustained efforts at improving them, draft after draft after draft. I am not embarrassed by the number of drafts I go through before I reach what I consider an acceptable standard. I admit to dismay in realizing that the initial writing itself, my sentences as I first put them on screen or paper, seem not to be improving in spite of all the years I have worked at this. Still, with the help of time, prodigious editing, and feedback from critic readers invited to review drafts at various stages, things usually end up OK.

I have never been preoccupied with quantity in my writing. I was astounded while being introduced to an academic audience overseas to hear that I had written "157 books and articles" until I realized that a busy administrator summarily recruited to introduce me had simply counted *every* entry on my curriculum vitae, whether book, article, panel presentation, or conference attended. I recommend turning a deaf ear to anyone who claims to know the number of books or articles required to achieve tenure, promotion, or fame. I am unimpressed by colleagues who "crank out" what amounts to academia's equivalent of motel art. I take great pride in my portfolio. On the other hand, although writing may be an art—and even the "primary art," as English poet Samuel Taylor Coleridge once claimed—my writing has not made an artist of me. What I have become is, I think, a skilled craftsperson. I have to *work* at it. My pride is essentially craft pride. Careful work, carefully presented, perhaps envious of art without any pretension of achieving it.

As to feedback from others, it certainly helps if among your invited critic readers you include some with technical knowledge about your topic, but not all your readers need to be specialists. One effective way to have nonspecialists help, and to recruit readers over objections that your work is "much too technical" (or some other excuse that can be taken more than one way), is to ask them to read your manuscript aloud to you. That will enable you literally to "hear for yourself" how your words look and sound to someone who shares neither your specialized knowledge on the topic nor your intimate knowledge about how your sentences are supposed to be read.

You are not likely to find anyone willing to read back every sentence of every draft, so you must learn to read your own sentences as though they are being read by a stranger. Imagine that stranger to be easily led astray by ambiguous references, convoluted sentences, or insufficient attention to headings, paragraphing, and punctuation. If I have any secret to reveal about my editing, it is that I try to attend to every sentence in search of possible traps for an unsuspecting reader. I don't mind writing a tricky sentence now and then, but I pore over my sentences to search out ambiguities and eliminate needless words. Writing has to communicate. Right?

Finding the appropriate level of detail is a major concern in preparing accounts derived from descriptive fieldwork. How much detail should we present, in what manner, to make our case without unduly burdening the account with inconsequential facts? To me, such questions get back to purpose, to that carefully worded (and pondered, and revised, and pondered some more) guiding statement intended to get us on track and to keep us there.

Style—panache—can neither cover for nor substitute for a problem with focus. Style is necessary but not sufficient. It is highly personal, a subset of every individual's "idiosyncratic human touch," most certainly an element of art rather than a practice of science. Even styles identified by their lack of style—academic writing, for example—become habits we acquire and observe without critical thought. There is too little testing of the boundaries, too little effort to employ a wider variety of styles appropriate to the topic and acceptable to an audience. Keep an eye out in your own journals to see if everybody is writing the same way. Do academic editors really insist on turgid prose, or do they publish turgid prose because that is all they receive?

Much has been written about style, but in seeking after it you are probably better off to spend time editing another version of your own work than devouring another style manual. If I had to pass along one bit of advice that strikes me as helpful, it is advice Joseph Williams offers in *Style*: "The secret to a clear and readable style is in the first five or six words of every sentence" (Williams 1990:52). Clear and readable style is the name of the game. If Williams insists, as apparently he does, that style is set and revealed in the first few words of every sentence, consider taking him at his word(s) and attend to your own "first few words." Then, just in case he has miscounted, attend to everything that follows, in that and every other sentence as well.

Giving special attention to the beginning of each sentence, paragraph, or section provides an excellent starting place for anyone serious about style. If you are not sure how to begin your editing, begin there, with beginnings. If more academic authors did that, we might end up with fewer sentences of the sort, "It can easily be understood, therefore, that in the present situation . . ." Style cannot save a manuscript any more than it can save a sentence, but it can greatly enhance the chances that a manuscript will go on to have a life of its own. A style-conscious author could delete all 11 words in my example, allowing author and reader alike to proceed more rapidly to the action or point of that sentence . . . should there happen to be one.

213

Having put so much emphasis on style, I may inadvertently have skipped over the haunting specter and crippling effect that not-being-able-to-get-*anything*-down-on-paper poses for the researcher who cannot, or will not, get the writing started. Surely the anxiety associated with not being able to start writing is fearsome, and one may succumb to some darker art in defense. Self-deception is one. Frequently such fear is camouflaged by endlessly extending time in the field or the library, under the pretense that there is still too much to be learned before one can be presumptuous enough to begin writing.

I do not know how to help anyone who simply cannot, or will not, start writing. That is a problem I do not have. I start by looking for a way to take a reader with me into the account, which also gets the writing process itself underway. Here I pass along some oft-repeated tips, accompanied by further reflections so they are not mere clichés:

- *Set aside time for writing each day.* I'm sure no one disagrees with this wonderful idea. I also realize it may not be practical for people whose writing must be sandwiched into busy schedules that preclude time for it. Nor is it likely to seem helpful to anyone who has experienced just "sitting there." You must admit, however, that you are unlikely to get anything written unless you have paper or a keyboard at the ready in front of you and have made writing your top priority for the moment. To overcome inertia, if you just can't get started, how about listing all the things that seem to be getting in the way and then examining each in detail—in writing—along with any ideas about possible ways to overcome each of them? Maybe your dilemmas themselves offer entrée to the account you are trying to present: "As I sat down to begin this account, I immediately realized several dilemmas that confronted me. . . ." Or, "From the moment I was first able to conceptualize the problem I address here, I realized I faced a comparable dilemma in bringing it before a wider audience. . . ." By the second or third draft you may even be able to drop those awkward beginnings and get to the point.

- *Begin writing "too early."* As already discussed, you should start writing soon, the sooner the better. Recognize that writing must be joined to the research; it is not a final step after everything else is finished. Write to discover what you have to say about what you are experiencing and how you are going to say it.

- *Write what you intend to use and use what you write.* Whether your note making is brief or elaborate, don't make every entry something that would have to be rewritten before you could incorporate it into your final account. Take particular care with your descriptive passages and the write-up of complete, richly detailed vignettes. Your own musings as your fieldwork proceeds warrant similar care and elaboration. Consider that such entries might find their way into the finished account at a later date, their location to be determined as the manuscript takes shape.

- *Begin writing at an easy place.* When you are ready to begin drafting sections of your final account, start with sections where the writing should come easily. Method, perhaps? How you happened to pose this problem? Some first impressions or common misperceptions? Draw together some purely descriptive sections, incorporating or expanding on original fieldnotes, as described above. It is never too early to *begin* writing the final draft.

Sometimes it is helpful to recognize, or to reaffirm, what you already should know: Your writing problems are not all that different from what others experience. I was surprised to learn that my set of private distractions was not all that unique: "clearing my desk" instead of turning immediately to writing, when I know that first-thing-in-the-morning is my most productive writing time; hitting the cheese and Triscuits early on; spending an unusually long time combing the cat. I would like to be able to report that I am so well disciplined that I write every day. In truth, the best I can do is to arrange "writing days" when I have a minimum of a full and uninterrupted morning. During those periods, if I am on a roll, I might not even answer the telephone.

Simply stated, the only antidote for not writing is to write. You can always improve what you have written, editing the good stuff and tossing the rest. Until you have words in front of you to edit, thoughts can jump around forever in your head in so abstract a form that they can neither be communicated to others nor sharpened to your own satisfaction. Of course I mull things over before I write, and I constantly jot down ideas, phrases, and questions as they pop into my head. But my best "mullings," like my best scanning for related ideas and relevant citations in the literature, seem to come *after* I start to capture my thoughts on paper, not before.

When you are *not* writing, be honest with yourself and others; don't make the claim to be writing unless some words are in place where you can actually look at them. If mulling ideas is the way you like to begin, don't let me rush you through that stage. Do whatever works for you that enables you to get the account written, one draft at a time.

This book serves as a good example of writing in order to find out, in this case "squeeze out," what I had to say on aspects of a topic I have not addressed previously. The entire volume is a think piece, a reflection of practice rather than a report of research. I originally believed that I could easily make the case for *the art of fieldwork*, and that the writing would simply "flow." Until I began to identify the various aspects I wanted to discuss (my tentative table of contents, subsequently revised and revised), I found myself working off of unbridled but also undisciplined enthusiasm. In this instance I wrote a complete draft before I discovered the need to make a crisper distinction between two complementary but distinct dimensions implicated by my title, one examining fieldwork as art, a *perspective* for looking at fieldwork, the other examining the art of *doing* fieldwork, much as one might talk about the art of conversation, fly fishing, or restoring antiques.

Once I began writing—rather than just ruminating—ideas began to form, to reveal their strengths and weaknesses, and, alas, to contradict each other. With writing came better questions that offered a better way to consult the work of colleagues, rather than reading or rereading "everything I could" about fieldwork before first attempting to capture my own ideas.

Let me note a certain comfort I gain from the realization that a book like this can also be revised *after* it is in print, should a subsequent edition seem warranted. I do not recall ever experiencing what I have felt during this writing, that even as work on the first version finally came to a close, I entertained hope that the opportunity to prepare a second, revised edition might someday present itself. For now, I have taken these ideas as far as I can go.

An important distinction can be made between revising a fieldwork-based account and revising an extended essay such as this one. I have never revised my field-based accounts, a conscious decision I made the first time the opportunity arose. It seems to me that fieldwork accounts are best left intact as historical documents, corrected only for errors of fact or abridged to meet publication requirements. New information, alternative or enhanced analyses and interpretations, and follow-up accounts can be appended or published separately, as with the chapter, "A Kwakiutl Village and School 25 Years Later" that I was able to add to my original *A Kwakiutl Village and School* (HFW 1967) when it was reissued in 1989. I think this has been standard practice, beginning perhaps with William F. Whyte's classic *Street Corner Society* (1943), whose second edition (1955), with the addition of an appendix on method, became an even more valuable resource for urban fieldworkers than the original publication. The reissue of many of the original monographs in the Spindlers' *Case Studies in Cultural Anthropology* in a subsequent *Fieldwork Edition* that now included an added section on method enjoyed similar recognition.

I do not feel the same about preserving essay-type works in their pristine form. The amount of revision or updating to be done helps me make decisions about whether or not to revise at all. I can imagine finding satisfaction in someday revising this book, but that will have to come after a period in which the ideas and the way of expressing them have had ample time to season. Meanwhile, I hope readers will engage in vigorous debate as to the direction those revisions should take and what else needs to be noted on behalf of preserving fieldwork's full potential.

Writing as Disciplined Activity

Admittedly, the emphasis I have put here on writing, and on early writing, gets words recorded, the process begun, without much quality control beyond your own criteria for what constitutes an adequate sentence. "No writing" at one extreme is faced off at the other by the excesses of overwriting, where writing processes get in the way rather than facilitate the reporting. One way this can happen is for wordsmithing to take over your work, so that style becomes a preoccupation, leading to "slick description" instead of "thick" (Sanjek 1990:404). Efforts at good writing need to be coupled with having something worthwhile to say.

Academic pressure to publish or perish interferes by insisting that whether or not you have something important to say, you had better get in print anyway. The system is not likely to change, so the best solution seems to be one suggested earlier, to address your research efforts toward topics of genuine importance. You'll need to be able to bolster your energy and morale as necessary to convince yourself that your work does matter and is worthy of your effort. Take personal responsibility for work that bears your name, and see that the work you do does bear your name. Consider your name on a manuscript as your hallmark.

In an effort to develop a personal style and to contribute original work, you may be distressed at the influence others can exert over your writing, especially if you had anticipated that, at long last, you would be "free," like any self-respecting artist, to do your own thing. Where you may have anticipated "so many possibilities," you seem instead to encounter such constricted choice. The message you wanted to tell seems lost or redirected, your own style subordinated to the preferences of your dissertation committee, editor, or sponsor. I must console with little consolation: Welcome to the club!

If it wasn't clear at the time, maybe now you realize why an early chapter (Chapter 3) examined art worlds and the cultural milieu in which artists work, so that you would realize that you are in good company. If your committee or an editor or publishing house interested in your manuscript offers little by way of options to their directives, you probably need to "knuckle under" and do what they ask you to do. A Chinese proverb suggests "When the door is low, bow your head." Survival is a first order of business not only in the field but in deskwork as well.

The "power" to withdraw a manuscript is about the only power you have, short of some overly dramatic action such as dropping out of a degree program or changing your career line. These are never attractive alternatives, especially if you have invested months on a particular project and some part of a lifetime acquiring competence at fieldwork. Withdrawing a manuscript may bring some personal satisfaction, but you are in a position to exert rather little force when virtually all journals have manuscripts

218

competing for space and all publishers have more on the table than they could ever print. In general, I recommend that you accede to whatever requests and suggestions you receive if they are likely to lead to having your work accepted. Just think of yourself as comparable to struggling artists in their art worlds, knowing what they would like to do but doing what they have to do.

On the other hand, always write for yourself *first*—the story you want to tell, the way you want to tell it. Be willing and prepared to make deep, painful changes when circumstances seem largely out of your control. Keep your original ideas and manuscripts intact, however. There may come a day when you will be able to return to your original manuscript, to compare your critics' comments with your own reassessment and decide whether you still wish to develop your material as you had planned.

Regardless of how heavy-handed they seem, most people who offer suggestions are well intended. Your immediate perception may be that others are placing roadblocks in your path, but it is more likely they are trying to help you with your writing (or, at worst, endeavoring to keep poorly written or poorly researched accounts from being circulated). Points conveyed as directives may be more negotiable than they appear initially; editors do not like to be accused of dictating to authors, especially authors writing for professional journals in their own field. Nonnegotiable items may reflect publishing house or institutional policies over which even your seeming adversaries have little control. You may feel the urge to challenge such policies, but consider doing so at an appropriate time in your career—such as *after* you get the degree or publish your book, not *instead* of it. (I could "hang tough" and insist on a footnote of explanation and apology with that editor who replaced my first person pronouns with his awkward third person ones, but that all took place 21 years after I completed my doctorate! There's a thought: See if you can enlist us old-timers to fight your battles for you.)

Your experiences with publishers and reviewers might also be of interest to colleagues; you may be able to vent your anger and turn out an insightful piece on academic publishing at the same time. And don't be surprised if, after the passage of time, a manuscript you once were willing to defend "tooth and nail" no longer looks as inviolable as you had insisted. One of the most difficult kinds of "objectivity" to achieve is toward what we ourselves have written. I noted that I take pride in what I write and enjoy rereading earlier pieces, but that is personal and subjective. In cold, hard fact, nothing I have written is destined to become a runaway best-seller.

Publishing, like everything else about fieldwork, can be highly political as well as a matter of chance and luck. The most effective way an author can exert a positive influence in getting a manuscript to the attention of an editor is to pay careful attention to the match between the material and the publishing source. Since this involves a certain amount of networking, newcomers can seek help from old-timers who may have a broader view of who is interested in publishing what. Be selective in asking others to help with the critical editing of a manuscript, but remember that it is not unreasonable to inquire whether a distant scholar might be willing to read your manuscript and render an overall judgment as to its suitability for publication and, if so, to suggest possible journals or publishers.

Along the lines of matchmaking, the best place to inquire is with a journal or publisher known to publish material similar to what you are preparing, much as artists exhibit where comparable works previously have been shown or performed. Although publishers and journal editors (like gallery and museum directors) may prefer to think of themselves as open to anything new and different, in fact they must specialize in order to define any audience at all. The journals most likely to publish a paper reporting a qualitative study are the journals that have been doing it all along. The journals most interested in an ethnographically- or an ethnomethodologically-oriented study will be the journals that have already published such pieces. You should be able to get some clue to likely journals from looking at the citations in your own reference section. If a journal you are considering is not already cited, look at recent issues and think about adding some "politically correct" references to your list. "Window dressing!" you cry. Perhaps it is. Window dressing is an art.

Sending material out for review brings another reminder that style alone is never enough. Academic reviewers are especially likely to regard a manuscript in hand as a *draft* (rather than the polished manuscript you intended it to be) that can be edited for style—if the problem focus and insights you offer seem to warrant. My experience is that the most prevalent problem with submitted manuscripts is the lack of clear focus, the author going off in too many directions rather than following a well-honed and logical argument or development of a case. So we end up full circle, back to the "problem problem" where we started. Well-begun is half done, indeed. Maybe more than half! ●

PART FOUR
FIELDWORK AS PERSONAL WORK

For many of its zealous practitioners, participant observation is an art form and almost literally a way of life appropriately constituted as an oral tradition.

—Danny Jorgensen
Participant Observation, 8

Implicit in most *Art of . . .* books is the assumption that as we discover how to do something, or how to do it better, we will derive greater satisfaction in the doing. Some *Art of . . .* books make that assumption explicit, as in Irma Rombauer's forever popular *Joy of Cooking*, its title calling attention to the pleasure to be gained rather than to the how-to-do-it nature of the book itself.

I am hesitant to write about the "joys" of fieldwork. Not everyone who engages in it has fun at it. Most who have a major engagement with it do so only once, in the course of conducting dissertation research, and some never quite get through, or over, that experience. The editors of a collection of essays presenting an "inside view of qualitative research" introduce the book with this stark appraisal:

> Fieldwork must certainly rank with the more disagreeable activities that humanity has fashioned for itself. It is usually inconvenient, to say the least, sometimes physically uncomfortable, frequently embarrassing, and, to a degree, always tense . . . Field researchers have in common the tendency to immerse themselves for the sake of science in situations that all but a tiny minority of humankind goes to great lengths to avoid. (Shaffir and Stebbins 1991:1)

Furthermore, I am not sure that those of us who do enjoy and derive personal satisfaction from fieldwork—at least in the recounting, if not necessarily on a moment-to-moment basis at the time—want to give our detractors more ammunition by suggesting that one reason we do it is that we like it. On the other hand, there has been an analytical cast to the discussion to this point, and I may have dwelt unduly on fieldwork's complex problems, contextual constraints, and paradoxical dilemmas. My intent has been to present a rounded view that meets fieldwork's frustrations, problems, and complications straight on, with a perspective drawn from the making of art rather than the doing of science. I have also tried to keep the discussion grounded in practical concerns. That may have given more of a how-to-do-it cast than I intended, although it underscores the doing of fieldwork as meticulous art and craft, not something "artsy-craftsy." In any case, I have devoted enough attention to matters of how-to-do-it and to considerations of what we can learn from looking at how artists working in other media for other audiences do it. Now it is time to ask "why," with a look on the bright side, touting some of the personal satisfactions in fieldwork.

Chapter 10, the major chapter in this final section, offers such a review. That chapter is followed with a brief coda that takes the book's title as its own, providing the kind of final passage that codas are intended to do to bring a work to a "satisfying" close.●

CHAPTER TEN
THE SATISFACTIONS
OF FIELDWORK

For some readers of ethnography—myself included—the apparent freedom from rigid methodological rules associated with fieldwork and the blissful disregard that many ethnographic writers displayed for high-flying abstractions in their papers and monographs seemed to provide a wonderful excuse for having an adventurous good time while operating under the pretext of doing serious intellectual work.

—John Van Maanen
"An End to Innocence," in
Representation in Ethnography, 2

The claim to attention of an ethnographic account does not rest on its author's ability to capture primitive facts in faraway places and carry them home like a mask or a carving, but on . . . the power of the scientific imagination to bring us into touch with the lives of strangers.

—Clifford Geertz
"Thick Description," in
The Interpretation of Cultures, 16

All art requires presentation and representation; nothing is exactly as it seems. Fieldwork joins other art forms in that regard; it, too, is necessarily partial and incomplete, sacrificing some elements to enhance others through presentation and representation. Its accomplishments are what we behold.

We do not expect to be regaled with every dilemma each fieldworker confronted, any more that we are bound to accept an artist's personal plight or unbridled enthusiasm when making our private assessment of the finished product. We no more seek out poor or incomplete reports of fieldwork than we seek out discarded manuscripts, canvases, or musical scores simply to gain a deeper appreciation of the good ones. On the other hand, we give undue attention to trying to discern the genius in, or isolate artistic elements of, the scores or manuscripts or canvases of famous composers, authors, and painters, just as we return repeatedly to a small corpus of fieldwork classics.

It may be reassuring for the novice practitioner of any art form to keep in mind that even the best of potters throws away some pots, the best painter paints over canvases that are unsatisfactory, the published author admits to poems or manuscripts that have never been and are unlikely ever to be published.

Failed fieldwork is more elusive still: It simply disappears. If there is no written record except in private notes, and the fieldworker makes no further mention of it, in the long run it may be of no more consequence than a forgotten summer holiday. As a result, the only models available to the beginner are of successfully completed fieldwork as reported in successfully completed accounts, and of those, perhaps unfortunately, the same few are held up to generation after generation of students. As with other art worlds, we, too, place the masterpieces on so high a pedestal that they tend to inhibit when they are meant to inspire. Consistent with his notion of the *integrated professional*, Howard Becker suggests that as a consequence "people tend to denigrate routine science and art work, when that's what practically all of it is" (personal communication, April 1995).

Three anthropologists who joined forces to edit a collection dealing with fieldwork as "the human experience" made this observation in the text they did produce about another text that "got away":

> It must be mentioned at this point that not all fieldwork has been successful: there have been failures. All anthropologists know about them through the cocktail circuit, but they are rarely written up. As editors we first wanted to do a book titled *Failed Fieldwork*, thinking that much could be learned from such a book, but we could not get anyone to contribute chapters. (Lawless, Sutlive, and Zamora 1983:xv–xvi)

In examining fieldwork for all that is or can be artistic about it, my intent has been to encourage researchers to become bolder in the art of their work just as they are admonished to become more exacting in its science. One might think of that part of the discussion as attending to the professional side of fieldwork. As a professional, the researcher self-consciously draws from both science and art to create a role unique to fieldwork itself. In this chapter, I review aspects more personal in nature that can make fieldwork not only professionally but personally satisfying.

I do not mean to divorce the personal from the professional; one attractive feature of fieldwork is the way it links the two. This is especially so for researchers who buy wholeheartedly into a mainstream work ethic, as I suspect most do. They find salvation in a correspondence between what they feel obliged to do professionally and something they find personally satisfying as well. Although fieldwork is not a career in itself, it can become the focal activity in a career heavily oriented toward research and writing.

The term *work*, embedded in the compound word *fieldwork*, suggests a productive, effortful activity, although outsiders find it a rather curious form of it. Most of us who pursue fieldwork have been called on to explain both to disbelieving relatives and to skeptics in our research settings exactly what the "work" part of it is. This is difficult to convey to those who restrict their definition of work to physical activity involving some degree of exertion. In practice, the term *fieldwork* is probably used most comfortably everywhere except when one is actually in the field. At a research site, the word *study* has always seemed more suitable to me. That term frees us from having to defend why we are not at a workplace of our own. How else can we explain why we are free to come and go from whatever else it is that we do, in some other place that is apparently not too insistent that we are there to do it, to join in the activities of others among whom we appear to have few obligations, no responsibilities, and often rather limited skill, including even the ability to communicate?

Qualitative researchers resent the suggestion that their methods are "easier" than quantitative ones; they are likely to insist that fieldwork is "hard." Of course, we don't mind when colleagues commiserate with us about the long hours, risks, inconveniences, and uncertainties associated with fieldwork. For anyone with a strong work ethic, those hours, risks, inconveniences, and uncertainties underscore claims that fieldwork means "hard work," if more of an emotionally stressful than a strictly physical nature.

Commiseration for all we go through in conducting our work is heady stuff for anyone who likes to be recognized as a hard worker. Yet I become uneasy whenever quantitatively oriented researchers assuage me by insisting that qualitative research is "even harder" than theirs. I prefer the argument that it is difficult primarily because it is fraught with uncertainty. As with explanations about teaching, it is not easy to communicate to a casual onlooker exactly what makes such hard work of it. Perhaps our most convincing argument deals not with fieldwork itself but with the concomitant responsibility of reporting it. Novice fieldworkers may share the same concern. They may anticipate the thrill of having an adventurous good time without a clue as to how one goes about "writing a book" about it afterward.

I trust that experienced old-timers will agree with me that *conceptualizing and reporting* are fieldwork's biggest bugaboos, but *any* aspect of the fieldwork process can strike terror in the heart of the inexperienced researcher. There is no end to a list of "What ifs . . .?" that can be proposed. Those who feel overwhelmed by *every* aspect are well advised to seek another line of work or to pursue their inquiries in more systematic fashion. But each step along the way also offers the potential of satisfaction to those who see opportunity rather than obstacles. I have singled out five such sources of satisfaction for discussion. One might regard the list as suggestions for deriving the most satisfaction out of the fieldwork investment. Better still, these might be thought of as guidelines for *living* the fieldwork experience.

Being—or Becoming—a Sociable Social Researcher

One interesting role we play (often inadvertently) is a strange combination in which we serve at once as *ambassadors for* and *detractors of* research. Our fieldwork excursions ordinarily take us among ordinary people likely neither to have been the subjects of research nor to have encountered researchers in action. What we do is not all that mysterious, and thus we give the uninitiated a peek behind the veil of science. They see research performed by, with, and "on" humans like themselves. Granted, they see a special type of researcher, quite different from their presumed image of someone in a white coat peering through a microscope. Our very presence on site detracts greatly from the mystery, in the same way that "government scientists" are demystified when we see one of them interviewed on TV.

I think it valuable for people to have this realistic glimpse into how research operates. It is, after all, a fallible human endeavor, neither totally trustworthy nor totally beyond any layperson's comprehension. We read often enough about researchers in high-stakes efforts who have falsified reports or announced results prematurely and not always their own. Although we are sometimes made painfully aware of fieldwork's own shortcomings, the breadth and depth of all knowledge should remain suspect. Too seldom is the public made aware of the huge leaps researchers sometimes make between what they observe and the *possible* implications for human safety or well-being. In a modest way, the on-site researcher performs a public service by exposing inquiry for what it is, rather than fostering its image as the mysterious doings of an unseen group of relentless truth-seekers referred to as "scientists." We bring research "to the people" in more ways than one.

Unquestionably there is an aura and a status associated with the term *researcher*, and an image as well. It is not the image of a fieldworker. Perhaps reflecting my own generation, the vision of researcher-at-work that appears in my mind is one of a white-coated chemist carefully pouring something from one test tube into another. (The liquid in one of the two vials should have a reddish cast.) Granted, that image is probably better suited to the local pharmacist. The only research chemist of my personal acquaintance sits in front of a computer most of the time. I do not envy the work, although paradoxically I, too, seem to spend a great deal of time sitting in front of a computer. I don't mind borrowing something of that aura and status. I do that by appropriating the label *researcher*, careful to emphasize—as though an obvious plus—that the kind of research I do is *not* in the laboratory but is conducted with *real* people in *natural* settings.

As with most qualitative researchers, there is an implicit equation in my mind: The *realness* of my settings compensates for the lack of a laboratory that might otherwise validate my claim. I conduct my inquiries in the real world, a world that the laboratory researcher attempts to manipulate, control, and now even replicate with computer capabilities ironically labeled "virtual reality." I study in real rather than virtual reality. My efforts are

229

devoted to describing and understanding that world "just like it is." And yes, that is research.

In the fieldwork part of fieldwork—that relatively brief period during the whole process in which the researcher is engaged with the individuals being studied—one can actually be in *role* as a social being while remaining totally immersed in one's work. For those naturally inclined toward sociability, that is about as near as one can come to having one's cake and eating it, too. For those not all that socially outgoing by nature, fieldwork provides—and to some extent demands—a level of sociability that they might envy in others but would not otherwise achieve on their own were it not for the requirements of the role. In short, fieldwork lauds natural sociability and insists on some effort at it among those for whom sociability does not come easily.

It is the *role* of fieldworker that is social. Humans are innately social, but those attracted to academic careers are not necessarily the most social of humans. The role sometimes helps fieldworkers achieve what they seem unable to achieve through personality alone. That may explain why fieldworkers who seem distant and aloof at home sometimes write with such fondness about "their people" or "their informants" at more remote field sites.

As part of my own fieldwork personality, the role has often necessitated my pursuing one social activity I particularly abhor: visiting. (I'm not much on attending weddings, graduations, or funerals, either.) I am perfectly capable of carrying on a conversation, but I go to great lengths to avoid having to "sit and visit," in no small measure because I am a listener and obsessive talkers seem to take advantage. Dignify such visiting as an essential element of fieldwork, however—small talk done in the line of duty—and I can do it. The knowledge that not only must I carry off the visit but will later have to write up my notes makes my effort all the more heroic. Such sacrifices—all in the name of research.

A Hint of Adventure

Fieldwork can provide an invitation to adventure underwritten with a sense of intellectual purpose. Admittedly, not everybody seeks adventure or wants to devote the time necessary to engage in it; fieldwork can be a terrible nuisance to anyone simply checking off the hurdles to academic tenure or otherwise anxious to get comfortably settled. Under such circumstances, it can make an already potentially unsettling experience even more so, literally and figuratively. But young people whose lives have been lived out essentially in schools, and tenured faculty feeling hopelessly trapped in the presumed security of their institutions, sometimes long to escape the deadening routine of too-settled lives. My impression of the academic career is that to get anywhere one shouldn't really *go* anywhere. Fieldwork offers an approved way out of that dilemma.

For the tenured academic, the opportunity to engage in fieldwork *throughout a professional career*, rather than only at the outset of one, can become a reality through the tradition of sabbatical leave. Sabbatical leave—ordinarily the seventh or sabbatic year of service—is surely one of the special dividends of a teaching career. For a field-oriented researcher, it presents not only an incredible research opportunity but also the possibility of a periodically *recurring* one. For faculty not financially dependent on summer teaching, sabbatical leave may be parlayed into as much as an uninterrupted 15-month period, making extended fieldwork a possibility even at mid-career. Of course, it is not all that easy to "drop everything" and take off for a year, even for those unencumbered with working spouses, children in school, and the invariable host of complicating factors in our complicated lives. Yet the sabbatical makes field research compatible with teaching and offers the possibility of adventure in an academic career that might not otherwise seem destined for it.

My fieldwork experiences have literally taken me around the world. An involuntary tour of duty in 1952–54 with a see-the-world army got me no farther from my home town of Oakland, California, than Fort Lewis, Washington, although at the time that seemed preferable to being sent to fight an unpopular "action" in Korea. Fieldwork conducted in British Columbia, Canada, for my doctoral dissertation, took me only a few hundred miles farther north. Subsequent periodic leave allowed for the major part of one year spent in Rhodesia (now Zimbabwe), another in Malaysia, and two in Thailand, made possible by the sabbatical tradition (and salary) augmented by other funds (two Fulbright awards to Thailand, and a subsidy from Daystar Communications in southern Africa).

Once actually in the field, words of a more mundane nature are soon substituted for the term *adventure*. Adventure is, in fact, something most fieldworkers would rather have happen to someone else. But both before and after (especially after), fieldwork experience tends to be glossed in a quasi-romantic fashion. I confess that my collective memories of fieldwork give pleasure far in excess of the day-to-day experiences themselves.

No matter how difficult living in the field—when and if it is possible and appropriate to make so total a commitment—or going to one's research site for repeated visits of a shorter duration, if that is the realistic alternative, it can come as a surprise to fieldworkers to discover ambivalence about departing. At the end of my initial 12 months spent among the Kwakiutl, I felt at once emotionally drained yet intellectually invigorated by the opportunity to have observed and participated, however marginally as a white male teacher in an Indian community, in a culturally different way of life. (For the record, I also departed without any idea of how I would go about writing it up. It was far too close as personal experience; the dissertation assignment was what had become unreal.)

Conversely, if the experience itself has brought the fieldworker little joy, sometimes the departure brings both joy and a sense of relief, and one's anger or frustration provides impetus for the reporting. Anthropologist Hortense Powdermaker described her joy at leaving Hollywood after the fieldwork on which *Hollywood, the Dream Factory* (Powdermaker 1950) was based:

> I was never totally immersed in Hollywood as I have been in other situations ... As I left Hollywood after a year and drove past a sign marking the boundaries of Los Angeles, I burst into song, as is my habit when feeling joy. But even that reaction did not make me realize how deeply I had hated the place. (Powdermaker 1966:224–225)

Whatever the outcome of the fieldwork itself—and negative experiences have proven as powerful as positive ones to motivate subsequent reporting— I think the critical test is how deeply one has felt involved and affected personally. If it is hardly surprising when ethnographers at their sites for a year or more feel this, I think the *nature* of fieldwork can produce it in even a modest project. I suggest to students in my classes that they will probably remember their brief fieldwork encounters long after they have forgotten the class sessions, the texts, alas, even the instructor.

Problem Setting as Intellectual Challenge

The conceptualizing that accompanies field research affords a major worry for some but a stimulating intellectual challenge for others. Fieldwork presents an unusual opportunity for the truly contemplative life, not only figuratively but literally through "living" fully contextualized research. Regardless of how the experience is later written up, the thinking that accompanies fieldwork must be one's own: Everything is filtered through what Geertz calls "I-witnessing" (Geertz 1988:73ff). The self becomes the referent against which all others' actions are played out, all others' meanings discerned.

There could be no more nurturing circumstances for the self-reflective individual than in the mindwork that must accompany fieldwork. The entire previous section examined fieldwork as mindwork; I will not elaborate here except to underscore that the conceptualizing that precedes, accompanies, and follows fieldwork can be highly satisfying, personally as well as professionally. Mindwork *is* the creative dimension in fieldwork, the reflective product of a maturing scholar. There are no child prodigies in this endeavor.

When engaging in fieldwork, we observe something that has never exactly occurred before and would not be an object of study now were we not doing it. Our work is *always* unique in time and place. Today many researchers are also breaking new ground by introducing qualitative inquiry in disciplines and professional arenas previously receptive only to rigid quantitative approaches. Even when our research topics are similar to what others have done or are doing— classroom studies of Whole Language approaches or bilingual students, or studies of new immigrants, the homeless, people suffering with AIDS—the exact combination of ourselves as observers and the specific settings in which we work stand as one-of-a-kind, a fleeting moment that we capture. Every start is a fresh start, rife with potential for seeing new possibilities, gaining new insights. We are, in a sense, freed from the onus of "replication studies" because we can never exactly replicate the conditions of a field-based inquiry. There is no excuse for fieldworkers to crank out motel art; every study reported ought to reveal something significant that expands our efforts at understanding. I so like to hear researchers embarking on their inquiries who say, genuinely, "I'm really excited about this study!" Why shouldn't they be? Why ever undertake what Margaret Mead described as the "deep involvement" of fieldwork without that sense of excitement?

> The ability to do good fieldwork still depends, as it always has, on a deep involvement with a task so exacting that no efforts, no amount of brilliance or imagination, no battery of technical aids, no depth of commitment and sense of responsibility will ever be enough to permit any individual to do what is there to be done. Those who are attracted by the inexhaustibility of the task, will continue to be so. (Mead 1970:258)

The fact that we continue for years to reflect on our fieldwork experience offers consolation, even compensation, for the inevitable frustration of finding ourselves unable to bring a study quickly to the level of sophisticated insight we would like to achieve. As discussed earlier, we "abandon" our studies rather than complete them. We come to a point where we must give them up and get on with other obligations. We need never *totally* abandon them, however. One's fieldwork experiences cannot help but be cumulative if they have been deeply lived. We have the opportunity to mull them over and over, bringing new understandings to bear on earlier problems, seeking fresh perspectives. I feel fortunate to have accumulated a rich lore of research experience that I continue to ponder. One way or another I "return" constantly to review the lessons from my field experiences and reflect on my efforts to draw lessons from them. As an envious office-bound colleague once reflected, "You fieldworker-types are lucky. You never run out of things to write about."

The Authority of Authorship

Writing is another facet fully as capable of providing satisfaction for some as it most assuredly brings a sense of panic to others. Writing is creative in two senses, its figurative one entailing an originality of thought and expression, its literal one of "creating" something in a new form through "re-creating" prior experience. Accomplishing the task cannot help but bring personal fulfillment as well as professional recognition (publish or perish) in watching the fieldwork cycle come to fruition. For myself, writing has become a fulfilling activity in its own right, part of my self-definition. Deferred gratification though it certainly is, I derive a sense of accomplishment from the writing I have done and an exhilarating sense of challenge while doing it. (Well, on most days, if not on every one.)

I do not suggest that fieldworkers must necessarily have a "love of words" or take particular delight in sitting at their desks forging sentences at their fingertips from ideas not all that clearly formed in their minds. Nor is there necessarily great joy to be gained from endlessly editing what one has drafted in the effort to generate sentences that better convey intended meanings. Rather, I think personal satisfaction is gained from *having something important enough to say* to warrant saying it well enough to call to the attention of others. This is not fieldwork's long suit—our accounts never signal dramatic breakthroughs of the kind that hit the evening news telecasts or morning papers. But it is heady stuff nonetheless to be able to report well on topics of social significance, literally to "bring them to life." However modestly, that is how we make our individual contribution toward human knowledge and understanding. And as researchers, that is why we try to get things right as well as get them written.

I noted that I have never heard of anyone who became a fieldworker simply to exercise his or her writing talents. Yet field research does offer an alternative way to sneak into a writing-dependent career without having to be validated through studies in journalism, becoming an English major, or taking courses like Scientific Writing. That may explain why fieldwork accounts are often tedious to read (a feature they share with certain literary classics), but it is gratifying to recognize a growing library of accounts that are as satisfying for their style as they are profound in their insight. And sometimes we come out well simply because we try to tell it like it is.

(I should point out that from the outset of this project I have been tempted—and urged—to identify some fieldwork classics. In so doing, however, I would have had to assume the role of critic. I have chosen instead to write about how our various critic audiences affect the fieldwork we do and the way we write it up. I do think the exercise of developing a list of our own choices is a fine idea, but it is an activity in which all can engage.)

When our efforts extend to *giving voice to others* while learning to mute our own, we sometimes succeed in bringing different voices into arenas where they would not otherwise be heard, offering support in evidence for claims of what we do and perhaps do best. "The art of the ethnographer," Paul Bohannan writes, "is to learn, then to translate, a foreign people's stories without inserting his or her own pattern" (1995:77). And, he continues,

> Fieldwork was a first attempt to recontext ideas as they are actually held in the real world . . . into the emerging world of social science. It is the best way so far discovered, in spite of the fact that it remains an art with many built-in traps. (P. 148)

Looking at Life

As a form of legitimated voyeurism, fieldwork can delight anyone hopelessly attracted to *people-watching*, in spite of the risk of censure for practicing a Darker Art. In its social science sense, voyeurism implies more than a preoccupation with sexual activity, referring in an inclusive way to the fact that fieldwork not only permits but requires one to observe other humans at work and at play. Consistent with their charter to examine all aspects of human life, fieldworkers have at least an *implied* license for doing what most people do only covertly—to study whatever they find intriguing about the activities of their fellow humans.

Most certainly, sexual behavior falls within that domain. An incidental dividend of fieldwork is that one is not only allowed but expected to have more than passing interest in matters sexual. In pursuit of that "intimate, long-term acquaintance" discussed in Chapter 4, fieldworkers have in fact often been conspicuously conscientious about detailing the sexual practices—or at least the stated beliefs—among whatever groups they have studied, while remaining conspicuously dispassionate toward discussing their own sexuality. Only lately has this topic been broached in the fieldwork literature, beginning with Karla Poewe's candid *Reflections of a Woman Anthropologist* (published in 1982 under the pseudonym Manda Cesara), most recently in a collection instructively titled *Taboo* (Kulick and Willson 1995).

One of my first impressions about the study of anthropology was that some of its sources were kept under lock and key in the library at UC Berkeley, a fact so tantalizing that it is a wonder my horny undergraduate fraternity brothers did not all become anthropology majors for at least long enough to be able to check those books out. One of the books so guarded must surely have been Malinowski's *Sexual Life of Savages*, its promising title endorsed in a preface contributed by Havelock Ellis. Even today, social scientists seem especially attentive to reporting whatever they can about sexual practices among the "natives." Michael Moffatt's *Coming of Age in New Jersey* (1989), for example, is a contemporary study of college students that seems to have been especially adapted for the market by devoting two of its seven chapters to that topic. (In an earlier day, I might have wondered why *only* two chapters were devoted to a topic so central to the life and thought of 20-year-olds.) My point is that our focus on natural settings is seen as giving us license to delve into sexual matters that might not otherwise be considered any of our business. We seem to delve into them with abandon.

We are probably not as subtle as we think in attempting to pass lightly over our interests in such topics. This was brought home sharply by the observation of a Thai social scientist who remarked to me in 1985, "We don't need any more researchers coming over here to do studies of Thai prostitutes. There are far more important issues that confront Thai society than that." Her observation kept me from revealing a topic I had considered for investigation, the life history of one or more young Thai *male* prostitutes. With the subsequent spread of AIDS in that population, perhaps I had a defensible topic after all. My underlying point is that fieldworkers do feel they can exercise far-ranging choice in the problems they address, or look at broad contexts in problems often more narrowly defined. They can indulge their whims in the line of duty.

It is problematic with all inquiry that researchers will find what they are looking for. My focus here is personal satisfactions in fieldwork; and finding something that one is interested in, and looking for, can indeed bring satisfaction. Such satisfaction need not get in the way, especially for researchers who also derive satisfaction from full disclosure in their reporting and for whom research is also a strategy for living their personal lives.

Another aspect of trying to figure out what human social life is all about, of being able to understand "something," is the pleasure many find in the role of a learner who actively regards others—others of all stations—as one's teachers. Fieldwork is not well suited for individuals who thrive on authority and expertise and feel they must know everything about whatever subject they touch. Nor is it comforting for anyone obsessed with maintaining control. On the other hand, fieldwork is wonderfully suited for those who

237

find satisfaction as life-long learners, ever appreciative of how much others know and have experienced, rather than in need of parading their own learning before an audience. An old adage advises us to learn as though we will live forever. That seems good advice—or fair warning—for fieldworkers. The human condition does not remain static long enough for the work to be completed, even for an instant.

Fieldwork is a learning experience, and neophyte fieldworkers need to recognize their own preferred learning styles in contemplating how best to make the experience a personally satisfactory one. Some people like to meet new experiences head on; others prefer a gradual immersion, anxious to gain both knowledge and experience before undertaking independent work. I do not think that "training" or formal coursework is absolutely essential preparation for fieldwork, for I do not think of it as a mysterious process as much as a matter of good sense and sound judgment. Still, there is no reason for anyone who seeks it not to get some guided experience, and it seems counterproductive to begin an inquiry without a clear sense of what others have learned. Surely not every neophyte fieldworker needs to reinvent or rediscover participant observation or interviewing all over again!

Courses and workshops offered today under such titles as Ethnographic Research, Field Methods, or Qualitative Inquiry provide an opportunity for guided practice in participant observation and interviewing. Funded research and large-scale projects also create opportunities for entry into fieldwork, with project staff working cooperatively on large issues and training assistants to continue or extend the work. Thus there are ways to acquire fieldwork skills through apprenticeships as well as formal coursework. Both approaches tend to focus on fieldwork *techniques*, but that is what novices are most concerned about, and there is nothing wrong with taking first things first. Note that in arranging the chapters in this book I followed the same logic: The "fieldwork part of fieldwork" was discussed first. But the essence of fieldwork is the mindwork that guides it, from inception to publication, and mindwork is mostly caught, not taught.

In the days before we became so self-conscious about *method*, there was usually help for the asking, with occasional complaining that supervision in the field was "excessive" even when handled entirely through correspondence. Written memos sent from the field force one to keep up with the reporting, however, and they may eventually find their way into the final report. Sometimes these exchanges of correspondence have provided substance for volumes in their own right (two examples already cited are the fieldwork dialogue between Kimball and Partridge, 1979; and the correspondence of Robert Redfield and Sol Tax compiled by Rubinstein, 1991). In the course of the fieldwork experience, many other students have established satisfying collegial relationships with their mentors, relationships that extended well into their careers. This may be especially prevalent in anthropology, where attention to kinship among the peoples studied has made anthropologists more aware, and more appreciative, of their own academic kinship. Although more than three decades have passed since I completed my doctoral studies at Stanford, George and Louise Spindler still exert an influence on my work through encouragement, ideas, and constructive critique. I trace more than twenty of my articles and books directly to their support, including my first two major fieldwork studies and the first two monographs in which they were reported.

Human social life itself is the focus of this work, and fieldworkers able to see themselves as learners and actors in the social settings they study, rather than hiding behind the role of distanced onlookers, are in the better position to realize the potential of the disciplined subjectivity the approach allows. Although fieldwork requires some sense of detachment, there is also a call for involvement, room for compassion and understanding. Ideally one ought to be able to escape "role" completely and just be oneself, participating in and enjoying life by experiencing how it is lived by others. Clearly the focus of field research ought to be on topics and groups where this potential can be realized. Those among whom you conduct research ought to be glad to see you each time you appear, and you ought to be glad to see them. A spirit of joie de vivre should prevail. Fieldwork is an activity one can engage in—with passion, without apology.

Writing enthusiastically on its behalf, sociologist Danny Jorgensen confesses that participant observation "is for me an abiding preoccupation— if not a way of life—and an important component of my social identity" (1989:8). Jorgensen does not insist that everyone must become so zealous a practitioner: "You need not make such a commitment, however, to use participant observation appropriately and profitably" (p. 8). He's right, you "need not make such a commitment." But why not make it anyway?

Fieldwork beckons, even dares, you to become part of what you study. That is the difference between observation and participant observation.

There is always the hope, and the ever-so-slight chance, that what we uncover and report from our fieldwork will in some small way enhance our understanding of the lives of others and of ourselves. Geertz describes this as "the power of the scientific imagination to bring us into touch with the lives of strangers" (1973:16), although my underlying premise here is that science alone is not equal to the task. The roles of emotion and imagination—viewed as essential elements in artistic endeavor—will be examined in the final chapter.

There is even the chance, perhaps slimmer yet, that we do actually help bring about beneficial change in the lives of those strangers, or even our own. We can't measure such outcomes, at least not in the full context and long term that really count. But there is a certain satisfaction that comes just from recognizing the high ideals to which we aspire. (Strange, that anthropological fieldworkers are often so hard on missionaries for their zeal, so apparently unaware of their own.)

I remember a comment offered by one of my earliest doctoral students, Ray Barnhardt, reflecting on what he had gained from the anthropological spin I had introduced into his studies as an educator, much the same way my mentor had done for me. On completing his dissertation, Ray took a faculty position at the University of Alaska, Fairbanks, where he has devoted some twenty-five years to programs creating new opportunities for Alaska's Indian and Eskimo populations. I imagined that he would extol the virtues of studies in cultural anthropology for the insights he needed. But he did no such thing. Instead, he reflected on how his studies in anthropology gave him insight and perspective *into his own life and work*. He could take it effectively from there. His perspective provided me with a fresh perspective of my own. We do well to examine the extent to which whatever we would like to see happening to and for others is happening to ourselves.●

CHAPTER ELEVEN
THE ART OF FIELDWORK

A work of art makes a selection of elements of experience, imagination, and emotion.

—Raymond Firth
Elements of Social Organization, 156

Imagination is more important than knowledge.

—Albert Einstein
On Science

Nonnative speakers of English have a difficult time with the articles *a*, *an*, and *the*. I have an equally terrible time articulating how I use them. I have wondered if the best advice I can give nonnative speakers is to tell them to use an article whenever they think they should not, and not to use one when they think they should. As a native speaker, I simply trust my "ear" in such matters.

However, my ear was not much help with word choice for my chosen title and topic *The Art of Fieldwork* as I came to realize the subtle distinction between declaring that fieldwork *is* art and stating more circumspectly that fieldwork is *an* art. On behalf of a concern I share with others that science might eventually overpower the quintessentially human quality of fieldwork, I set out to make the case that fieldwork *is*, or should be regarded as, art. I wound up instead making the case that there is an art to fieldwork and art in it, but that doesn't make Art of it, at least in an everyday sense. Max Gluckman credits Malinowski with raising fieldwork to a "professional art" (1967:xiii); perhaps we had best leave it at that.

Yet I am reluctant to leave the art metaphor without casting a final backward glance to review how fieldwork is *like* art, even if no claim is made that it *is* art. What is it that artists do that fieldworkers also do? Conversely, what is at risk of being lost through efforts to make fieldwork too scientific, or too systematic, denying elements of "experience, imagination, and emotion" that may be critical for understanding what human social life is all about?

In an essay titled "The Social Framework of Primitive Art" that appeared in his 1951 text, *Elements of Social Organization*, British anthropologist Raymond Firth (later to become Sir Raymond Firth) makes the statement quoted in the epigraph to this chapter. His reference is not to the art of fieldwork; rather, it is a generalization about what goes into all art, in all societies. In this final chapter, I take his observation as a starting point for reviewing what goes into the making of art and what an examination of the making of art has to contribute to fieldwork. I close with a look at why we do well to nurture that contribution.

I do not mean to suggest that Professor Firth has necessarily gotten it right—that art draws always and only upon the three elements he identifies: experience, imagination, emotion. Nor did I mean to suggest earlier that Feinberg has necessarily gotten it right, that the main task of art is the "assertion of the authority of intuition" as a counterforce to the authority of reason or logic (Feinberg 1987:147). But I am partial to examining things in terms of complementary threesomes, and a threesome that encompasses *imagination* and *emotion* in addition to *experience* not only suggests a useful perspective but also invites us to look at what must be added to, or combined with, fieldwork *experience* itself. Feinberg might proceed differently, searching instead for the source of intuition that he finds in a combination of the sensory and the intellect. I think the two approaches point in the same direction. No one has yet succeeded in getting it exactly right. Or ever will.

Experience, imagination, emotion. As likely a trio as any to embrace the dimensions on which artists draw. How then might, and do, fieldworkers draw on such dimensions to realize the artistic potential in their inquiries?

Imagination, seen as the creative dimension, draws attention to how experiences are joined together and subsequently revealed to the viewer or listener. Emotion opens the way for feeling tones necessary to temper a too-wholehearted embrace of scientific objectivity. We must not lose sight of the fact that fieldwork is essentially inquiry into *selves*, and thus of *ourselves*, our social selves in their cultural milieu. There is a point at which objectivity itself must become suspect in studying selves whose own objectivity is, at best, only relative.

An early chapter (Chapter 3) examined how a broad cultural milieu is reproduced as a context for the individual fieldworker just as it is for the individual artist. Since my purpose is to further the argument on behalf of the artistic potential in fieldwork, let me turn first to what we stand to gain—what the consumer "gets"—as a consequence of the artist's efforts. What does art do in *any* circumstances? And what then is the unique contribution that artistic endeavor offers to fieldwork that scientific endeavor cannot?

How Art Works

What art accomplishes under all circumstances seems for me best captured by the term *enhance*. When that which is enhanced has an otherwise practical use, we categorize the art as utilitarian. Art and craft can become hopelessly entangled as we ponder or argue whether some tool or other artifact has been artistically designed or only superbly crafted. Anthropologists have long recognized human efforts in going above and beyond what Felix Keesing describes as "utilitarian survival activities" (Keesing 1958:342). Keesing illustrated his point by noting that "an extra margin of symmetry and of neatness in flaking . . . shows even in occasional tools from the Lower Paleolithic," while the Upper Paleolithic is "marked by an extraordinarily elaborate flowering of graving, painting, and sculpture" (p. 343). Somewhere in that transition from symmetry and neatness to something "extraordinarily elaborate" we cross the threshold to the fine arts, where aesthetic expression becomes the prime objective, and achievement in terms of elegance or excellence is "defined by canons of aesthetic appeal" (p. 346).

The terms "above" and "beyond" appear often in efforts to define the skill and finesse that distinguish master craftspeople or artists from the routine—and sometimes to distinguish artist and craftsperson from each other. In reaching beyond the routine, artistic accomplishment may generate not only a sense of celebration or awe but as well a figurative (and sometimes literal) "lift" in the sense of a high, a rush, a "peak experience."

The nature and intensity of any such rush or high obviously depend on the medium, on one's personal disposition toward such things, and on culturally sanctioned ways to demonstrate approval or appreciation for particular forms of artistic achievement. We are expected to know how to "applaud" a lovely painting, a beautifully sung aria, an inspiring collection of poems, or a skillful pass by a matador; appropriate responses are not always interchangeable.

There are also personal dimensions to the ways each of us responds, in addition to culturally shared ones. To those for whom life seems a relentless cycle of pain and tragedy crushing with incessant routine, neither the most breathtaking of artistic accomplishments nor the most amazing of natural wonders may be sufficient to lift them out of customary doldrums. For those given to joyful appreciation, art serves to enrich and enhance what is perceived as good or beautiful to begin with. The exquisite becomes more so through artistic endeavor, whether one's own or that of others, bringing with it added wonderment or delight. At the least, one appreciates the effort, which is why imitative art is better than no art at all.

Art affects us in uniquely human ways that sometimes transcend our physical beings: Figuratively, if not literally, we are touched, perhaps overwhelmed, by an unexpected emotional "charge." The feeling is captured in the lyrics of an old song, when all of a sudden your heart sings; you gape or gasp at what you behold, or are otherwise struck by a sense of awe.

"Now hold on there," you may be thinking, "is he going to argue that this is what we should be striving for in conducting our fieldwork and writing up our accounts?" No, I am not going to insist that our written accounts should find readers gasping for breath, stomping their feet, whistling, clapping their hands, or hearing their hearts burst suddenly into song. But what do we already do, and what might we do more of, to realize the artistic potential of our work? Do we try to infuse our days in the field, and the accounts we render about them, with imagination and emotion, elements that Firth insists must be added to experience in order to achieve art? Do we sometimes miss opportunities to make more of the fieldwork experience itself, striving so hard to be good scientists and objective observers that we fail to recognize it as a lived experience for the fieldworker?

Those whom we study will not pass this way again. Are we always aware that neither will we?

Art in the Conduct of Fieldwork

In terms of producing the completed studies that are the raison d'être of qualitative inquiry, fieldwork can be viewed as a strictly instrumental activity. As such, it is an acceptable, valid, and well-regarded means to achieve a worthwhile end. With both the research process and the ensuing research product deemed a priori to be worthy, a caution heard frequently among fieldworkers is that one should never act in such a way that "the field" is left in disarray. No fieldworker should be denied access because of the actions of a predecessor; opportunity for future or further research must be safeguarded. The fieldworker of today fulfills an unwritten obligation to the fieldworker of tomorrow.

There is, concomitantly, the reasonable assumption that one's successful performance in the role of fieldworker will ensure good fieldwork results. My efforts in this writing have largely been directed toward that end: to encourage researchers not only to regard fieldwork as an opportunity to realize scientific potential but to capitalize on its artistic potential as well, and thus to reach beyond science rather than feel constrained by it. The temptations of scientific claims-making need to be counterbalanced by a conscious effort to do good art, or, stated more as a caution, not to be content doing only good science when circumstances call for imagination and feeling as well. One of the strange criticisms heard today of some of the early fieldworkers was their preoccupation with being "scientific" to the exclusion of other qualities humans can demonstrate.

Like art, science, too, can enhance; it can also be overdone. But perhaps we owe those intellectual forebears a debt of gratitude. In an earlier day, the clarion call was for good science, and that is what early fieldworkers endeavored wholeheartedly to do, consistent with the claims they wanted to make for their efforts. Today we enjoy the luxury of pondering whether fieldwork ever was or should be allowed to become only that.

A critical aspect of traditional ethnography that has been changing over time is time itself, both in terms of expectations for the overall duration of a research project and, especially, in the time actually spent on site. The early ethnographers tended to remain in the field once they got there. That may have been due in part to external factors such as the remoteness of their sites and the difficulties of travel. Nevertheless, the precedent was established that fieldwork was a long-term commitment, especially for one's initial foray.

Long-term fieldwork has a second meaning as well, referring to fieldwork conducted through repeated visits among one group of people extending over many years. On that score British social anthropologists have earned a reputation for outdoing their American colleagues. The latter are more likely to locate new settings and new "peoples" for their subsequent studies. The American practice has fostered comparisons between groups; the British practice, within-group comparisons over time. In either case, once researchers got into the field, they remained there and/or returned time and time again, becoming, at least to some extent, part of what they studied. (The French fieldwork tradition initiated in the 1920s provides something of an exception. It emphasized an *intensive* approach based not on long-term individual participant observation but on "multifaceted documentary team research, resulting in hundreds of sound recordings, textual accounts, and major collections of art and artifacts" [Tedlock 1991:83].)

That was how participant observation got started. Given that long-term commitment, one did not approach residents of one's intended research site as a survey researcher or one-time interviewer might do, but rather as a newly arrived neighbor eager to make acquaintances and learn one's way around the community. To me, this remains the basis of what genuine fieldwork is all about—a researcher who will stay long enough to learn something of the way some other group of people lives and thinks. That does not necessarily mean the fieldworker will make deep and lasting friendships, but it does mean that *some kind of relationship* and *some sense of involvement* will develop toward at least some people in the group. Fieldwork knowledge entails intimate personal knowledge of the contextualized lives of others. If there is no possibility of ever gaining such knowledge, and subsequently being able to use it to achieve some worthwhile action or academic purpose, then the research activity itself does not warrant a claim to be fieldwork.

I do not disparage social research that lacks the element of intimacy or is done in shorter time frames. Research itself is a process of discovery, and there is no canon insisting that discovery has to be a long-drawn-out process. Practical considerations increasingly make it necessary for today's qualitative researchers to be able to compete through more efficient data gathering means than their ethnographic forebears ever would have considered or condoned. I am in accord with the need recognized by anthropologists—and anyone else given to participant observation strategies—to be able to speed up the work when a traditional approach is too time-consuming. But the purposes of the research must be restructured accordingly; social contexts cannot be researched through opinion polls or rapid appraisals.

The time has come to tighten the definition of what we accept as legitimate fieldwork, restricting it to *on-site research conducted over a sustained period of time and requiring some degree of researcher involvement.* We need to introduce—or to reintroduce—a more dramatic contrast between *doing fieldwork* and *gathering data.* Data gathering often requires field research, but it assumes no level of involvement comparable to fieldwork, no minimum length of time, no appreciation for context. It is vulnerable to the criticism of being superficial (just as fieldwork is vulnerable to the criticism of being grossly inefficient and time-consuming), but the charge itself is irrelevant. If one is gathering data and knows what data are to be gathered, then once that is done, it is time either to go home or to make one's inquiry more profound.

The label *fieldwork*, on the other hand, ought to be reserved for research circumstances when depth *is* a reasonable trade-off for breadth (and speed), and when the accusation of being "superficial" is least justified, in spite of the realization that we can never get the whole story, write the "true" account, or reach perfection with our approach. "Finally," Bruce Jackson writes in his own treatise titled *Fieldwork*, "I should tell you that I've never had what I'd call a perfect field experience—a trip where everything went exactly as I'd planned and where I later thought I'd obtained everything I should've obtained" (1987:9). Perhaps it is just as well. Not all people regard reaching perfection as a wise thing to do. Native artists are known to introduce flaws into their handicrafts lest their time on earth be prematurely "completed" through the inadvertent attainment of perfection.

Nonetheless, becoming a *genuine participant* in at least some activities of a group over a period of time, or acting in slightly more reserved capacities such as *observing participant* or *privileged observer*, are far different ways of gathering far different data from the sorts of "neat" data most researchers seek and get. Fieldwork ought to be reserved to describe the efforts of those who pursue that different approach.

In proposing a sharper distinction between data-gatherers and field-workers, I am not trying to reclaim fieldwork as the exclusive domain of the cultural anthropologist. To some extent the reverse is true—old-fashioned, time-consuming fieldwork may soon become a style of research in which fewer anthropologists engage, while researchers in other fields are incorporating or adapting ethnographic approaches to extended on-site study in their own work. The basis for the distinction lies not in who the researchers are but what they seek to understand. For the traditional ethnographer, that has always been "culture," and as John Van Maanen observes, "Culture is not to be found in some discrete set of observations that can somehow be summed up numerically and organized narratively to provide full understanding" (1988:218). Fieldwork is ideally suited to the study of culture, but one does not have to be committed to the concept of culture to do fieldwork. There are other terms and ways to conceptualize and study the social contexts in which humans interact. No discrete set of observations leads to understanding those contexts without the play of imagination and emotion as well.

Whatever the assignment as it originates, a fieldwork-oriented researcher ought to think to himself or herself, or say aloud if someone else is organizing the research, "What about my joining this group in some of its routine activities, perhaps living among them for a while, instead of just dropping in with a survey or interview protocol?" Of course, the answer might very well be, "Whatever you might learn through that approach doesn't seem important enough to warrant the investment in time." Given that response, I would find myself inclined to agree!

Where in-depth study is not warranted, fieldwork should neither be selected nor touted as the research strategy. I would hope, nonetheless, that researchers of any persuasion avail themselves of any and every opportunity simply to "knock about" and get a feel for their research settings. When the nature of the inquiry warrants it and resources—especially time—allow for it, ah! what an opportunity fieldwork should provide, both as data source and lived experience.

Fieldwork is the more inclusive category. Data gathering can be done without fieldwork. Fieldwork cannot be done without gathering data, but it entails far more than data gathering as a process of sustained inquiry. During the course of fieldwork, the data gathering process itself needs to be scrutinized in order to assess its contribution to the research purpose. Data gathering lends itself too easily to the mindless and endless recording of inconsequential detail. In tightly designed studies, once the research approach has been conceptualized, there is little call for imagination and no need at all for direct experience; emotion is ruled out from the beginning. Data gathering offers unlimited opportunity for the rituals of systematic inquiry, and virtually no opportunity for the sensitivity of the artist.

There is at least one further opportunity for enhancement in the conduct of fieldwork: the opportunity fieldwork offers to enhance the lives of others through the interpersonal engagement on which it is based. We worry, rightfully, about "ripping off" our informants, about those "massive seductions" described earlier (Chapter 6), but I cannot make so lopsided a presentation that I overlook what fieldworkers *sometimes* bring to the lives of others. The courteous attention, the sincere (even if utilitarian) interest of the fieldworker, can be flattering in themselves, especially since our attention is most often addressed to everyday folk. The perspective we bring can be equally exalting to individuals who, like ourselves in other situations, lose track of what is noteworthy about their own lives, what is worthy of celebration. Each of us has a story to tell if the right person happens to come along to ask.

At times in my field research I have been that "right person" in the life of another individual or group. Whatever I was able to give back to those particular individuals was more art than science. They did not need me to underscore the cold hard facts of their lives; of those, as Becker puts it, they were "already pretty much aware" (1982:xi). They did seem to welcome the attention they received and the perspective on context I could offer, even if they doubted that I had quite gotten it right. And that brings us finally to art in the telling of the fieldwork story.

Art in Relating the Fieldwork Story

There are two stories to be told from the fieldwork experience. One is the somewhat idealized version of how things are for the individual or group being described. With the intent of achieving scientific objectivity, stories of this type have often been told impersonally, as though the fieldworker were not present except as a vehicle for the account to reveal itself. The other story is the story of the fieldwork, the fieldworker revealing something of himself or herself, at the extreme occupying center stage as in Geertz's notion of "I-witnessing" (1988:73ff). Van Maanen describes such stories as Impressionist Tales, accounts that inform readers "not about what usually happens but about what rarely happens" (1988:102). Accounts of the latter type are defended on the basis that fieldworkers ought at least to know what they are talking about when talking about themselves or describing what they have observed and experienced firsthand.

In an earlier day, this latter type of reporting tended to be played down, suppressed in favor of the more distanced, and thus satisfactorily "objective," presentation. The postmodern era turned things on their head; the subjective report became the authoritative account, the one we were to believe. The fieldworker's subjective experience was deemed to be the only experience to which the researcher had access. At the risk of summarily dismissing prior fieldwork done in a positivist vein, the new thinking did open the way for first-person accounts that invited social scientists to write more personally, more emotionally if not necessarily more imaginatively. Thus the way was cleared for drafting accounts drawn more artistically as well. Such efforts were often set cautiously apart from the bulk of the report, presented in a first-person style easily distinguished not only from traditional ethnographic reporting but often from the rest of the text.

Except for those few individuals whose lives are touched directly by the experience, the evidence for and consequences of the art of fieldwork are found essentially in the account that derives from it. If the success of such efforts is to be analyzed or otherwise assessed, that must be done by looking at how well artistic endeavor is realized in those published accounts. The criterion I have suggested here is their capacity to enhance, to extend or deepen our understanding, initially of the setting at hand, ultimately of our own lives as well.

Data can be analyzed, the techniques for gathering data can be analyzed, and various steps in the process can be taught and practiced, but in the end there is an elusive quality that allows some people to do more than others with virtually the same ingredients, and a few people to do what others recognize as truly remarkable. To return to the working definition of art proposed in Chapter 1 and make it "fieldwork relevant," fieldwork might be said to achieve the status of "art" when the addition of the fieldworker's idiosyncratic human touch is recognized by a discriminating audience as achieving in the completed account an aesthetic quality exceeding what can be achieved by attention to data gathering alone. Yet to reach so far in an effort to do art, we find ourselves introducing criteria into the fieldwork endeavor that are tangential to it. We want our accounts to be aesthetically satisfying and satisfyingly human, but those are not the end points of our reporting. So let me rewrite a definition that focuses on what attending to the art of fieldwork is intended to accomplish, without inadvertently setting us in pursuit of developing an art form:

> *The art of fieldwork is achieved to the extent a fieldworker is able to render from research-oriented personal experience an account that offers to a discerning audience a level of insight and understanding into human social life that exceeds whatever might be achieved through attention solely to gathering and reporting data.*

As "patrons" of the art of fieldwork, we do not insist on having an aesthetic experience, or being dazzled with the creative or idiosyncratic touch of the fieldworker, but neither do we want merely to "know about" some other lifestyle. We want to reach some new depth of understanding of our own as a result of *re*experiencing aspects of what the fieldworker has experienced, understood, revealed, and enhanced for us.

Becker observes, "Participants in the creation of art works, and members of society generally, believe that the making of art requires special talents, gifts, or abilities, which few have. Some have more than others, and a very few are gifted enough to merit the honorific title of 'artist'" (1982:14). We do not do fieldwork because we are artists at it, and we do not become artists through our accomplishments at fieldwork. But we should not hesitate to nurture and draw on whatever artistic talents, gifts, or abilities we possess that help us to achieve the full potential of a fieldwork approach.

It is hard to imagine anyone being naturally "gifted" in all the dimensions that fieldwork requires, from the ability to conceptualize a problem, negotiate a setting and entrée into it, handle all the logistical arrangements, get the necessary supporting data, organize and write up a superb account, satisfy all reporting obligations and commitments, find an interested editor or publisher, and simultaneously remain a compassionate ally to those in the field setting and meet all other obligations of a personal life and professional career. No one who takes on so much should hold back from attempting to infuse the work with adequate attention to its artistic as well as its scientific potential. And no one should refrain from finding ways to use natural gifts or develop requisite talents along artistic lines, just as we use and develop our capacities to become careful observers and provocative problem finders. Art and science alike are attainable in fieldwork. Neither must be gained at the cost of the other; there is room for more of them both.

Today's fieldworkers are under pressure to become more scientific, more efficient, more systematic, better focused. I think such ideals have their place and can be satisfied as necessary, *when it makes sense to meet them*, but I do not believe they are inherently praiseworthy. It is fieldwork's time-consuming, slowly focusing, sometimes convoluted and inefficient but always contextually rich, life-mirroring approach that needs to be protected in our age of efficient anxiety.

Conscious efforts to make fieldwork scientific need not detract from a corresponding effort to strengthen it as an art, grounded in experience enriched by the powers of imagination and emotion, the latter two qualities perceived as critical elements that enhance, rather than as obstacles to be overcome. Science and art become a threat to each other only if they are viewed as mutually exclusive, a threat to fieldwork practice only when fieldwork is regarded as consisting exclusively of one or the other, or of no more than the two. Fieldwork is fieldwork. It should neglect neither art nor science but transcend both. Science has much to contribute. Art has much to contribute. Fieldwork draws on both to make a contribution uniquely its own. ●

REFERENCES AND SELECT BIBLIOGRAPHY

Adler, Patricia A., and Peter Adler
  1994 Observational Techniques. *In* Handbook of Qualitative
    Research. Norman K. Denzin and Yvonna S. Lincoln, eds.
    Pp. 377–392. Thousand Oaks, CA: Sage.

Agar, Michael H.
  1980 The Professional Stranger: An Informal Introduction to
    Ethnography. New York: Academic Press.

Anderson, Richard L.
  1979 Art in Primitive Societies. Englewood Cliffs, NJ: Prentice-Hall.

Atkinson, Paul
  1990 The Ethnographic Imagination: Textual Construction of
    Reality. New York: Routledge.

Barnett, Homer G.
  1953 Innovation: The Analysis of Culture Change. New York:
    McGraw-Hill.

Barth, Fredrik
  1966 Preface. *In* The Social Organization of the Marri Baluch.
    Compiled and analyzed from the notes of Robert N. Pehrson
    by Fredrik Barth. New York: Wenner-Gren Foundation.
  1989 The Analysis of Culture in Complex Societies. Ethnos
    54:120–142.

1994a A Personal View of Present Tasks and Priorities in Cultural Anthropology. *In* Assessing Cultural Anthropology. Robert Borofsky, ed. Pp. 349–361. New York: McGraw-Hill.
1994b Comment on "Cultural Anthropology's Future Agenda." Anthropology Newsletter 35(6):76

Bateson, Gregory
1958 Naven. 2nd ed. Stanford University Press. [Originally published 1936.]

Becker, Howard S.
1980 Role and Career Problems of the Chicago School Teacher. New York: Arno Press. [Originally presented as the author's thesis, University of Chicago, 1951.]
1982 Art Worlds. Berkeley: University of California Press.
1986 Writing for Social Scientists. Chicago: University of Chicago Press.
1993 Theory: The Necessary Evil. *In* Theory and Concepts in Qualitative Research. David J. Flinders and Geoffrey E. Mills, eds. Pp. 218–229. New York: Teachers College Press.

Beebe, James
1995 Basic Concepts and Techniques of Rapid Appraisal. Human Organization 54(1):42–51.

Beer, C. G.
1973 A View of Birds. *In* Minnesota Symposia of Child Psychology, Vol. 7. Anne Pick, ed. Pp. 47–86. Minneapolis: University of Minnesota Press.

Benedict, Ruth
1934 Patterns of Culture. Boston: Houghton Mifflin.

Bernard, H. Russell
1988 Research Methods in Cultural Anthropology. Newbury Park, CA: Sage.
1994a Methods Belong to All of Us. *In* Assessing Cultural Anthropology. Robert Borofsky, ed. Pp. 168–179. New York: McGraw-Hill.

1994b Research Methods in Anthropology: Qualitative and Quantitative Approaches. 2nd ed. Thousand Oaks, CA: Sage.

Berreman, Gerald D.
1968 Ethnography: Method and Product. *In* Introduction to Cultural Anthropology. James A. Clifton, ed. Pp. 336–373. Boston: Houghton Mifflin.

Bidney, David
1953 Theoretical Anthropology. New York: Columbia University Press.

Blumer, Herbert
1969 Symbolic Interactionism: Perspective and Method. Berkeley: University of California Press.

Boas, Franz
1887 Social Organization and Secret Societies of the Kwakiutl Indians. Washington, DC: Government Printing Office.

Bohannan, Paul
1995 How Culture Works. New York: The Free Press.

Borofsky, Robert, ed.
1994 Assessing Cultural Anthropology. New York: McGraw-Hill.

Bosk, Charles L.
1979 Forgive and Remember: Managing Medical Failure. Chicago: University of Chicago Press.

Burgess, Robert G., ed.
1995 Howard Becker on Education. Buckingham, England: Open University Press.

Burke, Kenneth
1935 Permanence and Change. New York: New Republic.

Burns, Allan F.
1993 Everybody's a Critic: Video Programming with Guatemalan Refugees in the United States. *In* Anthropological Film and

Video in the 1990s. Jack R. Rollwagen, ed. Pp. 105–129. Brockport, NY: The Institute, Inc.

Carpenter, Edmund
1971 The Eskimo Artist. *In* Anthropology and Art. Charlotte M. Otten, ed. Pp. 163–171. Garden City, NY: Natural History Press. [Originally published as Comment to H. Haselberger, Method of Studying Ethnographic Art. Current Anthropology 2(4):361–363, 1961.]

Cesara, Manda [Karla Poewe]
1982 Reflections of a Woman Anthropologist: No Hiding Place. New York: Academic Press.

Chagnon, Napoleon A.
1968 Yanomamö: The Fierce People. New York: Holt, Rinehart and Winston.

Christensen, Garry
1993 Sensitive Information: Collecting Data on Livestock and Informal Credit. *In* Fieldwork in Developing Countries. Stephen Devereux and John Hoddinott, eds. Pp. 124–137. Boulder, CO: Lynne Rienner Publishers.

Clifford, James
1988 The Predicament of Culture. Cambridge, MA: Harvard University Press.

Clifford, James, and George E. Marcus
1986 Writing Culture: The Poetics and Politics of Ethnography. Berkeley: University of California Press.

Cooper, Patricia, and Norma Bradley Allen
1989 The Quilters: Women and Domestic Art. 2nd ed. New York: Anchor Press, Doubleday. [Originally published 1978.]

Coote, Jeremy, and Anthony Shelton, eds.
1992 Anthropology, Art, and Aesthetics. Oxford, England: Clarendon Press.

Crapanzano, Vincent
 1980 Tuhami: Portrait of a Moroccan. Chicago: University of
 Chicago Press.

Creswell, John W.
 1994 Research Design: Qualitative and Quantitative Approaches.
 Thousand Oaks, CA: Sage.

Crocker, William H., and Jean Crocker
 1994 The Canela. Fort Worth, TX: Harcourt, Brace.

Darwin, Charles
 1969 The Autobiography of Charles Darwin. Nora Barlow, ed.
 New York: W. W. Norton

d'Azevedo, Warren L.
 1958 A Structural Approach to Esthetics: Toward a Definition of
 Art in Anthropology. American Anthropologist 60(4):702–714.

Denzin, Norman K.
 1994a The Art and Politics of Interpretation. *In* Handbook of Qualitative Research. Norman K. Denzin and Yvonna S. Lincoln, eds.
 Pp. 500–515. Thousand Oaks, CA: Sage.
 1994b Review essay: Messy Methods for Communication Research.
 Journal of Communication. September.

Denzin, Norman K., and Yvonna S. Lincoln, eds.
 1994 Handbook of Qualitative Research. Thousand Oaks, CA: Sage.

Devereux, George
 1968 From Anxiety to Method in the Behavioral Sciences. The
 Hague: Mouton.

Douglas, Jack
 1976 Investigative Social Research. Beverly Hills, CA: Sage.

Eisenberg, Merrill
 1994 Translating Research into Policy: What More Does It Take?
 Practicing Anthropology 16(4):35–39.

Eisner, Elliot
1985 On the Differences Between Artistic and Scientific Approaches to Qualitative Research. *In* The Art of Educational Evaluation: A Personal View. Elliot Eisner, ed. Pp. 189–200. Philadelphia: Falmer Press. [Originally published in Educational Researcher 10(4), 1981.]

Eliot, T. S.
1950 Selected Essays. New York: Harcourt, Brace and Co.

Ellis, Carolyn
1991 Emotional Sociology. *In* Studies in Symbolic Interaction 12. Norman Denzin, ed. Pp. 123–145. Greenwich, CT: JAI Press.

Emerson, Robert M., Rachel I. Fretz, and Linda L. Shaw
1995 Writing Ethnographic Fieldnotes. Chicago: University of Chicago Press.

Epstein, A. L., ed.
1967 The Craft of Social Anthropology. London: Tavistock.

Erickson, Frederick
1984 What Makes School Ethnography "Ethnographic"? Anthropology and Education Quarterly 15(1):51–66.
1992 Post Everything: Notes on the Demise of Realist Ethnography. Paper presented at the American Educational Research Association, San Francisco, April 24.

Erickson, Kai
1967 A Comment on Disguised Observation in Sociology. Social Problems 14:366–373.

Evans-Pritchard, E. E.
1952 Social Anthropology. Glencoe, IL: Free Press.

Feinberg, E. L.
1987 Art in the Science Dominated World. J. A. Cooper, trans. New York: Gordon and Breach.

Fernandez, James W.
1994 Time on Our Hands. *In* Others Knowing Others. Don D.
Fowler and Donald L Hardesty, eds. Pp. 119–144. Washington,
DC: Smithsonian Institution Press.

Fetterman, David M.
1989 Ethnography Step by Step. Newbury Park, CA: Sage.

Fine, Gary Alan
1993 Ten Lies of Ethnography. Journal of Contemporary Ethnography 22(3):267–294.

Firth, Raymond
1951 Elements of Social Organization. New York: Philosophical
Library.

Fleck, Ludwik
1979 Genesis and Development of a Scientific Fact. Chicago:
University of Chicago Press. [Translated from the text originally
published in German in 1935.]

Flinders, David J., and Geoffrey E. Mills, eds.
1993 Theory and Concepts in Qualitative Research: Perspectives
from the Field. New York: Teachers College Press.

Fluehr-Lobban, Carolyn
1994 Informant Consent in Anthropological Research: We Are Not
Exempt. Human Organization 53(1):1–10.

Forge, Anthony, ed.
1973 Primitive Art and Society. London: Oxford University Press.

Foster, George
1969 Applied Anthropology. Boston: Little, Brown.

Fowler, Don D., and Donald L. Hardesty
1994 Others Knowing Others: Perspectives on Ethnographic
Careers. Washington, DC: Smithsonian Institution Press.

Freeman, Mark
1993 Finding the Muse: A Sociopsychological Inquiry into the Conditions of Artistic Creativity. New York: Cambridge University Press.

Galtung, Johan
1990 Theory Formation in Social Research: A Plea for Pluralism. *In* Comparative Methodology. Else Øyen, ed. Pp. 96–112. Newbury Park, CA: Sage.

Gearing, Frederick O.
1970 The Face of the Fox. Chicago: Aldine.

Geertz, Clifford
1973 The Interpretation of Cultures. New York: Basic Books.
1983 Local Knowledge. New York: Basic Books.
1988 Works and Lives. Stanford, CA: Stanford University Press.

Getzels, Jacob W., and Mihaly Csikszentmihalyi
1976 The Creative Vision: A Longitudinal Study of Problem Finding in Art. New York: John Wiley and Sons.

Gluckman, Max
1967 Introduction. *In* The Craft of Social Anthropology. A. L. Epstein, ed. Pp. vii–xx. London: Tavistock.

Gold, S. J.
1989 Ethical Issues in Visual Fieldwork. *In* New Technology in Sociology: Practical Applications in Research and Work. G. Blank, J. L. McCartney, and E. E. Brent, eds. Pp. 99–109. New Brunswick, NJ: Transaction Books.

Goldschmidt, Walter, ed.
1954 Ways of Mankind: Thirteen Dramas of Peoples of the World and How They Live. Boston: Beacon Press. [For the National Association of Educational Broadcasters.]

Green, Jesse, ed.
1979 Zuni: Selected Writings of Frank Hamilton Cushing. Lincoln: University of Nebraska Press.

Guba, Egon
　1981 Criteria for Assessing the Trustworthiness of Naturalistic
　　Inquiries. Educational Communication and Technology Journal
　　29(2):75–91.

HFW (*See* Wolcott, Harry F.)

Halverson, John
　1987 Art for Art's Sake in the Paleolithic. Current Anthropology
　　28(1):63–89.

Hatcher, Evelyn Payne
　1985 Art as Culture: An Introduction to the Anthropology of Art.
　　Lanham, MD: University Press of America.

Hawthorn, Harry B.
　1961 The Artist in Tribal Society: The Northwest Coast. *In* The
　　Artist in Tribal Society. Marian W. Smith, ed. Pp. 58–70. New
　　York: Free Press.

Henry, Jules
　1963 Culture Against Man. New York: Random House.

Henry, Jules, and Melford E. Spiro
　1953 Psychological Techniques: Projective Techniques in Field
　　Work. *In* Anthropology Today. Alfred L. Kroeber, ed.
　　Pp. 417–429. Chicago: University of Chicago Press.

Hilbert, Richard A.
　1980 Covert Participant Observation. Urban Life 9:51–78.

Hill, Michael R.
　1993 Archival Strategies and Techniques. Newbury Park, CA: Sage.

Homans, George
　1962 Sentiments and Activities: Essays in Social Science. New York:
　　Free Press of Glencoe.

Howell, Nancy
　1990 Surviving Fieldwork. Special Publication No. 26. Washington,
　　DC: American Anthropological Association.

Humphreys, Laud
    1989 The Sociologist as Voyeur. *In* In the Field: Readings on the
        Field Research Experience. Carolyn D. Smith and William
        Kornblum, eds. Pp. 128–133. New York: Praeger. [Adapted
        from Tearoom Trade: Impersonal Sex in Public Places, 2nd ed.
        New York: Aldine de Gruyter, 1975.]

Jackson, Bruce
    1987 Fieldwork. Urbana, IL: University of Illinois Press.

Jackson, Jean E.
    1990 "I Am A Fieldnote": Fieldnotes as a Symbol of Professional
        Identity. *In* Fieldnotes. Roger Sanjek, ed. Pp. 3–33. Ithaca, NY:
        Cornell University Press.

Johnson, John
    1976 Doing Field Research. New York: Free Press.

Jorgensen, Danny L.
    1989 Participant Observation. Newbury Park, CA: Sage.

Keesing, Felix
    1958 Cultural Anthropology: The Science of Custom. New York:
        Rinehart and Company.

Keesing, Roger M., and Felix M. Keesing
    1971 New Perspectives in Cultural Anthropology. New York: Holt,
        Rinehart and Winston.

Kimball, Solon T., and William L. Partridge.
    1979 The Craft of Community Study: Fieldwork Dialogues.
        Gainesville: University of Florida Press.

Kincheloe, Joe L., and Peter L. McLaren
    1994 Rethinking Critical Theory and Qualitative Research. *In* Hand-
        book of Qualitative Research. Norman Denzin and Yvonna S.
        Lincoln, eds. Pp. 138–157. Thousand Oaks, CA: Sage.

Kinsey, Alfred C., Wardell B. Pomeroy, and Clyde E. Martin
    1948 Sexual Behavior in the Human Male. Philadelphia: W. B.
        Saunders Company.

Kirk, Jerome, and Marc L. Miller
1986 Reliability and Validity in Qualitative Research. Beverly Hills, CA: Sage.

Kleinman, Sherryl, and Martha A. Copp
1993 Emotions and Fieldwork. Newbury Park, CA: Sage.

Kluckhohn, Clyde
1949 Mirror for Man: The Relation of Anthropology to Modern Life. New York: Whittlesey House, McGraw Hill.

Kluckhohn, Clyde, and Henry A. Murray, eds.
1948 Personality in Nature, Society, and Culture. New York: Alfred A. Knopf.

Kluckhohn, Florence
1940 The Participant-Observer Technique in Small Communities. American Journal of Sociology 46(3):331–344.

Kottak, Conrad P.
1994 Teaching in the Postmodern Classroom. Bulletin of the General Anthropology Division, American Anthropological Association 1:10–12.

Kubler, George
1962 The Shape of Time: Remarks on the History of Things. New Haven, CT: Yale University Press.

Kuhn, Thomas S.
1970 The Structure of Scientific Revolutions. 2nd ed. Chicago: University of Chicago Press.

Kulick, Don, and Margaret Willson, eds.
1995 Taboo: Sex, Identity and Erotic Subjectivity in Anthropological Fieldwork. New York: Routledge.

Lakatos, Imre
1978 The Methodology of Scientific Research Programmes: Philosophical Papers, Vol. 1. London: Cambridge University Press.

Langness, L. L., and Gelya Frank
1981 Lives: An Anthropological Approach to Biography. Novato, CA: Chandler and Sharp.

Latour, Bruno
1987 Science in Action: How to Follow Scientists and Engineers Through Society. Milton Keynes, England: Open University Press.

Latour, Bruno, and Steve Woolgar
1986 Laboratory Life: The Construction of Scientific Facts. 2nd ed. Princeton, NJ: Princeton University Press.

Lawless, Robert, Vinson Sutlive, Jr., and Mario Zamora, eds.
1983 Fieldwork: The Human Experience. New York: Gordon and Breach.

Layton, Robert
1981 The Anthropology of Art. London: Granada.

Leach, Edmund
1957 The Epistemological Background to Malinowski's Empiricism. *In* Man and Culture: An Evaluation of the Work of Bronislaw Malinowski. Raymond Firth, ed. Pp. 119–137. New York: Harper Torchbooks.

LeCompte, Margaret, Wendy L. Millroy, and Judith Preissle, eds.
1992 Handbook of Qualitative Research in Education. San Diego, CA: Academic Press.

Lee, Raymond M.
1995 Dangerous Fieldwork. Thousand Oaks, CA: Sage.

Lévi-Strauss, Claude
1993 Regarder Ecouter Lire. Paris: Plon. [See a review by C. Ghasarian in Current Anthropology 35(3):329–330.]

Lévi-Strauss, Claude, and Didier Eribon
1991 Conversations with Claude Lévi-Strauss. Paula Wissing, trans. Chicago: University of Chicago Press.

Lewis, Oscar
1961 The Children of Sanchez: Autobiography of a Mexican Family.
New York: Random House.
1965 La Vida: A Puerto Rican Family in the Culture of Poverty—
San Juan and New York. New York: Random House.

Lincoln, Yvonna, and Egon G. Guba
1985 Naturalistic Inquiry. Beverly Hills, CA: Sage.

Lindeman, E. C.
1924 Social Discovery: An Approach to the Study of Functional
Groups. New York: Republic.

Lorenz, Konrad B.
1950 The Comparative Method in Studying Innate Behaviour
Patterns. Symposia for the Society for Experimental Biology
4:221–268.

Maines, David R., William Shaffir, and Allan Turowetz
1980 Leaving the Field in Ethnographic Research: Reflections on
the Entrance-Exit Hypothesis. *In* Fieldwork Experience. W. B.
Shaffir, R. A. Stebbins, and A. Turowetz, eds. Pp. 261–281.
New York: St. Martin.

Malinowski, Bronislaw
1922 Argonauts of the Western Pacific. London: Routledge
1929 The Sexual Life of Savages. New York: Halcyon House.
1967 A Diary in the Strict Sense of the Term. New York: Harcourt,
Brace, and World.

Mead, Margaret
1953 National Character. *In* Anthropology Today. A. L. Kroeber,
ed. Pp. 642–667. Chicago: University of Chicago Press.
1970 The Art and Technology of Fieldwork. *In* Handbook of
Method in Cultural Anthropology. Raoul Naroll and Ronald
Cohen, eds. Pp. 246–265. Garden City, NY: Natural History
Press.

Medawar, Peter Brian
1969. The Art of the Soluble. Hammondworth, England: Penguin.

Miles, Matthew B., and A. Michael Huberman
  1984 Qualitative Data Analysis: A Sourcebook of New Methods.
  Beverly Hills, CA: Sage.
  1994 Qualitative Data Analysis: An Expanded Sourcebook. 2nd ed.
  Thousand Oaks, CA: Sage.

Mintz, Sidney W.
  1974 Worker in the Cane: A Puerto Rican Life History. New York:
  W. W. Norton. [Originally published 1960 by Yale University
  Press.]

Mitchell, Richard G., Jr.
  1993 Secrecy and Fieldwork. Newbury Park, CA: Sage.

Moerman, Michael
  1988 Talking Culture: Ethnography and Conversation Analysis.
  Philadelphia: University of Pennsylvania Press.

Moffatt, Michael
  1989 Coming of Age in New Jersey: College and American Culture.
  New Brunswick, NJ: Rutgers University Press.

Moustakas, Clark
  1994 Phenomenological Research Methods. Thousand Oaks, CA:
  Sage.

Murdock, George Peter
  1971 Anthropology's Mythology. Proceedings of the Royal Anthropological Institute of Great Britain and Ireland for 1971:17–24.

Nyberg, David
  1993 The Varnished Truth: Truth Telling and Deceiving in Ordinary Life. Chicago: University of Chicago Press.

Ottenberg, Simon
  1990 Thirty Years of Fieldnotes: Changing Relationships to the
  Text. In Fieldnotes: The Makings of Anthropology. Roger
  Sanjek, ed. Pp. 139–160. Ithaca, NY: Cornell University Press.
  1994 Changes over Time in an African Culture and in an Anthropologist. In Others Knowing Others. Don D. Fowler and

Donald L. Hardesty, eds. Pp. 91–118. Washington, DC: Smithsonian Institution Press.

Paul, Benjamin D.
1953 Interview Techniques and Field Relationships. *In* Anthropology Today. A. L. Kroeber, ed. Pp. 430–451. Chicago: University of Chicago Press.

Peacock, James L.
1986 The Anthropological Lens: Harsh Light, Soft Focus. New York: Cambridge University Press.

Pehrson, Robert N.
1966 The Social Organization of the Marri Baluch. Compiled and analyzed by Fredrik Barth. New York: Wenner-Gren Foundation.

Pelto, Pertti J., and Gretel H. Pelto
1978 Anthropological Fieldwork: The Structure of Inquiry. 2nd ed. New York: Cambridge University Press.

Plattner, Stuart
1989 Commentary: Ethnographic Method. Anthropology Newsletter 32:30,21. Washington, DC: American Anthropological Association.

Powdermaker, Hortense
1950 Hollywood: The Dream Factory: An Anthropological Look at the Movie-makers. Boston: Little, Brown.
1966 Stranger and Friend: The Way of an Anthropologist. New York: W. W. Norton.

Price, Sally
1989 Primitive Art in Civilized Places. Chicago: University of Chicago Press.

Punch, Maurice
1986 Politics and Ethics of Fieldwork. Beverly Hills, CA: Sage.

Rabinow, Paul
1977 Reflections on Fieldwork in Morocco. Berkeley: University of California Press (Quantum Books).

Rappaport, Roy A.
1994 Comment on "Cultural Anthropology's Future Agenda." Anthropology Newsletter 35(6):76.

Richards, Audrey I.
1939 The Development of Field Work Methods in Social Anthropology. *In* The Study of Society. F. C. Bartlett, M. Ginsberg, E. J. Lindgren, and R. H. Thouless, eds. Pp. 272–316. London: Kegan Paul, Trench, Trubner.

Romney, A. K., Susan Weller, and W. H. Batchelder
1986 Culture as Consensus: A Theory of Culture and Informant Accuracy. American Anthropologist 88:313–338.

Roth, Julius A.
1962 *Comments on* Secret Observations. Social Problems 9:283–284.

Rubin, Herbert J., and Irene S. Rubin
1995 Qualitative Interviewing: The Art of Hearing Data. Thousand Oaks, CA: Sage.

Rubinstein, Robert A., ed.
1991 Fieldwork: The Correspondence of Robert Redfield and Sol Tax. Boulder, CO: Westview Press.

Sanjek, Roger
1990 On Ethnographic Validity. *In* Fieldnotes. Roger Sanjek, ed. Pp. 385–418. Ithaca, NY: Cornell University Press.
1991 The Ethnographic Present. Man: The Journal of the Royal Anthropological Institute 26:609–628.

Sanjek, Roger, ed.
1990 Fieldnotes: The Makings of Anthropology. Ithaca, NY: Cornell University Press.

Sartwell, Crispin
    1995 The Art of Living: Aesthetics of the Ordinary in World Spiri-
    tual Traditions. Albany: State University of New York Press.

Schlechty, Phillip, and George W. Noblit
    1982 Some Uses of Sociological Theory in Educational Evaluation.
    In Research in Sociology of Education and Socialization, Vol. 3.
    Pp. 283–306. Greenwich, CT: JAI.

Seidel, John
    1992 Method and Madness in the Application of Computer Tech-
    nology to Qualitative Data Analysis. *In* Using Computers in
    Qualitative Research. Nigel G. Fielding and Raymond M. Lee,
    eds. Pp. 107–116. Newbury Park, CA: Sage.

Seidman, I. E.
    1991 Interviewing as Qualitative Research: A Guide for Researchers
    in the Social Sciences. New York: Teachers College Press.

Shaffir, William B., and Robert A. Stebbins, eds.
    1991 Experiencing Fieldwork: An Inside View of Qualitative
    Research. Newbury Park, CA: Sage.

Silverman, David
    1993 Interpreting Qualitative Data: Methods for Analysing Talk,
    Text and Interaction. London: Sage.

Siu, Paul C. P.
    1987 The Chinese Laundryman: A Study of Social Isolation. New
    York: New York University Press.

Slater, Mariam
    1976 African Odyssey: An Anthropological Adventure. Garden
    City, NY: Anchor Press/Doubleday.

Smith, Alfred G.
    1964 The Dionysian Innovation. American Anthropologist
    66:251–265.

Smith, Robert J.
1990 Hearing Voices, Joining the Chorus: Appropriating Someone Else's Fieldnotes. *In* Fieldnotes. Roger Sanjek, ed. Pp. 356–370. Ithaca, NY: Cornell University Press.

Spicer, Edward H., ed.
1952 Human Problems in Technological Change. New York: Russell Sage.

Spindler, George, ed.
1970 Being an Anthropologist: Fieldwork in Eleven Cultures. New York: Holt, Rinehart and Winston.

Spindler, George, and Louise Spindler
1965 The Instrumental Activities Inventory: A Technique for the Study of the Psychology of Acculturation. Southwestern Journal of Anthropology 21(1):1–23.

Spiro, Melford E.
1990 On the Strange and the Familiar in Recent Anthropological Thought. *In* Cultural Psychology. J. W. Stigler, R. A. Shweder, and Gilbert Herdt, eds. Pp. 47–61. New York: Cambridge University Press.

Spradley, James P.
1979 The Ethnographic Interview. New York: Holt, Rinehart and Winston.
1980 Participant Observation. New York: Holt, Rinehart and Winston.

Stake, Robert E.
1995 The Art of Case Study Research. Thousand Oaks, CA: Sage.

Stoller, Paul, and Cheryl Olkes
1987 In Sorcery's Shadow: A Memoir of Apprenticeship Among the Songhay of Niger. Chicago: University of Chicago Press.

Strickland, Donald A., and Lester E. Schlesinger
1969 "Lurking" as a Research Method. Human Organization 28(3): 248–251.

Tambiah, Stanley J.
1990 Magic, Science, Religion, and the Scope of Rationality. New York: Cambridge University Press.

Tedlock, Barbara
1991 From Participant Observation to the Observation of Participation: The Emergence of Narrative Ethnography. Journal of Anthropological Research 47(1):69–94.

Trueba, Henry, and C. Delgado-Gaitan, eds.
1988 School and Society: Learning Content through Culture. New York: Praeger.

Turnbull, Colin M.
1961 The Forest People. New York: Simon and Schuster.
1965 Wayward Servants. Garden City, NY: Natural History Press.
1972 The Mountain People. New York: Simon and Schuster.

Van Maanen, John
1978 On Watching the Watchers. In Policing: A View from the Street. P. K. Manning and J. Van Maanen, eds. Pp. 309–349. Santa Monica, CA: Goodyear.
1988 Tales of the Field: On Writing Ethnography. Chicago: University of Chicago Press.

Van Maanen, John, ed.
1995 Representation in Ethnography. Thousand Oaks, CA: Sage.

van Willigen, John, and Timothy L. Finan
1991 Soundings: Rapid and Reliable Research Methods for Practicing Anthropologists. NAPA Bulletin #10. Washington, DC: American Anthropological Association.

van Willigen, John, Barbara Rylko-Bauer, and Ann McElroy, eds.
1989 Making Our Research Useful: Case Studies in the Utilization of Anthropological Knowledge. Boulder, CO: Westview Press.

Wagley, Charles
1983 Learning Fieldwork: Guatemala. *In* Fieldwork: The Human Experience. Robert Lawless, Vinson H. Sutlive, Jr., and Mario D. Zamora, eds. Pp. 1–17. New York: Gordon and Breach.

Wax, Rosalie
1971 Doing Fieldwork: Warnings and Advice. Chicago: University of Chicago Press.

Weitzman, Eben A., and Matthew B. Miles
1995 Computer Programs for Qualitative Data Analysis. Thousand Oaks, CA: Sage.

Wengle, John L.
1988 Ethnographers in the Field: The Psychology of Research. Tuscaloosa: University of Alabama Press.

Werner, Oswald, and G. Mark Schoepfle
1987a Systematic Fieldwork. Vol. 1, Foundations of Ethnography and Interviewing. Newbury Park, CA: Sage.
1987b Systematic Fieldwork. Vol. 2, Ethnographic Analysis and Data Management. Newbury Park, CA: Sage.

Whyte, William F.
1943 Street Corner Society. Chicago: University of Chicago Press.
1955 Street Corner Society. 2nd ed. Chicago: University of Chicago Press.
1984 Learning from the Field: A Guide from Experience. Beverly Hills, CA: Sage.
1994 Participant Observer: An Autobiography. Ithaca, NY: ILR Press, Cornell University.

Williams, Joseph M.
1990 Style: Toward Clarity and Grace. Chicago: University of Chicago Press.

Wolcott, Harry F.
1967 A Kwakiutl Village and School. New York: Holt, Rinehart and Winston. [Reissued with a new Afterword in 1989 by Waveland Press.]

1973 The Man in the Principal's Office: An Ethnography. New York: Holt, Rinehart and Winston.

1974 The African Beer Gardens of Bulawayo: Integrated Drinking in a Segregated Society. New Brunswick, NJ: Rutgers Center of Alcohol Studies. Monograph 10.

1975 Feedback Influences on Fieldwork, Or: A Funny Thing Happened on the Way to the Beer Garden. *In* Urban Man in Southern Africa. Clive Kileff and Wade Pendelton, eds. Pp. 99–125. Gwelo, Rhodesia: Mambo Press.

1977 Teachers Versus Technocrats: An Educational Innovation in Anthropological Perspective. Eugene: Center for Educational Policy and Management, University of Oregon.

1981a Confessions of a "Trained" Observer. *In* The Study of Schooling: Field Based Methodologies in Educational Research and Evaluation. Thomas S. Popkewitz and B. Robert Tabachnick, eds. Pp. 247–263. New York: Praeger.

1981b Home and Away: Personal Contrasts in Ethnographic Style. *In* Anthropologists at Home in North America: Methods and Issues in the Study of One's Own Society. Donald A. Messerschmidt, ed. Pp. 255–265. New York: Cambridge University Press.

1982 Mirrors, Models, and Monitors: Educator Adaptations of the Ethnographic Innovation. *In* Doing the Ethnography of Schooling. George D. Spindler, ed. Pp. 68–95. New York: Holt, Rinehart and Winston.

1983a Adequate Schools and Inadequate Education: The Life Story of a Sneaky Kid. Anthropology and Education Quarterly 14:3–32.

1983b A Malay Village that Progress Chose: Sungai Lui and the Institute of Cultural Affairs. Human Organization 42:72–81.

1985 On Ethnographic Intent. Educational Administration Quarterly 21 (3):187–203.

1987a Life's Not Working: Cultural Alternatives to Career Alternatives. *In* Schooling in Social Context: Qualitative Studies. G. W. Noblit and W. T. Pink, eds. Pp. 303–325. Norwood, NJ: Ablex.

1987b On Ethnographic Intent. *In* Interpretive Ethnography of Education: At Home and Abroad. George and Louise Spindler, eds. Pp. 37–57. Hillsdale, NJ: Lawrence Erlbaum Associates.

1990a On Seeking—and Rejecting—Validity in Qualitative Research. *In* Qualitative Inquiry in Education: The Continuing Debate. Elliot W. Eisner and Alan Peshkin, eds. Pp. 121–152. New York: Teachers College.

1990b Writing Up Qualitative Research. Newbury Park, CA: Sage.

1994a Confessions of a "Trained" Observer. *In* Transforming Qualitative Data: Description, Analysis, and Interpretation. Pp. 149–172. Thousand Oaks, CA: Sage.

1994b Transforming Qualitative Data: Description, Analysis, and Interpretation. Thousand Oaks, CA: Sage

Wolf, Eric
1964 Anthropology. Englewood Cliffs, NJ: Prentice-Hall.

Woolgar, Steven
1983 Irony in the Social Study of Science. *In* Science Observed: Perspectives on the Social Study of Science. K. D. Knorr-Cetina and M. J. Mulkay, eds. Beverly Hills, CA: Sage.

Young, David E., and Jean-Guy Goulet, eds.
1994 Being Changed: The Anthropology of Extraordinary Experience. Peterborough, Ontario: Broadview Press.

Zelditch, Morris
1962 Some Methodological Problems of Field Studies. American Journal of Sociology 67:566–576.●

NAME INDEX

M

Maines, David R., 125
Malinowski, Bronislaw, 43, 44, 63, 69,
    77, 118, 125, 146, 164, 184,
    236, 241
Marcus, George E., 201
Martin, Clyde E., 103
McElroy, Ann, 136
McLaren, Peter L., 165
Mead, Margaret, 28, 43, 78, 117, 120,
    173–174, 180, 199, 234
Medawar, Peter Brian, 160
Miles, Matthew B., 74, 147, 202
Miller, Marc L., 19, 167, 168
Mills, Geoffrey E., 187
Mintz, Sidney W., 174–175
Mishoe, Shelley, 32
Mitchell, Richard G., Jr., 153, 194, 195
Moerman, Michael, 87
Moffatt, Michael, 237
Monette, Paul, 103
Murdock, George Peter, 182, 185
Murray, Henry A., 172–173, 175

N

Naranjo-Morse, Nora, 26
Noblit, George W., 131
Nyberg, David, 149

O

Ogan, Eugene, 45
Ottenberg, Simon, 41, 77–78, 99, 177,
    179–181, 185

P

Partridge, William L., 29, 30, 239
Paul, Benjamin D., 110
Peacock, James L., 170
Pelto, Pertti J., and Pelto, Gretel H., 169
Plattner, Stuart, 70–72
Poewe, Karla (pseud. Cesara), 236

Pomeroy, Wardell B., 103
Popper, Karl, 164
Powdermaker, Hortense, 232
Price, Sally, 44
Punch, Maurice, 147

R

Rabinow, Paul, 65, 67, 68
Radcliffe-Brown, A. R., 69, 118, 162
Rappaport, Roy A., 11, 20
Redfield, Robert, 76, 82, 109, 239
Richards, Audrey I., 69, 75
Rohner, Ronald P., 118–119
Romney, A. K., 110
Roth, Julius A., 153
Rowe, Neil, 45
Rubinstein, Robert A., 76, 83, 109,
    162, 239
Rylko-Bauer, Barbara, 136

S

Sanjek, Roger, 41, 43, 90, 99, 132, 167,
    168, 181, 184, 190, 210, 218
Sartwell, Crispin, 14
Schlechty, Phillip, 131
Schlesinger, Lester E., 153
Schoepfle, G. Mark, 29, 30, 41, 157, 196
Schram, Thomas H., 196
Seidel, John, 72
Seidman, I. E., 110
Shaffir, William B., 125, 223
Shaw, Linda L., 99
Silverman, David, 202
Siu, Paul C., 41
Slater, Mariam, 90
Smith, Alfred G., 49–50
Smith, Robert J., 206
Spicer, Edward H., 41
Spindler, George, and Spindler, Louise,
    41, 45, 46, 106, 155, 156,
    217, 239
Spiro, Melford E., 106, 131
Spradley, James P., 110, 112, 157

SUBJECT INDEX

ABOUT THE AUTHOR /
ABOUT THE BOOK

Harry Wolcott began doing fieldwork in 1962, began writing up fieldwork in 1963, began lecturing about fieldwork in 1967, and began writing about the doing of fieldwork in 1970. He has been variously engaged in these pursuits ever since. On completing doctoral studies at Stanford University in 1964, he accepted a position at the University of Oregon as a Research Associate in its newly funded Research and Development Center in Educational Administration. More than three decades of administrative changes later he is still at Oregon, today teaching and writing in semiretirement as Professor Emeritus in the Department of Anthropology. In addition to his ethnographic studies and extensive writing in the field of Anthropology and Education, he has written two books published by Sage, *Writing Up Qualitative Research* (1990) and *Transforming Qualitative Data* (1994).

The Art of Fieldwork is something of a complement to those two Sage publications, this time giving attention to fieldwork itself and to the essential mindwork that must accompany it. An important distinction is made here between the orderly activities of data gathering and whatever else is involved that makes fieldwork more than just that. This is not to insist that fieldwork *is* art, but rather to suggest that the doing of fieldwork calls for qualities we associate with the imaginative and creative work of the artist as much as it calls for the systematic efforts of the scientist.

The author expresses special appreciation to Mitch Allen for encouraging this writing and including it among the first publications under the new imprimatur of AltaMira Press, a Sage subsidiary. Appreciation is also expressed to colleagues and invited critics who shared ideas, read early drafts of particular chapters, or provided a critique of the entire manuscript in one of several major revisions: Howard S. Becker, Allan F. Burns, Az Carmen, Mary Dalmau, Norman Delue, Carolyn Ellis, Dianne Ferguson, Ben Hill, Min Kantrowitz, R. Barry Lewis, Thomas H. Schram, George and Louise Spindler, James D. Swartz, Mark Wohl, and Philip D. Young.●